Community Education

an agenda for educational reform

Innovations in Education

Series Editor: Colin Fletcher (Senior lecturer in the School of Policy Studies, Cranfield Institute of Technology)

There have been periods of major innovation in public education. What do the achievements amount to and what are the prospects for progress now? There are issues in each slice of the education sector. How have the issues come about?

Each author analyses their own sphere, argues from experience and communicates clearly. Here are books that speak both with and for the teaching profession; books that can be shared with all those involved in the future of education.

Three quotations have helped to shape the series:

> The whole process — the false starts, frustrations, adaptions, the successive recasting of intentions, the detours and conflicts — needs to be comprehended. Only then can we understand what has been achieved and learned from experience.
>
> *Marris and Rein*

> In this time of considerable educational change and challenge the need for teachers to write has never been greater.
>
> *Hargreaves*

> A wise innovator should prepare packages of programmes and procedures which ... could be put into effect quickly in periods of recovery and reorganisation following a disaster.
>
> *Hirsh*

Current titles in the series

Pat Ainley: *From School to YTS*
Garth Allen, John Bastiani, Ian Martin, Kelvyn Richards: *Community Education*
Bernard Barker: *Rescuing the Comprehensive Experience*
Julia Gilkes: *Developing Nursery Education*
Gerri Kirkwood and Colin Kirkwood: *Living Adult Education*
Herbert Kohl: *36 Children*
Julia Stanley: *Marks on the Memory*
Jan Stewart: *The Making of the Primary School*
David Terry: *The Tertiary College*
Paul Widlake: *Reducing Educational Disadvantage*

Open University Press
12 Cofferidge Close
Stony Stratford
Milton Keynes MK11 1BY, England

and

1900 Frost Road, Suite 101
Bristol, PA 19007, USA

First published 1987
Reprinted 1989

British Library Cataloguing in Publication Data

Community education : an agenda for
  educational reform. — (Innovations in
  education).
  1. Community education
  I. Allen, Garth   II. Series
  370.19′4   LC1036

  ISBN 0–335–10288–3
  ISBN 0–335–10287–5 Pbk

Library of Congress Cataloging in Publication Data

Community education, an agenda for educational reform.
  (innovations in education)
  1. Community education — Great Britain.
  I. Allen, Garth. II. Series.
  LC1036.8.G7C66   1987   370.19′3′0941   87–25026
  ISBN 0–335–10288–3
  ISBN 0–335–10287–5 (Pbk)

Typeset by Marlborough Design Services
Printed in Great Britain by M. & A. Thomson Litho Ltd.

Community Education

an agenda for educational reform

EDITORS
Garth Allen
John Bastiani
Ian Martin
J. Kelvyn Richards

Open University Press
Milton Keynes · Philadelphia

Contents

Tables and figures

List of contributors

GARTH ALLEN, Head of Applied Social Sciences, College of St Mark and St John, Plymouth

PAULA ALLMAN, Lecturer in Adult and Continuing Education, University of Nottingham

JEAN ANDERSON, Senior Lecturer in Applied Social Sciences, College of St Mark and St John, Plymouth

JOHN ANDERSON, Principal, College of St Mark and St John, Plymouth

JOHN BASTIANI, Lecturer in Education, University of Nottingham

DAVID CLARK, Senior lecturer with responsibility for Community Education, Westhill College, Birmingham

JOHN DAVIS, Evaluator, Parent Support Programme, School of Education, University of Liverpool

COLIN FLETCHER, Senior Lecturer in Social Policy, Cranfield Institute of Technology

DAVE GORBUTT, Head of Adult and Continuing Education, College of St Mark and St John, Plymouth

TONY JEFFS, Senior Lecturer in Social Policy, Newcastle upon Tyne Polytechnic

IAN MARTIN, Senior Lecturer in Community Studies, Chester College of Higher Education

GORDON MITCHELL, Lecturer in Education, University of Warwick

BOB O'HAGAN, Vice-Principal, Hind Leys School and Community College, Shepshed, Leicestershire

KELVYN RICHARDS, Senior Lecturer in Community Education, Trent Polytechnic

JOHN SAMUEL, Vice-Principal, Haringey College

Introduction

Education in the post-war period has seldom been as near the top of the political agenda as it is today. Community education represents one approach to analysis, critique and prescription. It is grounded in a fundamental commitment to public sector provision and the principles of comprehensive and continuing education. It is now firmly established in policy and practice in many areas and is currently under active consideration in many others. In spite of this, however, it has not yet made much of an impact on the public or academic debate about education. This is both because its institutional development to date has been somewhat sporadic and incremental, reflecting significantly different patterns of policy and practice, and because, albeit as a still rather disparate movement of educational ideas, it challenges the validity and relevance of much of the language in which this debate is conducted.

As an agenda for educational reform, the fundamental claim of community education is that we need to renegotiate and reconstruct the ways in which the education system relates to its constituent communities of interest and residence. People in the community are losing confidence in public services largely because public services are losing touch with people in the community. In this respect, the current crisis in education reflects a wider crisis in the welfare state as a whole, and it is a crisis of confidence and expectation as well as ideology and finance. To this extent, the present groundswell of interest in community education mirrors many of the problems and possibilities of a seemingly beleaguered commitment to social and educational welfare at a time of unprecedented structural change, political dissension and economic retrenchment. As the papers in this collection illustrate, community education takes many forms. These reflect not only different local circumstances and priorities but also spring from distinctive historical and ideological roots. Consequently, a confusing variety of models of policy and practice exists today. It is important that these are identified, compared and evaluated. We hope that this book has a contribution to make in this respect. Certainly, all the papers in it proceed from the assumption that the term 'community education' remains problematic and contested despite its widespread currency. On the other hand, they also claim in different ways that it constitutes both a problem and a response worthy of investigation and commitment.

Community education now exists not only in the long-established practices of some local education authorities, but also in increasing numbers of policy documents and discussion papers as well as generic initiatives across the statutory and voluntary sectors. However unfinished its messages, community education represents a significant attempt to redirect educational policy and practice in ways which bring education and community into a closer and more equal relationship. All the papers in this collection seek to explore the implications of this. In the process, they help to suggest the elements of an agenda for reform and to identify some of the obstacles which stand in its way.

Our main interest is in the more diffuse developments which reflect what we would regard as a general community-orientated approach to education. We would argue that community education should not be understood primarily in terms of any particular policy package or institutional setting, e.g. the designation of 'community schools'. Rather, we suggest that community education is essentially about how the education service as a totality relates to people in the community. On this view, the community education dimension should be an integral part of the way in which all broadly educational agencies do their work and interact with one another. This helps to explain why some of the papers that follow are sharply critical of certain established patterns of practice.

It is no coincidence that this kind of realignment of education is now being widely adopted as an approach to local policy making in many parts of the country where little enthusiasm has been shown for the more traditional versions of community education. This, we would suggest, is not because the long-term advocates of community education have suddenly got their message over. On the contrary, the current groundswell of interest is based upon the recognition that community education as a general approach and as a way of working with people is becoming an increasingly urgent necessity.

Community education offers a basis and rationale for positive, coherent and open-ended responses across the education service as a whole to the structural change and social polarization now being experienced in many communities. Education cannot 'solve' the problems of a rapidly changing and increasingly unequal society, but it must engage constructively with these problems at the local level, i.e. in the communities where people experience them and struggle with them. In this sense, there is a degree of continuity and progression in the history of community education because it has always claimed to be about responding positively to change in communities. But this can only be done by perceiving and continually redefining education in the context of community.

The community education agenda, however, cannot be bottled up and prescribed like some kind of universal patent remedy. Communities are by their very nature diverse, dynamic and pluralistic. Consequently, the papers that follow contain very little direct prescription or detailed reference to established orthodoxies. They are not primarily concerned with the specifics of 'good practice'. That would imply a degree of transferability and replicability which contradicts our understanding of the community education process. This has to be worked on and worked out with people at the local level. Nor are the contents of this book representative of the whole field of contemporary practice. Because women and black people, for instance, constitute distinctive communities of interest and experience in social, political and educational terms, they have a special claim on community education as any systematic survey of current practice would demonstrate. And yet they are not specifically represented in this collection. Nevertheless, the logic of several of these accounts is that some current versions of community education are fundamentally about articulating the distinctive voices of such communities.

We hope that the analysis, critique, commentary and proposals offered here can help community education to happen by suggesting some of the elements of an agenda for action. We would emphasize that all these papers are derived directly from the kind of issues that arise at the operational level, challenging community educators to extend and reconstruct the theories of practice which, explicitly or implicitly, inform their work.

Most of the contributors to this collection work or have worked in institutions of higher education. We share a common interest in commenting in an informed and critical way on what we regard as a significant yet academically neglected dimension of educational reform and innovation. All of us are actively involved, through teaching, research, in-service training and consultancy, in the development of policy and practice. We hope that the book makes a distinctive contribution to the growing literature of community education. It aims to offer both the general and the specialist reader a set of critical yet committed commentaries which range across the generic field of practice. In different ways they all seek to reflect and address the problematic realities of 'doing' community education in various contexts — which, we would insist, is much more than a matter of management techniques. It is a process that demands continuous analysis, critique and rethinking. We do not feel that there is enough of this at present and therefore hope that these papers help to fill a significant gap in the existing literature.

Inevitably, the book is a collection of widely differing accounts covering a broad range of subject matter. In this respect, it reflects community education on the ground. The papers incorporate different interests, philosophies and value positions. They employ different educational and academic perspectives, drawing upon a variety of experience. Nevertheless, the collection is held together by a number of common concerns. As these are often implicit rather than openly stated, it may be useful to review them briefly here.

Our commitment to community education is tempered by a general sense of disappointment about the way it has developed, and sometimes failed to develop. Community education has often seemed to promise much and to deliver little. Fine words have not always been turned into effective action. Some of the papers suggest why reality seldom matches rhetoric. Common ground between the contributors also includes a critique of, for instance, the authoritarian nature of schooling, the apparent failure of adult education and youth work to make any real impact on the education system as a whole, and a general lack of imagination in the development of appropriate educational forms and styles.

Such criticisms are counter-balanced by shared convictions about the need for new directions and alternative agendas for academics, policy makers and practitioners alike. These are not presented as a new orthodoxy to replace another that has become outdated, but as a collection of accounts which can be examined, in whole or in part, and assessed on their own merits. So readers will not find a crude blueprint for success or simplistic solutions to complex issues and problems. Rather, we hope they will find an awareness of the need for much basic rethinking coupled with the development of new ways of working with people which call for imaginative initiatives in education and training.

In some cases, the contributors wish to clarify an idea or to make sense of recent experience; in others, it seems important to bring something to the attention of a wider audience, to place an issue on the agenda or to challenge a prevailing view or a vested interest, particularly where these endorse attitudes and practices that are an obstacle to genuine progress. Finally, there are papers in which a key concern is to tease out the practical implications of particular perspectives or arguments and to rehearse ways of translating them into action.

This book does not hold out a particular brief for any one kind of knowledge or way of knowing, or wish to give it a superior place in the repertoire. In our view, theory, research, policy and practice represent different but equally important traditions and ways of ordering experience. This is not to suggest that each has made a comparable contribution, but rather to claim that they have the potential to do so. Theory and research, in particular, have made little impact on community education and at present occupy a rather marginal place in the field. Much development in community education has been either policy or practice led. We are committed to the view that the study and practice of community education should be seen as both the interrelated and mutually beneficial.

The first section of this book reflects the debate about the philosophy and values of community education and the implications of theory for practice. This entails an examination of key concepts and how they are used, together with a consideration of different ways of studying community education, analysing it and supporting it with evidence. The problem of definition and interpretation may not be resolved, but various explanations for the continuing debate are offered.

In contrast, the second section takes a critical look at some of the key forms of community education provision and practice. These papers demonstrate how issues are defined operationally and illustrate the conflicts of interest and dilemmas of choice that arise in reality. Any accounts of practice need to examine the relationship between rhetoric and action. These contributions present opportunities to assess the kinds of evidence that are used to support claims and judgements.

The papers in the final section focus on the ways in which power operates at different levels and consider some of the personal and political implications of community education as a way of working with people. They raise a number of fundamental and interrelated issues about, for example, the nature of professionalism, what counts as knowledge and the processes of individual and social change and development.

SECTION 1

Clarifying ideas

CHAPTER 1

Community education: towards a theoretical analysis

IAN MARTIN

This paper is derived from in-service work with students representing several different branches of current community education practice. Martin reviews the debate about the definition of community education. He suggests that this can be clarified by an examination of the historical and ideological roots of contemporary practice. These provide the basis for a typology of analytical models. At the same time, the theory and practice of community education must be continuously reconstructed to reflect and engage with the changing social reality of life in the community. A feminist model is used to demonstrate this process of redefinition.

Introduction

> It is a commonplace that the characteristic virtue of Englishmen is their power of sustained practical activity, and their characteristic vice a reluctance to test the quality of that activity by reference to principles.
>
> R. H. Tawney

On the whole, the development of community education in Britain reflects the kind of conscientious but essentially unreflective pragmatism which Tawney, in the opening paragraph of *The Acquisitive Society* (1921), identifies as a fundamental attribute of our national character, predictably, this has had both positive and negative consequences. On the one hand, localized and ad hoc development has produced a rich diversity of practice. This has now evolved into a substantial and significant movement of educational ideas an activity which cuts across geographical, social and professional boundaries in a unique way. On the other hand, a price has been paid in terms of lack of conceptual clarity and theoretical coherence. Consequently, 'community education' has a credibility problem.

Moreover, at a time of economic recession and educational retrenchment, the inherent ambiguity of the term provides a convenient cover for all manner of expedient re-interpretation. This may, for example, take the form of the 'rationalization' of services in a way that suggests to some youth and community workers and adult educators that community education is little more than a euphemism for cost cutting. Alternatively, it can apparently offer an instant rationale for doing something, almost anything, about a whole series of pressing new problems and demands: falling rolls and the cost-effective use of plant, the educational management of unemployment and so-called 'education for leisure', parent politics, pupil disaffection .... It is no coincidence that community education conferences now seem to be haunted by anxious head teachers looking for ways of keeping under-used schools going by searching out the new constituency of the 'community'. Many a new 'community school' is the product of the threatened survival of the traditional 'school community'.

Longer established advocates of community education, however, would insist that it is about much more than mere expediency — although they would probably admit, in the best traditions of British pragmatism, that this can be a quite legitimate starting point for significant change and innovation. Nevertheless, even these veterans seem to be a confusing mixture, claiming a variety of distinctive pedigrees; for example, the Henry Morris/ Stewart Mason axis and the integrated-campus village and community colleges of Cambridgeshire and Leicestershire; the 'quiet revolution' in British primary education following the Plowden Report (1967); a radical and largely autonomous tradition in adult education and social action with its roots deep in working-class history.

Community education therefore appears to be a bewilderingly broad church, and the problem of definition becomes more acute in direct proportion to the currency of the term. No wonder the correspondent of the *Times Educational Supplement,* reporting a recent conference of the Community Education Association, remained puzzled by what she described in a rather twee way as the ideological 'tussles 'twixt tweeds and leathers' that she witnessed in discussion groups (Caudrey 1985, p. 10).

The basic question to which this paper is addressed is how to set about making sense of an educational movement which seems to tolerate, perhaps even to encourage, such a confusing variety of interests, interpretations and applications. It deliberately considers community education in general terms, at a macro level, in order to reflect the generic and amorphous nature of contemporary practice. It should be emphasized, however, that this is a personal and provisional interpretation. On the other hand, it is based on several years' experience working with in-service students who are broadly representative of the diverse range of current interpretations and applications of community education. It is offered here primarily as a stimulus to discussion and debate so that we can begin to apply theory in a more systematic and critical way to practice in community education.

The essence of the argument is that it is possible to locate various distinctive patterns in the historical development of community education and that these differ significantly in ideological terms. It is suggested that the hidden agenda of implicit values in community education may provide a useful starting point for analysis and evaluation. At the same time, it helps to clarify the continuing debate about definition. It also poses significant dilemmas of choice for some practitioners. These tend to be glossed over in attempts to formulate holistic theories of community education, which may therefore limit their analytical value. But lack of analysis simply compounds the confusion. Without it, community education has an in-built tendency to degenerate into an 'all things to all men' formula, as a Scottish HMI report vividly confirms (SED 1977):

> In the beginning was the word and the word was community education, and there arose many prophets willing to interpret the word, but few to deny its veracity. So that community education became a self-fulfilling prophecy, for its tenets were not written down on tablets of stone handed down from on high. And since no man knew what either community or education meant as separate creeds, when they were joined together their offspring multiplied exceedingly, offering diverse avenues to salvation.

When the 'facts' are problematic, and confusing, it is necessary to construct systematic theories of practice to order, interpret and evaluate them. Community educators have been slow to theorize about their practice and to probe its coherence. In this sense, we may have become the unwitting victims of our own pragmatism. Much of the literature is descriptive and uncritical. It tends to be somewhat anecdotal and rather bland, or narrowly utilitarian. It is true that some useful and perceptive work is emerging on specific institutional/agency contexts of practice, e.g. Skrimshire (1981), Hargreaves (1982) and Sayer (1985) on secondary school-based community education, and Lovett *et al* (1983), Brookfield (1983). Fletcher (1980) and Kirkwood (1978) on community adult education. These, however, are deliberately focused accounts which make no attempt to tackle the generic and inter-disciplinary nature of the contemporary community education movement as a whole.

Functional ambiguity

The inherent ambiguity of the idea of 'community' is one of the reasons why a clearer analysis of community education is required. We would do well to cultivate some of Raymond Williams' scepticism about the cosy connotations of a word which has become a conveniently vague label in recent social policy (Williams 1976, p. 66):

> Community can be the warmly persuasive word to describe an existing set of relationships, or the warmly persuasive word to describe an alternative set of relationships. What is most important, perhaps, is that unlike all other terms of social organization (state, nation, society etc.) it seems never to be used unfavourably, and never to be given any positive opposing or distinguishing term.

We should start by recognizing some of the implications of functional ambiguity (bad sense). 'Community' is a notoriously slippery and contested concept — so much so that some commentators have advocated abandoning it once and for all (see Stacey 1969, Dennis 1968 and, more recently, Hargreaves 1985). Much has been written both asserting and challenging its continuing relevance. For community educators, however, the definition of 'community' is crucial because it implies a critical choice between an essentially hierarchical, socially regressive and static model of social relations and one that is progressive, emancipatory and dynamic. In this respect, as Raymond Plant (1974) argues, the ideological and evaluative dimensions of the community concept are much more important than its descriptive relevance. Unfortunately, however, community educators seldom have time – they also perhaps lack the inclination? – to 'explore a meaning' before they 'espouse a cause' (Plant 1974, p. 4).

'Community' has become a ubiquitous label partly because it affords those who pedal it the luxury of not being pinned down too precisely.

A brief consideration of how the prefix 'community' is used in official policy initiatives demonstrates not only its ambiguity but also its ambivalence. This serves to underline the importance of community educators being clear about what they stand for – and against. In recent years it has been applied to a dubious assortment of localized, relatively cheap and expediently ad hoc responses to fundamentally structural problems (e.g. community programmes for the unemployed, community development for the urban poor, community service for the offender) as education and the social services are squeezed in the vice of an increasingly narrowly conceived economic policy. The current debate in social policy about the pros and cons of 'community care' is particularly instructive. Given the primacy of economic goals, the scale of demographic change and the potential of mass unemployment as a source of cheap labour (and even cheaper volunteers), the fundamental question must be: in whose interests?, i.e. care in the community or care by the community? Too often the 'community' label is exploited as a smokescreen to fudge some of the key issues both about power, accountability and resource allocation at national, regional and local levels and about the critical distinction between 'personal troubles of milieu' and 'public issues of social structure' (Wright Mills 1970, p. 14).

So the basic point for community educators must be about recognizing the negative implications of a functional ambiguity that allows so much of the debris of social and economic policy to be swept under the carpet of 'community'. The warning of John Benington, at the time Director of the Hillfields Community Development Project in Coventry, remains pertinent (Benington 1974, p. 260):

> Sociologists in search of the meaning of 'community' have so far come up with ninety-four different definitions. Their diffidence has not prevented politicians and professionals from using it as a kind of 'aerosol' word to be sprayed on to deteriorating institutions to deodorize and humanize them.

In view of this, it is not surprising that some erstwhile enthusiasts of community-based approaches to education have deliberately retreated from the conceptual bog of 'community' to the firmer and clearer ground of 'class' (e.g. see Jackson and Ashcroft 1972).

Nevertheless, it is central to the argument of this paper that the idea of 'community' as applied to education can also be functional in a positive way. According to David Hargreaves, the essence of community education is the 'blurring of boundaries between educational establishments and their surrounding communities, as well as between teachers and students, and work and leisure' (Caudrey 1985, p. 10). In this sense, community education stands for a particular quality of relationships among the communities of collective interest and need, not only within the education system but also between educational agencies and their publics in the outside world.

The theme of decompartmentalization can be clearly illustrated by sampling currently advertised posts in community education. Its logic is echoed in the characteristic jargon of 'service coordination', 'home–school liaison', 'inter-agency collaboration' and even 'curriculum permeation'. At the same time, it demonstrates that community education cannot be adequately understood if it is regarded as the prerogative or monopoly of any particular profession or interest group in education. Apparently, teachers, parents, youth workers, adult educators, play leaders, community workers and activists in the voluntary sector all claim a share of the community education cake. This paper is theoretical for a very practical reason. It reflects the 'constructive confusion' (Martin 1985a) produced by trying to force community education to make sense with several groups of in-service students representing precisely this sort of range of interests and interpretations. As common property, community education should present a unique opportunity for inter-disciplinary initiatives in both fieldwork and in-service provision. But their success is largely predicated upon the development of theoretical perspectives that can help not only to define common ground by transcending the specifics of practice but also to explain significant differences of definition and application.

Functional ambiguity (good sense) therefore allows community education to be understood as inclusive rather than exclusive. For several reasons, however, it will always be a difficult term to grasp conceptually. First, it challenges the relevance of many of the traditional demarcation lines, specialisms and categorizations of education to the interests and needs of people 'out there in the community'. Second, good practice is, almost by definition, the product of what Eric Midwinter calls 'local diagnosis'. Third, the generic character of community education is both a reflection of, and a response to, continuous change in the community, i.e. the reality of the world that exists outside the traditional closed shops of the education system. It is now widely recognized, for instance, that education should be understood as much more than simply the traditional 'front-end model' of schooling. The logic of 'learning through life', however, is not only the progressive deschooling of education but also that it must increasingly become the business of everyone: students, parents and the wider public of the 'learning society' as well as professional educators. But if community education is essentially about 'breaking down barriers' between learning and living (Wilson 1980), it must also be about promoting new and more democratic forms of educational access, accountability and control. In short, community education should be about power. This in turn implies more flexible definitions of 'what counts as knowledge' in curriculum and of educational roles and relationships. If all this is to happen, the functional ambiguity of community education must be exploited in a purposeful and constructive way to promote active collaboration between different communities of educational interest.

Theory and practice

One of the reasons why community education remains comparatively neglected by academic commentators and many professional trainers may be that theory still lags behind practice in this field. Community educators are themselves partly to blame for this. Sometimes they seem to take an almost perverse delight in presenting themselves as what Richard Crossman (a practical thinker if ever there was one) once called 'common-sense fellows with little time for theorizing' (Crossman 1952). It is now some years since Keith Jackson, an astute but not unsympathetic critic of community education, suggested that 'the very combination of the idea of education with that of community may sharpen up the meaning in some contexts' (Jackson 1980, p. 39). But we have been slow to follow this up in any systematic way and, indeed, have more frequently been guilty of what Jackson, in a less sympathetic comment, dismissed as 'mindless ad hoc-ery'.

It is often said, and even more often forgotten, that 'there is nothing as practical as good theory'. But if we are to apply ideas with any rigour to the confusing variety of contemporary practice in community education, it is necessary to complement the descriptive and anecdotal with more critical and analytical accounts. In particular, it is important to clarify the different patterns of historical development in the evolution of community education and to assess the extent to which these reflect distinct philosophies about the relationship between education and community.

To what extent, for example, is the idea of 'community' still meaningful, and how can the definition of this peculiarly elusive concept both help and hinder our thinking about education and social change? Presumably, 'community' meant something very different in the rural Cambridgeshire of Henry Morris in the 1920s and 1930s than it did in the inner cities of the Educational Priority Areas and Community Development Projects of the late 1960s and early 1970s. In the mid-1980s it may at last be time to jettison once and for all the idea of the community (singular) as some kind of organic and consensual social entity and accept instead that it makes more sense to talk about communities (plural), whose identities may both reflect common patterns of interest as well as residence and also come into conflict with one another. Indeed, given the divisive and pervasive reality of mass unemployment, relative deprivation and racial disadvantage, it may well be more appropriate to speak of building local communities of endurance, resistance and struggle (see Jenkins 1985) than to try to reconstruct a broken consensus.

The remainder of this paper considers two basic questions about the relationship between theory and practice in community education. First, to what extent is it possible to detect any underlying thematic coherence in the work of community educators which transcends the particularities of context? Second, how can the historical development of community education be disaggregated so as to formulate analytical models which clarify the range and diversity of interpretation in practice? It is also briefly indicated how this kind of theoretical analysis can be used to stimulate further thinking about new variations on the community education theme.

Back to basics

Intrinsically, community education is a relatively meaningless term. It now has widespread currency but lacks any generally acknowledged definition. This is partly because until quite recently the application of the term of developments in education tended to be retrospective rather than prescriptive.

Nevertheless, it is suggested that the combination of 'community' with 'education' at the very least implies a readiness to renegotiate – perhaps even to reverse – some of the traditional role relationships between the 'us' and 'them' of the educational process, e.g. teacher and student, professional and lay person, producer and consumer. In this sense, 'community' represents the changing world outside the institutional cocoon of the professional worker, and 'community education' is about evolving more open, participatory and democratic relationships between educators and their constituencies. The reciprocal quality of these relationships is crucial; community educators claim to work with people – not for them, let alone on them. Community education should be about partnership and solidarity rather than paternalism or manipulation. This fundamental element of role redefinition and reversal has wide-ranging implications for the nature of educative relationships, the context of learning and the potential for the redistribution of educational opportunity (both vertically within the individual's lifetime and horizontally across the social structure).

The logic of such rethinking is often expressed in a basic commitment to the concept of 'lifelong learning'. Both the Community Education Association and the Scottish Council for Community Education, for instance, identify forms and varied contexts througout life, as the starting point for their interpretations of community education. Its essential purpose is therefore to translate the rhetoric of 'lifelong learning' into educational reality. School is only the beginning of a continuous experience of 'learning to be', i.e. to become more fully human (Faure *et al* 1972), or what Henry Morris called the 'art of living'. It should be emphasized that this is a radical and fundamentally iconoclastic perspective because it implies sustained educational engagement with the social reality of people's lives in the community. It therefore challenges not only dominant assumptions about the form and age-graded organization of the 'front-end' schooling but also the relevance of the narrow professional specialisms we have constructed to service our trained perceptions of other people's social and educational 'needs'. Time is on the side of community education in this respect. The technical demands of economic change and the social demands of increased leisure and demographic factors, for instance, will inevitably precipitate a radical convergence of traditional professional monopolies in educational and social service provision.

It is therefore significant that the Community Education

Association, which claims to represent the community education movement nationally, confers primacy on 'lifelong learning' in its attempt to define common ground among practitioners. The other key themes identified on its membership application form follow on from the recognition that 'Learning takes place in many and varied contexts throughout the individual's life'. This tenet provides a basic rationale for the Association's view of community education as both a practical and a philosophical commitment to:

- Developing strategies of social and educational redistribution which can help to create a more just and equitable society.
- Promoting closer coordination and collaboration between local agencies in both the statutory and voluntary sectors.
- Supporting local initiatives in community development which seek to give people more power and control over their own lives.
- Encouraging more open and democratic access to the human and material resources of the educational system.
- Redefining our notions of curriculum and learning process in such a way that education both 'generates individual autonomy and facilitates social cooperation' (Hargreaves 1985).

This kind of thematic approach is useful to the extent that it helps to identify a degree of commonality among community educators. The question is, of course, how such rhetoric is translated into reality. How are all these good intentions interpreted, prioritized and implemented in practical situations which are often complicated by competing needs and conflicting interests, different institutional expectations and constraints, and limited resources? To begin, in Tawney's words, 'to test the quality of our activity by reference to principles' we need to go further, to develop a more discriminating type of analysis.

A tentative theoretical analysis

> There is a limit to the amount of theorizing about definitions that is of educational use in, so to speak, a conceptual value vacuum.
>
> R. M. Titmuss

As already indicated, this paper reflects several years' experience of working with very mixed groups of in-service students and the demand imposed by them to make sense of community education in ways which reflect their own particular interests and concerns.

Once discussion moves beyond generalities, what is striking is the extent of disagreement – and this is more than simply a crude polarization of, for example, conservative teachers in 'tweeds' and radical community workers in 'leathers'. It is important therefore to stress that in our experience differences of interpretation are not just a function of particular contexts of practice: they are personal and philosophical as well as professional and institutional.

Recently three groups of students were asked to prepare brief statements beginning with the words, 'Community education is about ...'. The results of this exercise were both interesting and problematic:

1 Community education is about the accessibility of education to everyone so that people can achieve a fuller and more rewarding life. People need to be involved in controlling more of their lives, making decisions through discussion and debate.
2 Community education is about modifying the existing education system to the benefit of those who are considered disadvantaged or deprived. Its aim is to give people who 'miss out' a better deal.
3 Community education is about acting in solidarity with those people in society who have least power, enabling them to analyse their situation and to achieve political change. Power to the People!

How are we to explain the coexistence of such different perceptions of the nature and purpose of community education?

Dave Clark suggests that a review of current practice in community education reveals a continuum of five levels of interpretation ranging from the purely pragmatic to the overtly political (Clark 1985). These can be summarized as in Table 1.1.

Table 1.1 is a useful contribution to the continuing debate about definition because it demonstrates the difficulty of reaching any kind of meaningful consensus when the whole gamut of practice is considered. It also raises important questions about how far formal education institutions, especially schools, can accommodate the more radical versions of community education. Although Clark appears to confuse the issue by labelling the fifth model 'ideological', the sense of his argument is that all interpretations of community education (whatever their claims to neutrality or pragmatism) are value-based. Each is intrinsically ideological because each reflects a particular set of implicit values. The more unstated or taken for granted these are, the more systematically they need to be examined. It is now a truism that a policy of 'not

Table 1.1   Review of current practice, after David Clark

Model	Purpose	Community educator's role	Query
1 Dual use	Cost-effective use of plant	Administrator/ manager	No more than commonsense?
2 Community service	Meeting local needs	Multi-purpose provider	Educational rationale?
3 Networking	Sharing/exchange of local educational resources	Network agent	Control and direction?
4 Awareness raising	Analysis of key current issues	Enabler/catalyst	Nature of praxis?
5 Ideological approach	Political education and social action	Advocate/ change agent	Institutional tolerance?

taking sides' is in itself an ideological statement in favour of the status quo (see, for example, Sheppard 1983).

However, it is not clear from this account how and why community education has come to be defined in such different ways. This demands further investigation of the growth and anatomy of community education. The kind of analysis required involves a deliberate commitment to a particular type of study, whatever one's point of view or vested interest in the outcome (Fromm 1973):

> By radicalism I do not refer primarily to a certain set of ideas, but rather to an attitude ... an approach; everything must be doubted, particularly the ideological concepts which are virtually shared by everybody and have consequently assumed the role of the indubitable commonsensical axioms .... This radical questioning is possible only if one does not take anything for granted, and furthermore if one enlarges the scope of one's awareness and penetrates into the unconscious aspects of one's thinking.

The argument presented here is that community education needs to be subjected to this kind of 'radical doubt' in order to explain different patterns in its historical development and contemporary application. In generic in-service work such analysis can start by unpacking some of the personal and professional ideological baggage students bring with them to the group (see Martin 1985b).

Study of the history and the literature of community education reveals distinctive elements in its development, originating in particular social and political circumstances. Furthermore, historical enquiry leads naturally to ideological analysis because it inevitably raises questions of context, purpose and value. It can therefore be used to explore some of the hidden agendas that inform the practice of community education. But this necessarily involves a conscious effort to get under the surface to the implicit ideologies beneath. This may be neither obvious nor easy. Although few would now seriously argue that education can be regarded as a neutral process, we are often expected to act as if it were. Indeed, it may be true that in community education we have been inclined to use this as an excuse for burying our heads in the sands of unreflective, if well-intentioned, activity. It is no coincidence that some of the most cogent critiques of community education focus on its apparent coyness – or is it naivety? – about the values it stands for (see, for example, Merson and Campbell 1975, Lawson 1977).

At present therefore there is still a dearth of value-based or ideological analysis of community education as a generic and inter-disciplinary field. Keith Watson's distinction between what he identifies as 'evolutionary' and 'revolutionary' models in the development of community schooling provides a useful starting point (Watson 1980). It certainly begins to disentangle the web by recognizing the Plowden Report as an important watershed in both educational and social policy. However, it is too narrowly school-based to apply to the wider spectrum of community education as a whole.

In working towards more systematic theories of practice, much can be learnt from the academic literature of applied social studies and community work where value-based analysis is used extensively. We need to be more open and eclectic in our thinking about community education, as well as more tolerant of untidiness and contradiction. It may well be, however, that at the end of the process we join Ralph Ruddock in saying, 'I am still confused ... but my confusion is now on a higher level' (Ruddock 1972, p. 19).

Perhaps the lack of analytical material on community education is partly a consequence of our reluctance to become constructively confused about what we mean by it.

The typology presented below is the product of mutual confusion I have shared and enjoyed with several groups of in-service student collaborators. It was originally developed as a conceptual framework to guide reading, promote inter-disciplinary study and suggest in a tentative way some of the reasons for contested interpretations. It is essentially an attempt to fill what Titmuss calls the 'conceptual value vacuum'. By organizing historically derived material in ideological terms.

A survey of twentieth-century developments appears to reveal three major strands in the evolution of community education in Britain. First, the secondary school-based village/community college movement pioneered by Henry Morris in Cambridgeshire (e.g. see Rée 1973 and 1985); second, the trend towards community primary schooling in some urban areas following the Plowden Report (1967) and experimentation in the Educational Priority Areas (e.g. see Midwinter 1972 and 1975 and Halsey 1972); third, innovative work in adult education and community development undertaken in some of the Home Office sponsored Community Development Projects in the late 1960s and early 1970s (e.g. see for example, Lovett 1975 and 1983). It is suggested that each of these were formative interventions in the historical development of community education and that all of them are still reflected in current practice. For the purpose of analysis they are significant because they imply quite different value assumptions and therefore premises about the relationship between education and community. Along the lines advocated by Erich Fromm above, it is these implicit 'ideological concepts' that are used to construct a value-based analysis.

It should be emphasized that the typology is intended to represent a spectrum of qualitatively different ideologies of community education, not some kind of crude historical or chronological continuum starting from the 'primeval soup of Cambridgeshire' (O'Hagan 1985). In fact, contrary to the received wisdom of the mainstream community education movement, it can be argued that in a strictly historical sense the consensual 'village college' tradition is the relative newcomer. Both the other models can be shown to have deeper, if now somewhat obscure, roots. For example, the 'reformist' and 'radical' models connect respectively with the original university settlements and early youth clubs and with the working-class self-education movement which is strongly associated with the emergence of indigenous, pre-Marxist socialism (see Simon 1974, Johnson 1979). In this respect, the typology as it is presented here can be misconstrued because reference is restricted to twentieth-century developments in what has only quite recently come to be known as 'community education'.

The analysis is eclectic in origin. In particular, however, it owes much to collaboration with students and to Bob Ashcroft's still seminal paper 'The community school as a base for community development' (Ashcroft 1975) and early Community Development Project work on concepts of social change at the local level (CDP 1974) (see Table 1.2).

It must, of course, be emphasized that these models (Table 1.2) are abstractions. Their aim is explanatory and heuristic. Such 'ideal-types' are exploratory rather than definitive, analytical rather than descriptive. Their value is therefore instrumental to the extent that they help to confer critical distance and disentangle the complex and often contradictory nature of reality:

> The purpose of model building is not to admire the architecture of the building, but to help us to see some order in all the disorder and confusion of facts, systems and choices.
>
> (Titmuss 1974, p. 30)

In this account key historical currents in the development of community education are identified and defined ideologically, essentially in terms of the assumed concepts of community they imply. It is this hidden subtext of social and, ultimately, political values which makes each model distinctive and coherent in social and educational terms. The point about the ideas and concepts behind these key interventions is precisely that they were largely unconscious, or certainly not articulate in any explicit way, at the time. Looking back, however, we are able to use the advantage of hindsight to contextualize, differentiate and compare the 'brute facts' of history. But this requires a conscious effort to 'expand the mental grid which decides what will fall into our field of perception' (Smith 1983, p. 44).

Although there has been considerable dilution and cross-fertilization in practice, each model is distinguished by particular and characteristic contexts of community education at the local level in different ways, and combine both to enrich and confuse the national scene. All three models have left their mark on the

Ian Martin

Table 1.2 Models of community education

	Universal model	Reformist model	Radical model
Implicit model of society/community	Consensus	Pluralism	Conflict
Premise	Homogeneity and basic harmony of interests	Heterogeneity and inter-group competition	Class structure, inequality and powerlessness
Strategy	Universal non-selective provisor for all age/social groups	Selective intervention to assist disadvantaged people and deprived areas	Issue-based education, equal opportunities and social action
Initial focus	Secondary school/community college	Primary school/home/neighbourhood	Local working-class action groups
Key influences	Henry Morris	Eric Midwinter, A. H. Halsey	Tom Lovett, Paulo Freire and deschoolers
Twentieth-cent. origins	Cambridgeshire and Leicestershire village/community colleges	Plowden Report (1967) and Educational Priority Areas	Community Development Projects, innovative adult education and community work
Dominant themes	Lifelong learning Integrated provision Openness and access Decompartmentalization Rationalization Co-ordination Voluntarism Neutrality Cooperation	Positive discrimination Decentralization Participation Social relevance Home–school links Preschooling/play Informal adult education Self-help Partnership	Redistribution/equal opportunities Community action power Redefinition of priorities Local control Political education Learning networks Structural analysis Solidarity and collaboration
Organization	Top-down (professional leadership) Formal Programme Institution Reactive		Bottom-up (local leadership) Informal Process Locality Proactive

contemporary movement and claim their adherents among practitioners. The 'universalists' are particularly concerned to sustain and reinterpret Henry Morris's vision of education as a 'cradle to grave' process that is relevant to all aspects of communal life and can be promoted through open-access and integrated local provision. On the other hand, the 'reformist' position, originally associated with the now somewhat discredited rationale of 'compensatory education', continues to reflect the concern of many community educators to discriminate positively on behalf of those who are regarded as socially and educationally 'disadvantaged' in society. However, the negative notion of 'cultural deprivation' built into early versions of compensatory intervention is rejected in favour of a positive definition of the educational potential of home, neighbourhood and local culture. The emphasis is therefore on active educational partnership at the local level, the importance of which is now widely recognized at all levels of this compulsory education system. Finally, the 'radicals' continue to use the relative autonomy enjoyed in some forms of non-traditional adult education and community work to develop with local people political education and social action focused on concrete issues and concerns in the community. Although the idea of education as a means of redistributing power remains an important theme in the thinking of many community educators, in practice this kind of work is vulnerable to its own subversive logic and marginality. Nevertheless, it represents a significant reaffirmation of a venerable and largely autonomous tradition.

In reality, of course, most community education takes place in the blurred areas between the theoretical models. In this sense, they are neither mutually exclusive nor exhaustive. Given their ideological differences, however, cross-fertilization will produce a degree of tension or incompatibility of the kind that is often evident in practice. The applied value of ideological analysis is that it can help to explain this and to clarify the dilemmas of choice which frequently confront practitioners.

In generic in-service work this typology provides a conceptual framework for studying a terrain where there are few clear signposts. We have found it particularly useful in three respects. First, it can be used as an introductory guide to both the history and literature of community education enabling students with very different backgrounds and expectations to locate their own interests. Second, it encourages self-critical thinking about the value assumptions and preconceptions we all bring to the study and practice of community education. In particular, it helps to clarify the relationship between *how* we think and *what* we think. In this

sense the typology is an instrument of *praxis* because it provides a
structure of ideas within which to move from action to reflection
and back. The consequences of this self-examination may be
unpredictable. As one highly politicized and overtly 'radical'
student put it (Martin 1985b, p. 28):

> Inside every hardliner there is a little liberal struggling to get out. I
> found some people, whom I had regarded as my enemies, were
> actually on my side. On the other hand, my prejudices were more
> often confirmed than contradicted.

Third, the typology helps to relate personal views about
community education to the situational variables of work, the
spectrum of practice as a whole and the wider issues of society. In
this way, it may be used to identify areas of tension and conflict as
well as agreement. In the process, we can begin to clarify both
connections and contradictions between the personal, professional,
institutional and political dimensions of practice. It is significant
that although the typology is not intended to be used in a directive
way, it has in some cases provoked or consolidated quite radical
rethinking.

There are, of course, limitations and pitfalls in any such attempt
to make sense of the development of practice in a theoretical way.
Ideological analysis, for instance, can be misinterpreted as
propaganda. It must therefore be stressed that the purpose of the
typology is not prescriptive – even though it does demonstrate that
practice is always political in terms of choices and priorities. Nor
does it pretend to offer blueprints for action. In reality, institutional
expectations and constraints may well predetermine the
community educator's scope. On the other hand, multi-purpose
posts, such as that of school-based 'community tutor', often ...
involve conflicting demands and these need to be clarified
theoretically before they can be confronted practically. Finally, the
historical derivation of the typology may restrict its relevance to
the full range and diversity of current developments in community
education. Part of the educative purpose of such models, however,
is to probe their inadequacies and construct alternatives. If this
analysis provides an initial focus for applying theory to practice, it
is also meant to be a starting point for further thinking. As
indicated below, a group of feminist students has recently used it in
precisely this way.

Generating further thinking

The dynamic and always problematic relationship between education and the changing reality of life in the community should be at the heart of community education. This may help to explain why some local education authorities with no previous commitment to community education are now expressing an active interest in it as a way of developing positive educational responses to the impact of structural change at the local level – and, in the process, attempting to resurrect the lost vision of comprehensive reform (e.g. see Newham 1985, St Helens 1985). At a time when the beleaguered state sector of education is being forced on to the defensive in so many ways, it is significant that community education is seen as offering a way forward into an uncertain future on the basis of a renegotiated partnership between education and community. These new versions of community education deliberately seek to reflect the changing and often grim reality of people's lived experience and to engage purposefully with it. Education must now, for example, be about the social, economic and political implications of new patterns not only of education, work and leisure (including, for the time being, mass unemployment), but also of demography, race relations, family life and gender roles (in both the domestic and public spheres). If community education is to remain relevant to the experience and expectations of people in the community, it is essential that it is continually redefined and reconstructed to reflect the changing reality of their lives. It may therefore be useful to give one example which illustrates how new theoretical perspectives are being generated in an attempt to articulate and examine current trends in practice.

In recent years some feminists have taken an interest in community education because, they argue, women constitute a particular community of interest in terms of their social experience. It is therefore important that feminist community educators should develop their own theories of practice (see, for example, Thompson 1983). The feminist perspective has recently been used by a group of students to extend and at the same time challenge the original typology. The model of community education they have derived from a feminist premise is quite distinctive (Dodd *et al* 1985) (see Table 1.3).

Table 1.3 Radical feminist model of activity

Implicit model of society / community	Radical feminist
Premise	Gender-related inequality Oppression of women
Strategy	Positive discrimination / action Gender role analysis Separate provision Reconstruction of female knowledge and reality
Initial focus	Girls' / women's groups Women's studies Feminist education
Key influences	'Discounted' women in history Mary Wollstonecraft Virginia Woolf Jane Thompson
Twentieth-cent. origins	Suffragette movement World Wars I and II Modern birth control 'Sexual revolution'
Dominant themes	Separatism / collectivism Control / autonomy Nature of oppression Family, education and work Personal politics Nature of learning process Excavation and analysis of women in history Redefinition; female continuity, identity and knowledge

The purpose of this extension of the original typology is to articulate a distinctively feminist understanding of community education reflecting the interests and experience of particular students, and in the process to stimulate discussion and debate about a significant trend in contemporary practice (e.g. separatist experimentation in schooling and youth work, women's studies and health groups, positive discrimination/action in adult education, women's aid, self-help initiatives). The main point here, however, is that although the ideological premises of the master (sic) typology have been rejected, the analytical framework is retained and used to generate a new, theoretical perspective on a specific current development in community education. This helps to ensure a degree of equivalence and thus to facilitate comparison. Presented in this way, the feminist argument may at least be given more serious and systematic consideration than it often receives in general discussion. We all have something to learn from the unique insights and methods that feminists are bringing to the theory and practice of community education.

A group of black students is now working on a similar project. Again, what matters is that they see community education as an opportunity to express a particular view of education and to control the learning process in a way that reflects the distinctive history, experience and aspirations of the black community.

Community education must be responsive to this process of continual extension and reconstruction if it is to remain relevant to change in society and changing definitions of 'community'. Perhaps the acid test of this relevance is the extent to which we regard the development of alternative interpretations as legitimate contributions to the continuing debate about definition.

Conclusion

Life is a swallow, theory a snail.

R. H. Tawney

Too often discussion about the meaning of community education takes place in a theoretical vacuum. The argument presented in this paper is that it can be more firmly located historically and ideologically. The analysis offered here is the product of collaboration with community educators who represent the generic nature of contemporary practice. We have found this approach useful as a way of explaining and thinking through some of the underlying reasons for contested interpretations and differences of emphasis. In this way, it provides a frame of reference for reflexive thinking, dialogue and constructive disagreement.

It is, however, no more than a tentative and provisional statement of some of the apparent connections and contradictions in community education. Its primary purpose is to stimulate discussion and further thinking and to encourage the elaboration of alternative analyses which reflect the continually changing contexts of practice. The ultimate test of the value of such abstract models may be that they enable us to theorize about practice with enough confidence to abandon them and construct alternatives.

References

Ashcroft, R. (1975). 'The school as a base for community development' in Centre for Educational Research and Innovation (CERI), *School and Community*, OECD.

Benington, J. (1974). 'Strategies for change at the local level: some reflections' in Jones D. and Mayo M. *Community Work One*, Routledge & Kegan Paul.

Brookfield, S. (1983). 'Community adult education: a conceptual analysis' in *Adult Education Quarterly*, 33, 3, Adult Education Association of the USA, Washington.

Caudry, A. (1985). 'Community tussles 'twixt tweeds and leathers' in *Times Educational Supplement*, 5 April.

Clark, D. (1985). 'Definitions defined' in Community Education Development Centre, *Network 5*, 1 January.

Community Development Project (CDP) (1974). *Inter-Project Report 1973*, CDP Information and Intelligence Unit.

Crossmar, P. H. S. (1952). *New Fabian Essays*, New Turnstile Press.

Dennis, N. (1968). 'The popularity of the neighbourhood community idea' in Pahl, R.E. (ed.) *Readings in Urban Sociology*, Pergamon.

Dodd, G., Harrison, B., and Martin, I. (1985). 'Community education: a feminist perspective' in *Journal of Community Education 4*, 3 December.

Faure, E. *et al* (1972). *Learning To Be: The World of Education Today and Tomorrow*, UNESCO.

Fletcher, C. (1980). 'The theory of community education and its relation to adult education' in Thompson J. (ed.) *Adult Education for a Change*, Hutchinson.

Fromm, E. (1973). Introduction to Illich I., *Celebration of Awareness*, Penguin.

Halsey, A. H. (ed.) (1972). *Educational Priority*, HMSO.

Hargreaves, D. (1982). *The Challenge for the Comprehensive School*, Routledge & Kegan Paul.

Hargreaves, D. (1985). in Ranson, S. and Tomlinson, J. (eds), *The Government of Education*, George Allen & Unwin.

Jackson, K. (1980). 'Some fallacies in community education and their consequences in working-class areas', in Fletcher, C. and Thompson, N. (eds), *Issues in Community Education*, The Falmer Press.

Jackson, K. and Ashcroft, R. (1972). 'Adult education, deprivation and community development: a critique', paper no 7, Conference on Social Deprivation and Change in Education, University of York.

Jenkins, D. (1985). 'A theology for the liberation of tomorrow's Britain', (report of 1985 Hibbert Lecture, BBC Radio 4) in *Guardian*, 15 April.

Johnson, R. (1979). 'Really useful knowledge': radical education and working-class culture, 1790–1848' in Clarke J. *et al* (eds), *Working-Class Culture: Studies in History and Theory*, Hutchinson.

Kirkwood, C. (1978). 'Adult education and the concept of community', in *Adult Education*, 51.

Lawson, K. (1977). 'Community education: a critical assessment', in *Adult Education*, 50, 1.

Lovett, T. (1975). *Adult Education, Community Development and the Working Class*, Ward Locke.

Lovett, T. *et al* (1983). *Adult Education and Community Action*, Croom Helm.

Martin, I. (1985a). 'Ideology and practice in community education', in CEDC *Network*, 5, 2 February.

Martin, I. (1985b). 'From practice to theory and back: inter-professional in-service provision in higher education', in Sayer, B. (ed.), *Outlines 2*, CEDC.

Merson, M. and Campbell, R. (1975). 'Community education: instruction for inequality' in Golby, M. *et al* (eds), *Curriculum Design*, Croom Helm/Open University.

Midwinter, E. (1972). *Priority Education*, Penguin.

Midwinter, E. (1975). *Education and the Community*, George Allen & Unwin.

Newham Education Committee. (1985). *Going Community: Community Education in Newham*, London Borough of Newham.

O'Hagan, B. (1985). 'The contradictions of universalism' in CEDC, *Network*, 5, 7 July.

Plant, R. (1974). *Community and Ideology: An Essay in Social Philosophy*, Routledge & Kegan Paul.

Rée, H. (1973). *Educator Extraordinary*, Longman.

Rée, H. (1985). *The Henry Morris Collection*, Cambridge University Press.

Ruddock, R. (1972). *Sociological perspectives on Adult Education*, Department of Adult Education, University of Manchester.

Sayer, J. (1985). *What Future for Secondary Schools?*, The Falmer Press.

Scottish Council for Community Education (SCCE). (Undated). *Discussion Paper no. 1* SCCE.

Scottish Education Department (SED). (1977). *Community Education, Occasional Paper no. 6*, HMSO., Edinburgh.

Skrimshire, A. (1981). 'Community schools and the education of the "social individual"' in *Oxford Review of Education 7*.

Sheppard, D. (1983). *Bias to the Poor*, Hodder & Stoughton.

Simon, B. (1974). *The Two Nations: the educational structure, 1780–1870*, Lawrence and Wishart.

Smith, A. (1983). *Passion for the Inner City*, Sheed and Ward.

St Helens Community Education Department. (1985). *Discussion Paper: Community education*, Metropolitan Borough of St Helens.

Stacey, M. (1969). 'The myth of community studies' in *British Journal of Sociology* 20, 2.

Tawney, R. (1921). *The Acquisitive Society*, G. Bell and Sons.

Titmuss, R. (1974). *Social Policy: an Introduction*, George Allen & Unwin.

Thompson, J. (1983). *Learning Liberation: Women's Response to Men's Education* Croom Helm.

Watson, K. (1980). 'The growth of community education in the United Kingdom', in *International Review of Education* XXVI, UNESCO.

Williams, R. (1976). *Key-words*, Fontana.

Wilson, S. (1980). 'School and community' in Fletcher, C. and Thompson, N. (eds), *Issues in Commuity Education*, The Falmer Press.

Wright Mills, C. (1970). *The Sociological Imagination*, Penguin.

CHAPTER 2

The meanings of 'community' in community education

COLIN FLETCHER

Applied community studies conducted by research students provide the case material for this account. Fletcher uses this to reassert the relevance and significance of both the idea of community and the practice of community education. He also shows how different dimensions of local people's experience of life in the community lead to distinctive forms of philosophy and practice. It is important to note that these may involve the community educator in issues of conflict and crisis both within and between the institution/agency and its constituent communities. In this sense, the politics of practice are seldom as cosy or consensual as some community education's advocates, or critics, seem to suggest.

Introduction

I want to define and develop the meanings of 'community' in community education. The reasons for doing so are related to my past and present experiences. To begin with, I arrived in community education in 1976. For the next five years my work was to chronicle and encourage the development of Sutton Centre in Nottinghamshire. This task involved explaining a community education centre to the town of Sutton in Ashfield and vice-versa. There were many studies to report and stories to tell.[1] There were projects about the community shared with students, staff and local people. I learned to do different kinds of community studies.[2]

When the Sutton Centre research contract finished in 1981 I was most fortunate to get a job and became a teacher of post-graduate studies for mature professionals at Cranfield Institute of Technology. In this way I was freed from the container of doing a case-study and could foster all manner of community education researches. I am learning to work alongside teachers, tutors and organizers from the inner cities, from outer suburbs, from market towns and new towns. Almost all of our community education students want to begin with a portrait of 'their own place'. We have developed some techniques together for describing local communities.

Now, with the Sutton Centre experience behind me and with the fresh evidences of more recent endeavours, I want to reply to criticisms of 'community' in community education rather than continue to avoid them.

The first criticism is that 'community' cannot be defined or that there are so many definitions that there is a medley of meaninglessness. Hillery is often quoted. He wrote that he had found 94 different definitions in the literature and that was in 1955![3]

The second criticism is that this is the age of disguising 'dirty work' by giving it a 'community' label – community homes, community police and community relations officers. The software of social control, it is said, has been ingratiating itself with a veneer of politeness. 'Community' labels are like string gloves on steel fists. Images are thus piled on insults. Community educators are 'policing the crisis'[4] even if they are some steps back from the riot shields. Community educators are weaving fine threads: like Lilliputians tying down Gulliver, they immobilize the resistance to gigantic deprivation and exploitation.

The third criticism came from a more passive cynicism. Communities are in eclipse, ran the argument. Thus, the warm rays of community have only been felt since the eclipse has been obvious to all.[5] Major social thinkers from the 1890s onwards have been saying that the bonds are breaking up. The solidarity of 'organic relations' is changing to a calculating materialism. Thus, concluded this criticism, community education is a movement for resuscitating village life – it is a mouth-to-mind resuscitation.

My first response to these colourful charges were simply defensive. Straight away, I thought, 'Yes, I *can* define community!' It is a sense of 'us' combined with a specification of 'place'. Even Hillery had found these two features in some form within 56 of the definitions which he had marshalled. I did not think that such a sense of 'us' had to be warm and cosy feeling. The bonds could be of enmity. Hazlitt had written years ago that all country people hate each other! Secondly, I also thought that community 'labels' have encouraged inter-agency cooperation like a rare chink of common sense through the fortified walls of local authorities' bureaucracies. I have seen clear instances of both pooling resources and of reducing the victimization of problem families. Thirdly, I had also shared in the growth of local responsibility and in community development. I did not think that the 'sunrise industries' of education were sponsoring new interest groups. Communities might be changing but they were a long way from collapsing.

It was this last defensive thought which gave rise to a second and deeper set of responses. I needed to make my assumptions plain. These assumptions were (and still are):

1 Community is defined by one's relationships with people. It is not a finite idea, a yardstick or a Beaufort Scale for measuring the strength of winds which a collection of people can create together. How 'community' changes as a consequence of one's relationship with people becomes an urgent problem.
2 Attaching 'community' as a label to education is not equivalent to hitching up a trailer. It is indicative of the fact that education can innovate and does change. Even now, education is not a totally dominated and determined activity. How community education is innovative becomes a high-priority issue.
3 There are specific visions of 'community' in community education and these can be traced to the moral principles from which they actually derive. We rarely get the chance to trace principles systematically and so can often feel weakened and a long way from where we wish to be. How such moral principles reach into practices becomes the intellectual responsibility of professionals and practitioners alike.

These three assumptions are obviously related. They turn one's attention away from the many examples of good educational practice and towards questions about 'community'. It is proposed here that three kinds of relationships with community – looking at social conditions, sharing people's meanings and learning through social movements – virtually produce three kinds of definition of community, namely a social fabric made up by *either* individual aspirations *or* interest groups *or* residents in stress.

I face a dilemma at this point in shaping my argument. On the one hand I feel I should explain the details of these definitions more fully before giving some examples. On the other hand I want to show how working with community educators who were researching their communities made me realize that their day-today relationships with local people were actually giving rise to their definitions of community. It is significant that these practitioners were as unhappy with 'pure' definitions as they were without them! They did not begin with a neat argument about what community meant and proceed at an orderly pace with their analysis. No, they struggled with the meaning and the immediate fieldwork difficulties at the same time.

So rather than present the definitions and then give their details I have chosen to take each type in turn as it can be found in recent practitioners' researches. I open with questions which community educators ask and then show how one practitioner has set about these questions using their own words as much as possible. I am working towards the summary given in Table 2.1 on page 45. The point is that the meanings of 'community' refer to determinations *and* difficulties. The question is how they do so.

Type A: Looking at social conditions

Imagine: A primary school teacher watching parents collecting their children and thinking, 'How old are these people? Where do they work?'

Or: A secondary school teacher thinking about a student who can barely keep awake and wondering: 'How cramped and crowded are the homes in this neighbourhood?'

Or: An adult educator reading the local newspaper and seeing drama and music societies advertising their preformances and AGMs; and asking: 'What leisure groups meet hereabouts?'

How do they find out what they want to know?

To get some answers they might cooperate with those who already have answers to hand: the administrators, planners and auditors who regularly collect data on the economy, the demography and on voluntary organizations.

Work statistics they can get from a rates department. Every shop, factory, office and farm returns a form stating their full-time and part-time male and female employment. Planning departments have boxes of print-outs on the replies to the ten-yearly census. The main census gives ages, numbers of people in households, and the breakdown into private ownership and rented property. The

10 per cent household census goes into much, much more. Area education officers have tables on all their secondary and primary schools. There's an Aladdin's cave for those who would slowly amass a fortune of findings, who would build up a picture of more than guesswork and gossip.

Social conditions data come in tables, graphs and charts. The shape of community is a profile or a lot of profiles. There are shocks for those who survey thoroughly – 27 per cent of the national profile are adult couples without children. That is more than the 19 per cent who are adult couples with children. They find the number of elderly over 80 nearly as big as the number over 65 just twenty years ago.

Shirley Jones' fieldwork[6] included a close look at the three neighbourhoods of a Nottingham City secondary school's catchment area. She wrote:

> Census material was analysed as fully as possible to give both the present situation and the extent of change, which the area, within its separate parts and as a whole, has undergone in the last fifteen years.

Having discussed the figures she summarizes each area in words. Manvers, St Anne's Area, has the following key elements:

- Over the ten-year period the population has decreased by over a third.
- The majority of the population is in the 25–64 age group.
- There are fewer 'under fives'.
- There is an increase in the number of elderly people by over a third and there are more older women than older men.
- Household size is relatively small.
- The number of single persons, pensioner and one-parent family households in increasing.
- The majority of housing is rented from the council and the housing amenities are good.
- There is an increase in unemployment particularly among men.
- Thre is an increase in the number of women looking for work and in the percentage of women working.
- In the course of their work few are in a managerial or supervisory capacity or self-employed.
- There is a small percentage of car ownership.

Asking profile questions and looking for these kinds of answers takes community educators into surveying for themselves. In a survey of voluntary organizations questions can be asked about fees, membership strength, meeting places and times, and further needs for space or resources. Secretaries are accustomed to receiving letters and usually reply. Some write, 'Sadly we have been in decline since the Second World War'. Others will proclaim proudly: 'We have grown to 180 model engineers in a five-mile radius'.

Surveying projects can extend to samples, knocking on doors and telephone interviews. But these are costly and so rarely undertaken. In addition to costs, looking at social conditions to describe 'community' also has the difficulty of keeping up to date with all the changes. Nevertheless, this type of approach does have the strengths of being scientific. Shirley Jones expressed her purpose as:

> to create a deeper understanding of the area in terms of its social fabric, past and present, and to develop an insight into future development and growth and questions of priority and popular need. To try to connect the problems, priorities and possibilities highlighted not in terms of counting heads but in such a way as to enable to assess the building not the bricks.

Type B: Sharing people's meanings

Imagine   An adult educator asking herself: 'What am I doing for the elderly, or the physically handicapped?'

Or   A school teacher considering how Shakespeare's 'Seven Ages of Man' are recognizable in the surrounding villages and could feature in the curriculum?

Or   A community education worker thinking about supporting the long-term unemployed.

How do they inform themselves about the people they wish to know more intimately?

To get their answers they cooperate with those who already have a complementary piece of the jig-saw: the professionals in health, welfare and law enforcement. All these professionals go in and out of people's homes, drive around their streets; connecting, counselling, cautioning and collecting. They have files on people as well as deep impressions. They have casework knowledge.

The community educator is asking two kinds of questions. Firstly: 'If I begin with common deprivation or deficiencies what is the nature of that priority group? What are their needs?' Secondly: 'Are there any existing networks which I can plug into and help in a way in which I am qualified to do?'

In order to share both priorities and patterns of existing care the worker becomes a participant as well as an observer. The process of attending meetings, volunteering and establishing trusted friendships are all tributaries along which 'intelligence' flows. Some persons are identified as 'key informants' because they have a wealth of connections and they have a similar interest in understanding the whole picture.

Eamonn Cahill, Deputy Head (Community) at Stantonbury Campus, Milton Keynes, has been particularly concerned with disability.[7] He wrote:

> Milton Keynes is a city that attracts many disabled from all over Britain. The shopping precinct is built on one level, completely covered with wide access 'to all shops'.

> The rate of employment in this group is low and with more disabled people being relocated in Milton Keynes, their frustration in relation to unemployment is growing.

> Mary Older is remarkable. She is spastic and deaf. Her speech is badly distorted and her upper body is in a state of continuous involuntary motion. She is confined to a wheelchair … Mary has spent her 35 years of life striving for independence.

Mary Older was one of the study's 'key informants'. Her typed reply to Eamonn Cahill's question about classes included the following:

> As far as Stantonbury reaching out for education for the handicapped goes as to whether we integrate, or have a private class, it depends on the individual. I mean, some people would benefit from studying in a large group whereas others would not. I, personally, when it comes to studying for an exam would prefer to be in a private class or small group because of my hearing problem, whereas, if it was a general class on art and craft, then it would not matter so much. Other disabled people without hearing problems, would be able to integrate into a large class. If the class is large or small, it does not have to be primarily all disabled people in that class, it can, and must, if possible, be a mixed group of disabled and able-bodied people. Not only does integration help the able-bodied person come out of himself and get used to the disabled person, but it helps the disabled person become less disabled minded, and forget about being disabled.

> Yours sincerely

> Mary Older
> Typed by toes

In time, having learned from fellow professionals and key informants, the ideas of priority groups and networks become inseparable. The substance of the community is seen as being its characters and its self-help friendships.

On the minus side there can be struggles of conscience over knowledge of law-breaking behaviour. There are some shocks, too, from meeting the opposition of local worthies. Say a group of glue-sniffing skinheads is taken on a trip to the seaside. It will not be long before there are mutterings about 'wasting public money'. Or if a group of severely handicapped are integrated into a drama class, it will not be long before there are comments about 'them being better on their own together than with able-bodied people'.

The difficulties of sharing people's meanings are personal, professional and political. It is demanding intellectually and emotionally. There is the 'image armour' of the educator to lay aside. And there is the 'politics with a small "p"' of that loaded question, 'Why are you bothering with *these* people?'

Eamonn Cahill concluded his study by making links between adult education, adult networks and priorities:

> Adult education participants have established networks in which they interact. They are also the participants of many other service agencies. To what extent adult education has influenced these networks is not known but it is often the first 'port of call' for people moving to the area.
>
> The high involvement of adult education students in the many clubs, societies and activities on the campus site could indicate that enrolling unknown in an adult education system was just a form of introducing oneself to an informal interest group network. The short stay experienced by most adult education students since the formal provision and the very large growth in informal groups would tend to confirm this. If adult education has played a part in the successful development of the professional communities by helping to establish informal networks based on interest groups, could the way forward be to decentralize and informalize the way these introductions to these interest groups are made? It is time to acknowledge the facilitating role of the adult educator as opposed to that of provider?

Type C: Learning through social movements

Imagine   An adult educator asking how can any course or event hold anything for the poor?

Or   A secondary school teacher determining not to reinforce
            the contemporary relations between the social classes.
Or   A primary teacher wanting to combat racism.

How do they connect with the forces which they want to confront?

To get their approach they cooperate with local people for whom
such matters are already an issue and who are organizing for
change.

One image for the nature of local issues is that of 'techtonics'.
The issues are like layers in the earth's crust, pressing up through
each other and grating against each other. Racism and sexism are
such layers as are the alienations of wage slaves and the workless.
Here, though, there are tensions within tensions.[8]

Take anti-sexism as a social movement. Just as there are
'traditional family values'. So the community is understood to be
structured by its conflict rather than its contents or its culture.
Within the community there are struggles for justice and for
preventing justice from even being an item on the public agenda.

Mary Stacey's study of parental involvement in primary schools[9]
notes:

> Tizard (1981) has suggested that community values may be
> completely at odds with the school's; it may be difficult or even
> impossible for schools to come to terms with the community values.
> Milward (1983) sees community education as tending towards
> 'notions of communal good life' and a consensus view. Where
> schools find themselves challenging such issues as sexism, she
> suggests, they may find themselves challenging the 'keystone of
> community' – the family.

Where social stratification and social class are recognized as an
issue, struggles are piled high. For the nouveau riche there is the
struggle to stay on the winning side; they sense that the 'elite' is
contracting and the 'mass' outside can expect more hardships.
There is fear, if not terror, in the eyes of the nouveau riche – their
obsession with attainments drives other values out. Even so, for
educationalists, the nouveau rich can also look like the arrival of the
cavalry at the long-besieged fort.

Mary Stacey describes the experience of city primary schools as
follows:

> The divisions amongst parents and how to deal with these,
> concerned many teachers, in some cases deterred them from initiating
> or making explicit new ideas or policies. In the London schools,

there were often at least twenty different ethnic groups with varied cultural and educational backgrounds. Teachers talked about the cliques that could arise, the dominance of certain groups and the difficulty of getting a real cross-section of parents to take part in school activities. In several schools, the type of parents and children coming in had changed considerably in the last few years. As inner city areas were becoming more popular with middle-class people, so more of them were using the schools. For some teachers, these parents were threatening or, it was felt, over-anxious and pressurizing. Some head teachers, however, saw them as a new force in the neighbourhood who would take political action and get things done for the school.

Stacey also gives some telling examples of the stresses which can come from resourcing groups in conflict:

In one school, the community teacher was running a group for women who had relatives in prison or had had bad experiences with the police. The head teacher was worried that this group with its particular needs was not integrated into the school, that they would not accept newcomers and did not want the community policemen to visit the school. In another school, black parents asked to set up a group specifically for them; in another, a group for single parents was set up. The head teachers in both schools had to accept a considerable amount of criticism from other parents who felt excluded.

Similarly, combatting the evil of racism has given rise to explicit tensions in anti-racism. Stacey's study of primary schools discusses how anti-racism can antagonize whites and blacks alike. She writes:

One of the greatest concerns, was the racism which manifested itself amongst parents and staff and how to challenge this. Some heads said they were criticized for doing everything for non-whites, although in reality, in most schools, it was the white groups who were dominating the parents groups and management committees. Most schools had anti-racist policies, some of which were printed in the school booklet. But some teachers feared that they would alienate parents if they challenged racism or taken-for-granted assumptions too overtly.

Against this white backlash is the intense black dislike of eyewash – a possibility which educators themselves ruefully recognize:

[One] ... head teacher emphasized the way 'celebrations' could be meaningless. He has expressed this view ironically in writing:

'There are enormous spin-offs from this hierarchical form of culturalism. The minority parents turn out to provide food, costumes, artefacts, etc. and appear to be eternally grateful. At the end of all such events staff and parents say "namaste" to each other, and the school reverts to its celebration of white, male, middle-class experience. The parents return to their own experience.'[10]

Anti-racism, of course, includes employing people with ethnic origins. Thus conflicts can occur over employment, as Stacey observed:

> In several schools I visited, Asian women were employed as ancillary teachers to help interpret and to work with class teachers. Several of them had teaching qualifications from their country of origin which were not recognized over here; however, there were those who would have been willing to do some more training over here if appropriate courses had been available. It did seem in certain schools that there was a danger of getting a two-tier system of white 'qualified' teachers and other ancillary teachers.

It can seem that the school's anti-racist policy is also a refusal to take ethnic minorities' aspirations seriously.[11]

The welling up of ancillaries' feelings here was a crisis of racism in miniature. The observation that there are real crises in and for the community leads to the second major component of learning through social movements. The closure of a major factory, the demolition of whole streets and estates and the construction of new shopping centres are all critical moments, critical events for all those who live in an area. There are times when a power struggle between business interests gets far more attention than the struggle between those interests and people's wants, needs and aspirations. Such events are rarely, if ever, 'spontaneous' and they are the hottest political topics for educators to include in the learning to which they give guidance.

Working with organized local people reveals grating layers of conflict and a seething lava beneath.[12] These are the confusions and unanticipated consequences of action. As the worker pushes on with projects it is more likely that such projects have local people in their 'star roles'. Taking a back seat and avoiding the limelight demands considerable self-discipline. To add to the difficulties of the shared meanings there are the inner conflicts of failed, half-baked, initiatives and the outer danger of becoming an exposed activist on the edge of victimization or atually embroiled in it.

The themes reviewed

There are, then, three faces or forms of 'community' which come from one's actions as a community educator. The Type A relationship with community is looking at social conditions with a dispassionate scientific eye. The Type B relationship is sharing people's meanings with individuality and with sympathy. The Type C relationship is learning through social movements as a politically committed activist (see Table 2.1). Each relationship has its 'facts' about 'community' and each personal preference is strongly affected by the opportunities and obstacles to the development of community education pursued by the educator.

Can all three relationships exist together in any community education initiatives at any one time? For whilst a community educator's strongest feelings may be as a scientist, a realist or an activist they may not be felt to be exclusive personal ideologies.

Two quotations from principals of community education centres could help to show the bringing together of types which can occur in people's thinking.

First:

> The problems of society today can only be solved when society has become a community. Community occurs when a common predicament is shared. Sharing requires sympathetic understanding which in turn is the beginning of wisdom or the desired end of education. [13]

This position could be read as a combination of A and C types of perspective. Compare, then:

> Community implies a group of people sharing together despite many individual differences in a common major purpose. [14]

This position could be read as a combination of A and C types of perspective. But can types of relationship really be combined to produce working definitions in this way? For example, Type A's demographic profiles may be used to mark off priority groups. Indeed the census's categories could be adopted directly so that the 'old' are 65 years old or older. Similarly it may be thought that developing black or women's groups *is* combatting sexism or racism.

But deeper down these elisions do not work. Age cohorts are not social groups. Planners' perceptions and people's self-conceptions rarely, if ever, match. The elderly, in fact, are those who feel old, frail and vulnerable. Racist issues are not within black groups, they are related to the 'criminalization' of whole neighbourhoods and *all* young black people; to the cattle-prod treatment of 'sus' laws and

Table 2.1 A summary of relationships with community in community education

Relationship of:	Type A: Looking at social conditions	Type B: Sharing people's meanings	Type C: Learning through social movements
A focus on:	Profiles	Priority groups	Pressures
Expressed through:	• Economic activity • Population statistics • Housing • Voluntary organizational life	• Deprivation • Deficiencies • Networks of mutual care	• Sexism • Racism • Class relations • Poverty • Economic and physical crises
By co-operation with:	Administrators	Professional colleagues	Local, organized people
In methods of:	Surveying	Participant observation	Participatory action
And the difficulties of:	• Costs • Changes over time	• Tokenism • Politics with a small 'p'	• 'Causing' antagonisms to be expressed • 'Inviting' reactions from the powerful
Through the personal ideology of:	Being scientific	Being realistic	Being political
On the moral basis of:	Equality	Civility	Justice

later regulations; and to the conflict of attitudes implied in seeing a riot as a breakdown of a community rather than as an uprising of a community learning to trust each other in open struggle.

The types of relationships which define community are not merely different, they are in opposition to each other as conflicting sectional interests within professions and community alike. Each relationship – be it with profiles, priority groups or political pressures; whether it is developed through cooperation with administrators, professional colleagues or local leaders – looks towards innovation in community education.

The Type A community relationship offers the prospect of a comprehensive service. Its facts and figures lead to arguments about access for all.

The Type B community relationship orchestrates the provision of a quality service. It makes claims for priority people to have fresh opportunities for personal growth.

The Type C community relationship organizes the potency of a critical service. It pushes for a commitment to oppositions held in common by residents in struggle.

There are, too, the foundations of community education's models – moral bases for them becoming more widely professed and practised. Such moral bases argue yet more strongly that the types of relationship are firmly different and separate.

The moral bases of community education's meanings of 'community'

By 'moral base' is meant principles which are publicly avowed and affirmed. The three approaches to community have already been expressed in moral terms. Now is the moment to do so more explicitly. All three types of relationships share a common opposition to centralization, be it of political control over communities or administrative control over local opportunities for learning. So, too, I feel, they share a common opposition to chauvinism whether it be male or military. These are the oppositions to wastefulness and to being dispossessed, disenfranchised and even destroyed.

The principles themselves are those of equality, civility and justice. The Type A approach and its ideology of a comprehensive service with equal access rests upon a broader belief in equality.

The principle is of equality of access and an equality or resources throughout life and for all walks of life. The dry statistics are an argument, in skeletal form, for lifelong learning.

In accordance with this principle there should be an evenness and virtual uniformity in the distribution of resources. Such 'fair shares' depend upon the availability of more statistics. Staffing, buildings and spaces, equipment and capital need to be counted and the 'drift' towards the "better-off" reversed. Equality applied to profiles of classes, sexes, ages and races opposes the inequalities of ownership. There is an inverse law of educational resources that is exposed by two sets of statistics: the first column shows the wealth and property from the most to the least; the first column shows the wealth and property from the most to the least; the second column shows the proportion of the public purse for education which they receive. The Type A relationship is a commitment to institutional justice and to distributional justice. Without doubt it is no easy or straightforward matter to up-end the inverse law which has achieved inevitability in public education.

The Type B approach and its ideology of a quality service derive from the principles of a sensitivity to culture being the hallmark of a civilization. The 'breakthroughs' for individuals and groups are an acceleration of 'progress' in this respect. Civility is grounded in respect for persons and for their rights as autonomous individuals. This respect is expressed in appropriate treatment and concern, the key to which is the recognition that people are different. People's rights lie in having their own culture and in having contact with the best or highest cultural achievements. The Type B relationship is a commitment to protected projects with special people – a moral principle often expressed as positive discrimination.

The Type C approach and its ideology of a critical service derives from principles of breaking bonds together, releasing learning and, through action and reflection, taking more responsibility for our own lives. In the words of Myles Horton it is 'organizing as learning'. In the dream of Martin Luther King it is to be 'free at last'.

Each phrase holds a summary of the relationship and varies its emphasis upon causes, events or effects. Breaking bonds depends upon the oppression. The politics of personal predicament and social movements have to be understood. There are fears and falsehoods to get rid of. But there are repressed truths to be recognized as well, learning which can be let out, said and shared. And action does not come along later; learning is in action and through action as well as about action. Justice demands a power struggle and the courage necessary to transform the society for which one has an equal responsibility. Under oppression it is moral to resist and to rebel. The Type C relationship goes from individual to educational principles; it is a commitment to the oppressed and conditioned by our learning in action against oppression.

Such then are the visions of community education, its dreams and its determinations. These are the visions which make community education a uniquely but not uniformly moral education in which, for the time being, there will be three faces, forms and futures for 'community'.

Notes

1 See Colin Fletcher. (1983) 'The challenges of community education: a biography of Sutton Centre 1970–1981', Department of Adult Education, University of Nottingham.

2 There was a development towards participatory research here. The first stage was to contrast background characteristics with the revelations of dramatic upheavals (Colin Fletcher (1977) 'Context maps and critical incidents', SCUTREA Conference Papers, University of Hull).

　　The second stage was to involve adult students in researching their own situation (Colin Fletcher (1980), 'Community studies as practical adult education', *Adult Education*, vol. 53, no. 2, pp. 73–8)

3 Hillery, G. A. Jnr. (1955). 'Definitions of community: areas of agreement', *Rural Sociology*, vol. 20, pp. 110–121. See Colin Bell and Howard Newby (1971), *Community studies*, Unwin, especially pp. 27–9.

4 Stuart Hall, Chas Cricher, Tony Jefferson, John Clarke, Brian Roberts. (1978). *Policing the Crisis*, Macmillan.

5 Maurice Stein. (1964). *The Eclipse of Community*, Harper & Row.

6 Shirley Jones. (1985). 'The role of the community teacher', unpublished MPhil thesis, Department of Social Policy, Cranfield Institute of Technology.

7 Eamonn Cahill. (1984). 'Adult participation and needs: an appraisal of issues in a new city', unpublished MSc thesis, Department of Social Policy, Cranfield Institute of Technology.

8 Fein puts this relativity in the following way:

　　Against the image of the study cohesiveness and grass roots democracy of the small town we must juxtapose the image of the oppressive censorial, anti-libertarian small town. Both sets of terms describe the same phenomenon. The choice depends largely on the perspective of the beholder rather than the character of the phenomenon.

In Fein, L. (1977). 'Community control and political theory' in Ragatt, P. and Evans, M. (eds), *The Political Context*, Ward Lock/Open University Press.

9   Mary Stacey. (1985). 'Parent/teacher partnership: from rhetoric to reality (A study of parental involvement in primary schools)', unpublished MPhil thesis, Department of Social Policy, Cranfield Institute of Technology.

10   Mike Mulvaney. (1984). 'The impact of an anti-racist policy in the school community' in Martin Straker-Welds (ed.), *Education for a Multi-Cultural Society*, pp. 27–33, Bell and Hyman.

11   I asked Kawa what he meant by self-development. His reply was:

> Thirty years of freedom have not freed our village from false values, rivalries and imported goods at the expense of village crafts. Many have become unemployed because this new system has created literate but uneducated people; because an educated man not only knows how to read and write, but is also disciplined and hardworking.
>
> If we are to rebuild our villages we have to begin at the beginning where we have to depend on ourselves.

Ariyaratne, A. T. (1985). 'Are you happy? I asked the farmer', *Convergence*, vol. 18, nos 1–22, 63–6. From the chapter 'Sharing of labour' in A. T. Ariyaratne, *Collected Works Volume*, edited by Nandasena Ratnapala, 1979, Sarvodaya Research Institute.

12   All these points, and the full force of the principle can be found in the task setting at Ulster People's College, Belfast.

13   Philip Toogood. (1980). 'Tomorrow's community education institution' in Colin Fletcher and Neil Thompson (eds), *Issues in Community Education*, Falmer, pp. 155–164.

14   Ron Mitson. (1980). 'Resources for learning in community education' in Colin Fletcher and Neil Thompson (eds), *Issues in Community Education*, Falmer, pp. 101–114.

Aspects of work by Shirley Jones, Eamonn Cahill and Mary Stacey can be found in their articles for the *Journal of Community Education*, vol. 5, no. 1, 1986.

I wish to thank the members of the Advanced Diploma in Community Education courses at Homerton College and CEDC as well as the Clwyd Branch of the CEA for the opportunity to discuss and develop this paper.

CHAPTER 3

The concept of community education

DAVID CLARK*

'Community' is a notoriously disputed and nebulous concept. It has even been suggested that the conditions of modern urban living render it either an anachronistic irrelevance or a convenient diversion from more fundamental and divisive issues. For Clark, however, community education is fundamentally about education for community. By this he means a distinctive and essentially moral quality of relatedness which transcends the familiar conflict in education between competition and cooperation. It is important therefore for community educators to redefine the idea of community in a way which provides a philosophy and a core rationale for their practice.

Community: a keyword?

When those who have been deeply involved in the field of community studies for many years come to the conclusion that their best-loved concept is all but useless, there is need to take note.

Doubts about the term 'community' seem first to have arisen from Hillery's discovery of 94 different definitions of the word, less than a quarter of which produced anything like a common formula, and at least 16 of which contained mutually exclusive elements (Hillery 1955). In more recent times, Pahl has argued that 'the word "community" serves more to confuse than illuminate the situation in Britain today' (Pahl 1970, p. 107).

Yet the concept of community is still very much with us. Indeed

* This paper was originally published in *The Journal of Community Education*, vol. 2., nos. 3 and 4.

Williams includes it as one of the 'keywords' (Williams 1976, pp. 65–6) in his examination of the social vocabulary of English people today. As he states in another context, the complexity as well as importance of the concept derive not from the word itself but from the meanings projected onto it over the years (Williams 1976, p. 81).

Thus, though the term may present us with many difficulties, its constant appearance and the emotive energy it generates mean that it cannot be ignored. A useful way forward, as Williams suggests, is to set the development of the concept in a historical context and to move on from there to discover some form of operational definition relevant to our concerns today.

Ferdinand Tönnies

The concept of community really came into its own in the nineteenth century. Its rise to prominence was due to 'the sense of immediacy or locality' which it came to represent 'in the context of larger and more complex industrial societies' (Williams 1976 p. 65).

This was particularly so in Germany where there was a powerful reaction by leading social theorists of the day to industrialization and urbanization which brought with them a division of labour threatening social fragmentation, to increasing bureaucratization and the impotence of the individual, and to a fear that secularization was fast undermining an ethical order still based on the influence of the Church in everyday life. 'The contrast, between the more direct more total and therefore more significant relationships of *community* and the more formal, more abstract and more instrumental relationships of *state*, or of *society* in its modern sense, was influentially formalized by Tönnies ...' (Williams 1976, p. 66).

In this complex book Tönnies singled out two forms of human will which he believed to be the basic ingredients of one or other ideal type of wider corporate relationships – natural will (typical of Gemeinschaft) and rational will (typical of Gesellschaft).

Plant summarizes Tönnies' two types as follows:

> In Gemeinschaft, human relationships are intimate, face to face and not discrete and segmented – they are with the whole man, not with a man under a particular description or acting from within a particular role .... Each person knows the others in the round. Because a community shares its values there can be no fundamental moral conflicts, roles and relationships cohere and cannot conflict. The community is stable in that physical mobility between one place and

another is not of any importance within this kind of society and there is very little or no mobility in terms of status. The ethic is very much of the 'my station and its duties' type.

On the other hand Gesellschaft relationships are characteristic of large-scale modern societies and institutions. The dominant image of relationship here is that of contract and not habit or customary observance. The authority of such a society is not traditional, indeed it is based upon the opposite – the legal, rational notions of consent, volition and contract, a view which implies a radically individualistic account of the genesis and authority of the legal order.

(Plant 1974, pp. 23–4)

Tönnies' ideal types have become the foundations on which a great deal of thinking about the concept of community is still based – though often Gemeinschaft and Gesellschaft are explained by other terms such as 'primary group' or 'secondary group'. It is, therefore, important to examine the limitations of Tönnies' analysis and to suggest ways forward which might minimize these.

The problem with Tönnies' approach is two-fold. On the one hand, he appears to reify his types turning them into actual realities rather than clusters of possible attributes. For example, Tönnies states; 'The study of the house (home) is the study of the Gemeinschaft as the study of the organic cell is the study of life itself' (Tönnies 1955, p. 60), and, 'The city is typical of Gesellschaft in general' (Tönnies 1955, p. 266). Tönnies' analysis thus implies that society is facing the eclipse of community. For example, he states 'The entire culture has been transformed into a civilization of state and Gesellschaft, and this transformation means the doom of culture itself if none of the scattered seeds remain alive and again bring forth the essence and idea of Gemeinschaft, thus secretly fostering a new culture amidst the decaying one.' (Tönnies 1955, p. 270).

Tönnies' concretization of his types, and the inference, (at times assertion) that 'real' community can only exist within Gemeinschaft has unfortunately left us with a concept very hard to utilize positively and creatively in a world very different from even nineteenth-century Germany. For it is clear that whatever else has happened to community it has neither 'decayed' nor been 'eclipsed'. Community could never be destroyed or civilization itself would collapse. Half a century ago MacIver in his major work on community accepted this when he wrote, 'Life is essentially and always communal life. Every living thing is born into community and owes its life to community'. (MacIver 1924, p. 209).

The concept of community, therefore, must be so defined and operationalized that it is of use in the urbanized, technological and highly mobile society of today. The term has to be meaningful within the life of the metropolis as well as that of the village.

Tönnies' analysis highlights one particular issue which is of great importance in relation to the pedigree of the word 'community'. The latter has for many years been a concept exposed to what Plant describes as the ambiguities of 'fact and value' (1974, p. 8ff). This does not mean that a definition in purely descriptive terms is impossible; it does mean that it is difficult, and, as I argue later, not necessarily helpful. To rob the concept of community of its evaluative and more dynamic meaning would severely restrict its usefulness. However, what matters above all is that in using the term we are as clear as possible about where fact gives way, and where value comes to the fore. Tönnies' problem, and that of many later students of community, was that description and evaluation were so interwoven that Stacey, after many years working in the field, was compelled to talk of 'the myth of community studies' (Stacey 1969).

Current approaches to the concept of community

The investigation of community has had five main points of entry, all of which have encountered the difficulties which Tönnies and his followers faced. The focus of attention has been on:
1 Participants
2 Territory
3 Social activities
4 Social relationships
5 Feelings

All these entry points and emphases are important. Where one comes to the fore, the remainder will inevitably need to be considered. Nonetheless, the question remains as to which of the five indices is *the* key to understanding what community is all about.

1 Community as a human collective
Certain of the earliest definitions of community refer to 'the common people' or 'the people of a district' (Williams 1976, p. 65).

The emphasis was on a group of people sharing a corporate life. This category presumed to embrace all ages, sexes and (often) social classes who are identifiable as a 'total group' through their daily encounters over many years.

This is a frequent starting point for the study of community. Despite its limitations there is about this perspective the sense of totality and inclusiveness which has made the concept attractive to many today. Nevertheless, to talk of community simply as a human collective remains so ill-defined as to be virtually meaningless unless other perspectives are immediately added to it. It fails to deal with the fact that the word 'community' is often used of groups which are not all-embracing in membership, do not necessarily share all things in common, and do not last for a lifetime.

2 Community as territory

Over the last two centuries community has regularly been taken as synonymous with a particular kind of place (notably the rural village).

More recently, the same idea has been transferred to the urban scene where the so-called 'neighbourhood unit', conceived by Clarence Perry in the late 1920s, was optimistically believed to open the way to 'villaging the city'. In post-war Britain certain investigations of close-knit inner city areas, such as Bethnal Green in East London and Barton Hill in Bristol, were regarded as classic community studies.

The main difficulty in using place as the starting point for a definition of community is, however, that nobody has a very clear idea of what that place should now be. Williams, for example, in his study of Gosforth, has a chapter on 'Community' which obviously pitches the concept at the level of the village (Williams 1956) whilst Willmott calls his survey of Dagenham (with a population of 90,000) *The Evolution of a Commuity* (Willmott 1963). And the confusion has continued. To take community as synonymous with some territorial unit per se now raises great problems as to which unit should be chosen and what makes it a community anyway.

3 Community as shared activities

A number of community studies over recent years have sought to approach the concept by way of activities which people share. This has resulted in some famous investigations, such as the Lynds' first Middletown enquiry in the 1920s (Lynd and Lynd 1929). These

enquiries have often been long on detailed description but short on
analysis; community has been assumed rather than discerned and
qualitatively assessed.

More recently Frankenberg has attempted to be more selective
by concentrating on 'dramatic occurrences' (special events,
ceremonials or customs;) (Frankenberg 1966a) which are supposed
to reveal a great deal about community life. But this approach is in
danger of going to the other extreme and placing too much
emphasis on the 'dramatic' as against the ordinary activities of a
group. Furthermore, one is left wondering just who decides which
'dramatic events' are communally of most consequence.

4 Community as close-knit relationships
A fourth entry point for the investigation of community has been
through the study of social relationships, especially of a close-knit
or 'primary' type. It is often assumed that groups wherein a strong
kinship network exists, or wherein the extended family holds pride
of place, are par excellence 'communities'. Once again, however,
we are left asking which patterns of relationships are to be regarded
as most communal – extended family ties can become unbearable
for certain of their members. Is it only as the traditional/rural end of
the continuum that communal relations can genuinely exist?

5 Community as sentiment;
The only way to minimize the problem just described is to attempt
to begin where people begin. And more often than not this starting
point is within the arena of feelings – in the 'gut' rather than in the
head. Simpson sums up this emphasis as follows:

> It should now be obvious that community is no circumscribed
> sphere of social life, but rather the very life-blood of social life.
> Community is not simply economic, nor simply political, nor
> simply territorial, nor simply visceral. Nor is it all these special
> elements added together. Ultimately, it is a complex of conditioned
> emotions which the individual feels towards the surrounding world
> and his fellows ... It is to human beings and their feelings,
> sentiments, reactions, that all look for the fundamental roots of
> community.'   (Simpson 1937, pp. 97, 71)

The advantage of this point of entry is that, whatever steps need to
be taken later to operationalize the concept, it gives community the
emotive dynamic it deserves and grounds it in the experience of the
actors. Descriptively and evaluatively this is a far better starting
point than an approach which simply assumes, on the basis of the

researcher's own predispositions, what the form and content of community should be.

Feeling, or the term preferred here 'sentiment', is a global concept. Its communal components need to be distinguished. The communal sentiment which has received almost universal acclaim is that of we-feeling, defined by MacIver and Page as 'the feeling that leads men to identify themselves with others so that when they say 'we' there is no thought of distinction and when they say 'ours' there is no thought of division' (MacIver and Page 1961, p. 293). We shall call this sentiment 'a sense of solidarity'. It is this association with a sense of solidarity which has made community, in Williams' view, such 'a warmly persuasive word' and one which 'unlike all other terms of social organization (state, nation, society, etc.) seems never to be used unfavourably (Williams 1976, p. 66).

Yet a sense of solidarity is insufficient in itself to do justice to the concept of community. Indeed, only the extreme determinist would claim that the movement of society towards the Gesellschaft end of the continuum has occurred simply through the inexorable march of the impersonal forces of history. What has given impetus to Gesellschaft, amongst other factors, has been the demand that the potential and rights of the individual, slowly emerging from the rigid status system of feudal society, be recognized. Thus the concept of community, to be meaningful in our time, must embrace not only we-feeling but what MacIver and Page term role-feeling too. The latter we call here 'a sense of significance'.

This sense of significance is defined by MacIver and Page as 'the sense of place or station' experienced by group members 'so that each person feels he has a role to play, his own function to fulfil in the reciprocal exchanges of the social scene' (MacIver and Page 1961, p. 293).

To adopt this approach, not only offers us a concept open and flexible enough to apply both to past and present, rural and urban societies, it enables us to get to the heart of a vital matter concerning the nature and expression of community in human affairs – the relations of the individual to the group and vice versa. The central issue is well put by Plant as follows: 'Is there some way of understanding community which will enable the freedom of the individual and the cooperation and fraternity of the community [we would use the word 'group' here] to be meaningfully held together?' (Plant 1974, p. 32). It is an issue of prime importance for the future of our 'global village'. As such any concept of community which does not take it on board is severely weakened.

COMMUNITY AS FACT AND VALUE

The approach to the concept of community via feelings requires the actors to assess the sense of solidarity and significance they feel in relation to any grouping of which they are members.

Such an entry point into the discussion of community has important advantages. It stresses present rather than past reality, which means that the researcher and educator can deal with communal concerns as they are now, rather than always having to take their bearings from some golden age long since past (though this is not to presume that the sense of community experienced by the actors themselves will not be influenced by their own upbringing and socialization).

Another major advantage of this starting point is that it can assess not only the presence but the strength of community. Such assessment may not be measurable to a precise degree but participants within any human group can usually say quite clearly whether they experience a weak, moderate or strong sense of solidarity or significance, and the overall response of members of any given collective can thus give a good indication of the extent to which the latter is communally meaningful (Clark 1969). Our definition of the concept of community based on this approach is thus as follows:

> The strength of community within any given group is determined by the degree to which its members experience both a sense of solidarity and a sense of significance within it.
>
> Clark, August 1973, p. 409

People's own sense of community is an important and sobering starting point for sociologist and educator alike. But to leave the concept of community there would still be of limited usefulness. For community is not the possession of any one group; it is the warp and woof of all societies within which many groups contend for scarce resources from the standpoint of differing ideologies. Thus once the role of the researcher gives way to that of active participant or intervenor, not least the role of educator, description proves inadequate and values enter the field. For 'community' can be strong without being 'healthy'. The members of factions, sects, gangs, criminal elites; all these no doubt experience a powerful sense of solidarity and significance, but have frequently threatened the very basis of social life itself. Thus, though the degree of community sentiment can help to tell us where groups *are*, it cannot indicate where they *should be*, in order that other collectives besides their own can experience the strongest possible sense of community consistent with the well-being of the whole.

The educator has to attempt to place community in an ethical context. What matters is not his doing this but his realization that the move from (the sociological) fact to (the ethical) value is being made. He thus needs to recognize and to state openly his personal ethical position and not just presume his own evaluative definition of commuity to be fact.

COMMUNITY AS VALUE: THE QUALITATIVE APPROACH

Community as value means adopting a view of solidarity which fosters the health of society, literally 'as a whole', and does not allow the intensity of feeling within certain groups to threaten the life and welfare of others. If solidarity is to be not only a sustaining and creative sentiment for particular collectives, but for society and the world beyond, then community as value must have a good deal to do with the nature of social boundaries.

A term is required to indicate that the quality of solidarity sought is that which is based on an acceptance of man's common humanity. Thus although a sense of solidarity is necessary to give the group a sense of cohesion and unity, in the context of community as value, it has to be a sentiment which is as open to and inclusive of the needs of others as possible. The word we choose to represent this qualitative dimension of solidarity is 'ecumenicity'.

'Ecumenicity' is frequently used of the modern movement towards the recovery of unity by different Christian denonimations. However, we are employing the word in its wider and original secular context to indicate a solidarity whose boundaries relate to the communal requirements of society and mankind as a whole. Ecumenicity appreciates the necessity of fostering a sense of solidarity within particular groups, regions or the nation itself but realizes that this must be a solidarity which enables people to feel themselves part of, and not hostile towards, wider society.

To work for such an open-ended sense of solidarity is a formidable undertaking simply because the sense of community which gives many groups security and confidence is that which can so easily turn inwards as a force for fanatic self-protection or the destruction of others. As Simpson put it in the troubled years of the 1920s:

> The problem is that of communalizing those who conflict. That is a large problem. It is the problem of carrying over the ideals of the primary or face-to-face group which is the most easily communalized, to the larger groups, and ultimately to nations and international action.
>
> (Simpson 1937, p. 39)

As with community descriptively defined, so with community as value; ecumenicity must be complemented by its equivalent in relation to the component of significance. The wholeness of society must be complemented by the wholeness of the individual.

Many words have been used to give an evaluative dimension to a sense of significance: dignity, individuation (as Jung), independence, etc. A term is required which validates the person yet does so in relation to the significance of others. The word we choose to represent this qualitative aspect of community is 'autonomy'.

Considerable debate has taken place in recent years concerning the concept of autonomy, linked especially to a discussion of the morally mature individual. Our main reference point, is the work of Wright who defines his most morally mature individual as possessing an 'altruistic-autonomous character' (Wright 1971, pp. 222). Such a person is autonomous in the sense that 'he chooses the rules he lives by, and feels free to modify them with increased experience' (Wright 1971, p. 222). This state is what the theologian Tillich terms 'the courage to be oneself' (Tillich 1962, pp. 114–151).

At the same time the attitude and behaviour of such an individual are 'Altruistic', that is 'dictated by the desire to help another person' (Wright 1971, p. 127). This is not to say that the motivation of the altruistic autonomous character is selfless; indeed it could be argued that a powerful component in all forms of altruism is 'enlightened self-interest'. But it is to affirm that his response to life consistently takes in to serious consideration the welfare of others. When we use the term 'autonomy' we shall be doing so in this context.

We can now redefine the concept of community, as fact *and* value, in the following way:

The strength of community within any collective is demonstrated by the degree to which its members relate and act in an ecumenical and autonomous manner.

Unless we state otherwise it is to this understanding of the concept which we shall be referring when using the term 'community' in future, and when speaking of the qualitative approach to its expression.

Community education as curriculum development

Community is by definition an educational endeavour. It has many affinities with the interventionary basis of social work and even more directly with community work. Indeed the boundaries have become increasingly blurred over recent years causing not only theoretical but professional confusion. Nonetheless, it is important to maintain the distinction between the social work orientation of what Klein calls 'responding to need' (Klein 1973, p. 9) with the emphasis on an immediate response to some crisis situation, and the educational aim of 'working for autonomy' (Klein 1973, p. 9) (we would add 'and ecumenicity'), the latter concern being with a long-term process of personal and social growth in relation to both individual and group.

Because community education is an educational undertaking, education for community must be concerned amongst other things with 'curriculum development', though the nature of that curriculum and how it is developed will need further consideration. For curriculum lies at the heart of education and unless its purpose, content and methodology are clearly thought through and agreed, chaos rather than community can be the result.

Curriculum development is no less value-free than community. Indeed the past two decades have seen in this country an increasing tempo in the vigorous debate about the hidden agenda of curriculum development (Bantock 1980; Galton 1980; Lawn and Barton 1981). Our own concern, however, is to find a theoretical approach to curriculum development which achieves the best 'fit' with our definition of community, and to make this explicit.

In this context we would opt for what Reid calls 'the deliberative approach to the study of the curriculum' (Lawn and Barton 1981, pp. 160–182). The deliberative approach sets aside both mechanistic views of curriculum development and 'grand theory', in favour of an ongoing exchange of experience and views between all those involved in specific educational situations. Deliberative theory 'allows for particularity, is under the control of people and regards them as acting in morally committed ways' (Lawn and Barton 1981, p. 174). It 'is evolutionary in its social philosophy and pragmatic in its conception of how knowledge should relate to policy and action' (Lawn and Barton 1981, p. 168).

A deliberative approach to curriculum development is thus optimistic in orientation. To the charge of naivety, Reid replies: 'How can it be good for people to act on theories that take a pessimistic view of human nature?' (Lawn and Barton 1981, p. 178). Though it must be added that others have argued that pessimism is at least as realistic a starting point as optimism.

Be this as it may, the value of Reid's approach for us is that it affirms both the value of the individual and the importance of the group in the context of their own definition of the situation. It is thus true to the qualitative aspect of community as we have defined it. At the same time it offers an open-ended model of curriculum development which accords with our understanding of community education as dynamic developmental process, the full potential of which cannot be pre-determined. This is not to ignore the more particular aims of objectives of community education. It is to make them available for critical review by all participants and to set them in an empirically realistic framework.

THE PRIMARY AIM OF COMMUNITY EDUCATION

Aims and objectives in curriculum development have not always had a good press. (The term 'aim' is used here to refer to ultimate and long-term, and the term 'objective' to particular and shorter-term, levels of purpose.) Lawton states that they can be simplistic on the one hand, or downright confusing on the other (Lawton 1973, pp. 13–16). But given a greater awareness of the wider social and ideological context in which aims and objectives must be set, and an appreciation that they should be constantly seen as provisional and open to debate, they still seem essential, as Hirst and Whitfield argue (Galton 1980, pp. 9–19, 21–32), for any intervention of an educational kind.

Consistency requires that the primary aim of community education has to accord with our earlier qualitative definition of community. It is, therefore, of great importance not to slip back into an approach to the concept of community which creates more problems than it solves. The main aim of community education is

not to erect a certain kind of social centre to organize a wide range
of activities and events. These entry points for intervention *may* be
involved but they are not in themselves the key concern of
community education. The main aim of community education is
not even the creation of a strong sense of solidarity and
significance, though this is the next most important concern after
the primary one.

The primary aim of community education is to enable the
members of any collective to become increasingly ecumenical and
autonomous. This is not a dual aim. As with the quest for solidarity
and significance, the search for greater ecumenicity and autonomy
is a total process enabling individual and society to become more
fully human. There is an inevitable tension already indicated
between those who put the emphasis on the member per se and
those who put it on the group, in all spheres of life not least in
education. As Lawn and Barton state, 'A vital concern for
curriculum studies, particularly in the contemporary context, is the
dynamic relationship between individual and collective.' (Lawn
and Barton 1981, p. 14) But just as community itself is seen as
essentially and qualitatively holistic, so is community education.
Though the latter may need to be approached from different
perspectives and via different techniques, ecumenicity and
autonomy are complementary aspects of a process converging on
the maturity of individual, group and eventually society itself.

OBJECTIVES

1 The validation of experience
One of the objectives of the community educator working for
ecumenicity and autonomy is to help those concerned validate the
experience of others and be able to empathize with them. It is also
to enable people to validate their personal experience and to have
insight into their own feelings, creative and destructive.

Wilson, in his seminal work on moral education, developed a
number of 'moral components' (Wilson, Williams and Sugarman
1967, pp. 192–5) which have since met a good deal of criticism for
their high level of abstraction. Yet Wilson's components of PHIL
and EMP relate closely to this first objective of community
education. 'PHIL refers to the degree to which one can identify
with other people, in the sense of being such that other people's
feelings and interests actually count or weigh with one, or are

accepted as of equal validity to one's own', whilst 'EMP refers to awareness or insight into one's own and other people's feelings; i.e., the ability to know what those feelings are and describe them correctly. A distinction might be drawn between self-awareness (AUTEMP) and awareness of others (ALLEMP).' (Wilson, Williams and Sugarman 1967, pp. 192–3). The validation of experience, therefore, would seem to be closely associated with so-called 'consciousness raising' in relation to the individual's awareness and appreciation of his own and others' interests and feelings.

2 Greater knowledge and experience of community in theory and practice
A second and related objective of community education is increasing knowledge and promoting experience which open windows to new dimensions of community itself. Such knowledge will mean being informed about other people's ideas and views, i.e. community as value. But it will also relate to actual collectives and their practical demonstration of community life, i.e. community as fact.

The art of community education is to provide those involved with 'a rich and varied experience of the interhuman' (Wright 1971, p. 24) in a way which can widen horizons and increase openness to new opportunities. This means as deep an understanding as possible of community making as a developmental process, both personally and socially. Thus if there are, as Kay believes, stages of communal maturity through which societies themselves move (taboo, legal, reciprocal, social and autonomous) (Kay 1970, p. 73ff), then awareness of these should be a matter of concern for the community educator. The task involves constantly searching for and providing practical examples of ecumenicity and autonomy which enable the learner to grow in understanding and appreciation of what community is all about.

Such understanding and appreciation, however, come more as a result of first-hand experience than second-hand report. As Davies and Gibson say of social education with relation to young people, so it is with community education for all:

> Social education cannot go on in detachment as an intellectual exercise. It demands young people's *involvement* in the relevant situations and interrelationships, it demands that they know first-hand and feel personally how common interests and shared activities bring and keep people together and what causes them to drift apart.
> (Davies and Gibson 1967, p. 13)

An understanding of possibilities, both realities and hopes, must also encompass an appreciation of the means of change and its consequences. The search for communal maturity is not a smooth or irreversible process, as references to 'growth' and 'development' might imply. It is about competition and conflict and many actual setbacks. The community educator, therefore, has to be alert to ideologies and theories of change, and their practical outworkings in relation to ecumenicity and autonomy. Community education must therefore embrace many aspects of political as well as social education.

3 Model building

A third objective of community education is model building; constructing mental pictures of how things might hold together, in this case of collectives demonstrating qualities of ecumenicity and autonomy. One value of such model building is the opportunity to rearrange bits of real life in a way that indicates new communal possibilities beyond those immediately in evidence. This objective requires the ability of the learner to define and utilize key concepts such as solidarity and significance, ecumenicity and autonomy.

4 Application

A fourth objective is enabling the student to apply his validation of self and others, his new knowledge and experience, and his models, in a way which can in practice reshape social reality in the direction of a greater degree of communal maturity. This objective necessitates facilitating not only the formulation of principles and guidelines on which to act, exploring resources and constraints, but making decisions and trying them out in the real world of people. It will require evaluation in relation to the action taken and an ability to make fresh decisions and reshape practice in the light of hard experience.

THE ROLE OF THE COMMUNITY EDUCATOR

1 The authority issue

Education for the community educator is of necessity an open-ended process. It is more appropriate to see community education as drawing on a range of educational approaches which can coexist within the aim of enriching community life. Indeed if communal maturity is a developmental process, different educational approaches will be necessary at different stages of the journey.

Hull discriminates between certain aspects of what he calls 'general education' (Hull 1975, pp. 53–75). 'Training recognizes the authority of the mechanical necessity which makes a sequence of operations invariable'. It is the necessary manipulations and reproductions of these sequences which have to be taught and learnt. 'Instruction' is about imparting 'a body of knowledge received or on authority', the intention being that students 'master the content' and 'cover the syllabus'. 'Nurture' is about supporting and befriending the student; it 'guards, protects and guides in the traditionally accepted way'.

Hull contrasts training, instruction and nurture with a further category of general education which he terms 'specific education'. The latter is especially concerned with teaching basic *principles* which can lead to the acquisition of knowledge and understanding in the widest sense. It is to do with the rationality of facts, 'with their relevance to the emerging personhood of the pupil, and with their intrinsic authority'.

The only form of socialization which Hull rules out of court is 'indoctrination' which deliberately avoids pupil assent and the criticizing of its own content. 'The indoctrinator deliberately deprives or seeks to deprive people of part of their humanity, reconstructing their self-hood along the lines prescribed solely by the indoctrinator.' Indoctrination is, however, an aspect of socialization which community educators frequently encounter in one guise or another and against which they need to be constantly on guard.

Hull's specific education, with its many affinities to the community education process, is very much related to the issue of power and authority. The community educator in particular has to understand and handle power and authority correctly if he is to succeed in his task. Figure 3.1 adapted from Kolb, Rubin and McIntyre, may help to illustrate the main issue involved (1971, p. 240).

Figure 3.1   The locus of authority in teacher/student relations

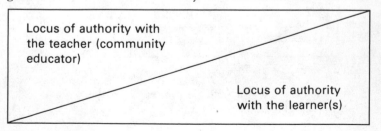

The community educator seeks to move the locus of authority in the learning encounter along the continuum from A towards B. How and when this is done depends on what stage of 'readiness' the learner has reached. But the gradual movement towards students taking greater responsibility for their own learning is of crucial importance. Other modes of general education (training, instruction, nurture) may not demand this.

Meighan and Roberts (1979, pp. 53–67) describe this approach to the learning encounter as 'autonomous study' and usefully distinguish a range of theories associated with different aspects of learning (for example, a theory of knowledge, of teaching, of resources, of assessment and so on). They thus begin to demonstrate how moving responsibility for learning from teacher to student may be worked out in practice.

Shifting the locus of authority relates not only to the relationship of community education and pupil but to the meaning of community education for the social system as a whole. Figure 3.2 indicates how, ideally, this relationship needs to be operative within every learning environment.

Figure 3.2   The locus of authority for community education in the social system

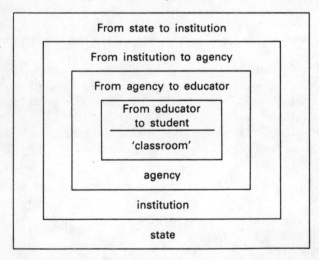

The community educator must work for the autonomy of the student, the agency for the autonomy of the educator, the institution for the autonomy of the agency, the state for the

autonomy of the institution. And because, for that to happen, there must also be a deep commitment to the development of ecumenicity, the two complementary processes should work together for the creation of a richer quality of community life throughout society as a whole.

2 Commitment and neutrality

One further aspect of the role of the community educator relates to the question of values. It is the issue of what Hulmes, in connection with religious education, calls 'commitment and neutrality' (Hulmes 1979). A view has emerged in recent years that professionalism, not least in education, demands 'neutrality'. The assertion is the more dangerous not because it is obviously wrong, but because it is misleading.

The truth is, Hulmes writes, 'that all teachers, whatever their starting point may be, have a commitment for which to account' (Hulmes 1979, p. 9). To assume one is, or worse still pretend to be, 'neutral' is even more deceptive, as our hidden agenda of personal values will then eventually emerge as manipulation. What should be realized, is that the teacher's commitment is a resource just because the aims and objectives of community education provide little inherent impetus unless powered by the conviction that ecumenicity and autonomy are vital for the building of a more human society and world. If community is value as well as fact, community education cannot be true to itself unless the educator is personally committed to promoting ecumenicity and autonomy. Without this commitment he can communicate little about the fundamental components of community education either in theory or practice. It is furthermore, an asset and not a liability if the commuity educator's values embrace both hope and reality. For s/he is engaged in perhaps the most demanding and difficult educational process of all. As Mannheim once put it, 'The complete elimination of reality-transcending elements from our world would lead us to a "matter-of-factness" which ultimately would mean the decay of the human will'. (Mannheim 1936, p. 236)

If there is some element of 'neutrality' involved, it lies in the community educator's validation of the experience of others and his openness to their expanding his own awareness as well as he developing theirs. Such openness in no way compromises commitment. Indeed, as Hulmes remarks, 'Far from being set in opposition to commitment, openness allows for its fullest expression' (Hulmes 1979, p. 29). It permits the community educator to make his commitment explicit, legitimately to relate it to his own developing experience of community. It is this stance that Reid takes in relation to his approach to curriculum development, mentioned earlier as especially relevant to community education, and which prevents educators falling into the trap of 'relativism' on the one hand or 'monism' on the other (Lawn and Barton 1981, pp. 179–180).

In this context the role of the community educator is to enable his learners to move towards more informed commitment for themselves. As Lawton states, 'Education is not concerned with changing behaviour ... but with making a change in behaviour a possibility.' (Lawton 1973, p. 74) The community educator by focusing on the nature and importance of informed commitment helps turn possibilities into realities.

References

Bantock, G. H. (1980). *Dilemmas of the Curriculum*. Robertson, Oxford.

Clark, D. B. (1969). *Community and a Suburban Village*. University of Sheffield, (unpublished Ph.D thesis), Sheffield.

Clark, D. B. (1973). 'The concept of community; a re-examination', *Sociological Review,* vol. 21. no. 3. pp. 397–416, August.

Davies, B. D. and Gibson A. (1967). *The Social Education of the Adolescent*. University of London, London.

Frankenberg, R. (1966a). 'British community studies: problems of synthesis', pp. 123–154, in Banton, M. (ed.), *The Social Anthropology of Complex Societies*. Tavistock, London.

Galton, M. (ed.). (1980). *Curriculum Change: the Lessons of a Decade*. Leicester University Press, Leicester.

Hillery, G. (1955). 'Definitions of community: areas of agreement', *Rural Sociology* vol. 20, no. 2. pp. 111–123, June.

Hull, J. (1975). *School Worship: an Obituary*. SCM Press, London.

Hulmes, E. (1979). *Commitment and Neutrality in Religious Education*. Geoffrey Chapman, London.

Kay, W. (1970). *Moral Development*. revised edition, Allen & Unwin, London.

Klein, J. (1973). *Training for the New Helping Professions: Community and Youth Work*. Goldsmiths' College, University of London, London.

Kolb, D. A., Rubin, I. M., and McIntyre, J. M. (1971). *Organizational Psychology: an Experimental Approach*, Prentice-Hall, New Jersey.

Lawn, M., and Barton, L. (eds). (1981). *Rethinking Curriculum Studies*, Croom Helm.

Lawton, D. (1973). *Social Change, Educational Theory and Curriculum Planning*. Hodder & Stoughton, London.

Lynd, R. S. and Lynd, H. M. (1929). *Middletown*. Constable, London.

MacIver, R. M. (1924). *Community*. Macmillan, London.

MacIver, R. M. and Page, C. H. (1961). *Society*. Macmillan, London.

Mannheim, K. (1936). *Ideology and Utopia*. Routledge & Kegan Paul, London.

Meighan, R and Roberts, M. (1979). 'Autonomous study and educational ideologies: a review of some theoretical and practical issues with special reference to the Schools Council General Studies Project', *Journal of Curriculum Studies*, vol. 11, no. 1. pp. 53–67, January–March.

Pahl, R. E. (1970). *Patterns of Urban Life*. Longman, London.

Plant, R. (1974). *Community and Ideology*. Routledge & Kegan Paul, London.

Simpson, G. (1937). *Conflict and Community*. Liberal Press, New York.

Stacey, M. (1969). 'The myth of community studies', *British Journal of Sociology*, vol. 20, no. 2, pp. 134–147.

Tillich, P. (1962). *The Courage to Be*. Fontana, London.

Tönnies, F. (1955). *Community and Association,* translated and supplemented by Loomis, C. P., Routledge & Kegan Paul, London.

Williams, R. (1976). *Keywords*. Fontana, Croom Helm, London.

Williams, T. M. (1956). *Gosforth*. Routledge & Kegan Paul, London.

Willmott, P. (1963). *The Evolution of a Community*. Routledge & Kegan Paul, London.

Wilson, J., Williams, N. and Sugarman, B. (eds.). (1967). *Introduction to Moral Education*. Penguin, Harmondsworth.

Wright, D. (1971). *The Psychology of Moral Behaviour*. Penguin, Harmondsworth.

CHAPTER 4

Community education in Britain: some myths and their consequences

BOB O'HAGAN

In this iconoclastic review O'Hagan challenges the 'myth of neutrality' which he perceives to be at the heart of the conventional wisdom of much community education literature. In contrast to this, he emphasizes that his account is firmly grounded in the dilemmas of choice and conflicts of value which arise in practice. In order to understand and resolve these, however, it is first necessary to develop more systematic theoretical analysis. This can be used to identify the implicit value premises that both inform and constrain practice. O'Hagan suggests how this can be done by exposing and demystifying some of the key dominant assumptions embedded in contemporary community education.

Received wisdom within community education derives from a set of assumptions which have remained largely uncontested until relatively recently.[1] There is no orthodox 'general theory' of community education, but the claims and the assumptions contain a number of oft-repeated falsehoods and half-truths which this article sets out to question.

In the main, the promulgation of these claims and assumptions can be understood in two ways. Firstly, they have been written as clarion-calls to policy-makers, intended as general arguments in favour of 'going community'. It may not, therefore, be fair to criticize any one of them in analytical detail, since they may be said to overstate their case in the same way as any other polemic may be expected to do. Secondly, they have been written almost exclusively by non-practitioners and non-recipients of community education, by which I mean those whose *main* task is not engagement in community education. I include here administrators and head teachers who, however much they may claim that their main functions cannot be separated from community education, undoubtedly have a different perspective, on the whole, from that of those whom I call practitioners. If the orthodox assumptions come from non-practitioners, they may similarly fail to take into account the detail of relationships and activity within community education encountered by the practitioner or the recipient.

The reason why it is important to question these assumptions is not for the sake of theoretical exactitude, but because, taken as a whole, they are associated with, if not constituents of, a particular ideology – reformist in nature – which has been dominant within community education during the 1970s and early 1980s. Yet as assumptions laying claim to universality, they conceal their ideological base.

According to this reformist ideology, the purpose of community education is to re-establish cohesion within a disintegrating society. It is frankly aimed at minimizing interpersonal conflict by social engineering which will bring people together and change their negative attitudes.

The community, rather than the institutions of society, must adjust, albeit through the deployment of additional resources. Above all, community education should address itself to social, rather than industrial, economic or political issues. Education is essentially a social tool. If the assumptions identified below are congruent with this ideology, their unchallenged persistence will reinforce this reformist ideology at the expense of alternative ideologies, whether conservative or radical.

New improved education with blue whitener

The first assumption is that community education stands in contrast to 'normal', 'traditional' or 'old-fashioned' educational practice or philosophy. It is even described as being 'radical' in its nature.[2] While its form may indeed be different from previous practices, for example the emphasis on an integrated delivery to a wider, all-age consumer group, the structure of education remains unchanged. Thus, orthodoxy stresses the importance of involving the whole community in education, but any sort of involvement is seen as valuable – the issues of what the nature of the involvement is (curriculum etc.), on whose terms (pedagogy) and for what purposes (ideology and control) are not explicitly recognized as contentious questions. By moving the debate from structure to form in this way, and by divorcing community education from 'normal' or 'traditional' education, the orthodox assumption takes the issue of ideology off the agenda.

In fact, community education is not, in itself, radical, except in the most limited meaning of the word. The debate within 'normal' or 'traditional' education has long recognized ideology as central. Throughout the first half of the nineteenth century, radical socialists struggled with both liberal reformists and conservatives concerning the structure of a popular or mass education.[3] This struggle has continued in Britain after the 1870 Education Act and throughout the twentieth century up to the present day.[4] Indeed, community education has been informed both in its theory and its practice by similar ideological differences.[5] The structural differences between alternative educational ideologies are at least as important as the particular form the education takes, and to hide the similarities between mainstream education and community education serves to cut the latter off from the roots which feed its development. Any attempt to take ideology off the agenda in fact serves to promote the one which is dominant at the time – a reformist ideology in the case of community education.

Community education becomes comprehensible when it is located firmly within the overall struggle for popular or state education, reflecting the same conflicts and collaborations and suffering similar assaults and setbacks. From this perspective, many of the researchers concerning broad educational matters can be applied to community education to yield useful results.

Rallying round the flag

The second, and related assumption is that community education is a 'broad church', that while it displays a bewildering diversity of practices, all are unified around an agreed general approach. Since there is general agreement concerning its aims and objectives, attention can be focused on the variety of case studies, not as individual specimens to be dissected and analysed, but as examples of 'good practice' to be copied more or less wholesale. In recent years, this has become most notable with the establishment of the Community Education Development Centre in Coventry, a central aim of which is the dissemination of good practice.

With the assumption that study should be directed towards good practice rather than analytical examination or theoretical construction, we are encouraged to spend so long looking at the spokes that it may come as a surprise to realize that they are not all joined to the same hub. The fact is that there is no unity concerning the approach; nor, more seriously, concerning its fundamental purpose. In consequence, examples of practice may conflict in their real purposes, since they may derive from differing ideological foundations. And since the ideological sources may not be clarified, the practical examples may even suffer from internal contradictions. Just as before, the assumption that community education is a broad church with a common aim but diverse practices, actually reinforces the dominant ideology of the moment, since it discourages critical examination of purposes.

But if the failure to identify and clarify different ideological sources leads to conflict and contradiction in practice, how has this come about? Why is there not more coherence within community education in Britain? Community education, and particularly community schools, have been relatively successful in policy terms as opposed to theoretical terms. That is, well over half of the local education authorities have invested resources to varying degrees in one form of community education or another since the Second World War. One reason for this is that it has rarely become a party political issue. This is because proposals for practical social policy need not be founded on highly articulated theory. Furthermore, community education and particularly community schools can be formulated practically as either conservative, liberal or radical proposals and thus a particular policy proposal may be supported by different political parties for entirely different reasons, because the theoretical implications are not clearly articulated.

Most frequently, in order to be implemented as policy, community education initiatives have had to be capable of gaining support from different parties. This has required a certain amount of ideological fudging in order to achieve a policy coalition. And it is precisely because community education policies have depended on coalitions of this kind that once the fragile policy is actually implemented, the practitioners find themselves unable to maintain them, since the ideological contradictions become exposed in the transfer from written proposals to practical application. Hence,

community education initiatives are often riven by key
contradiction which find expression in practical conflicts either for
the practitioners or the recipients.

The community education carnival

The third assumption is that community education is largely a
matter of painless fun, concerned with 'healing' and 'unifying',
with 'bringing people together in a common purpose'. But people
don't all have a common purpose any more than a common
interest. Communities, just like societies, are riven by
contradictions, contrasts and conflicts, and these do not stem
merely from a lack of understanding. Their causes are more
complex and more deep-seated, and suggestion that social conflicts
are in essence no more than individual or cultural differences,
ignores crucial issues of power and resources, and their unequal
distribution in society.

In the actual practice of community education then, it is not
possible to simply unify and heal the differences between sections
of the community or of society. For community education, no
matter what the actual practice, cannot promote the interests of
those with little or no access to power – political, economic or
educational resources – without harming the interests of those who
currently monopolize them.

As long ago as 1975, Stuart Maclure exposed this myth, though
it seems to have been overlooked since:[6]

> Radical community school developments are by definition, open-
> ended and unpredictable and produce situations of considerable
> strain for most of the people who become engaged in them.
>   There is plenty of evidence from the United States to show just
> how explosive and painful may be the consequences which follow
> determined efforts to transfer power and initiatives from the
> professionals to the laymen – especially if this also means, from
> white to black and from rich to poor.

In the long term of course, practitioners may be concerned with
unifying society by eradicating the sources of social divisions, but
most practitioners find themselves engaged almost day by day in
practical struggles of some kind, and they find it anything but a
painless activity.

If accepted, the orthodox emphasis on harmony and unity can

create feelings of guilt among practitioners, for failing to heal the differences between individuals and groups.

In contrast, many practitioners find themselves constantly having to fight for what they believe in, and this means that they must take sides, create alliances or join federations of individuals and groups working towards similar ends. These make them stronger in their common struggles, and in practice are more useful than the constant and unattainable pursuit of harmony and unity.

'Come on down!'

The call for 'participatory structures' or 'partnership in management' is a proposal that has emerged as a response to a particular set of historical circumstances.

The theme of participation offers the promise of reducing the destructive impact of rapid social change. There is little doubt that the 1960s and 1970s witnessed very rapid technological change with its uncomfortable social concomitants. Industrial re-structuring led to unemployment combined with rapid inflation, as well as large-scale re-housing, educational re-organization, fashion-led cultural change and so on. Understandably, there were increasing signs of social discontent such as public demonstrations and worsening police–public relations.

Participation was appealing. In the first place, taking advice from the public would reduce the danger of unnecessary harmful changes. Secondly, by involving the potential leaders of the movement of discontent, greater understanding of the reasons and need for change might be disseminated, helping people to cope better with its effects. Participation was mainly concerned with improving the two-way communication between administrators and public.

But systems of participation beg more questions than they answer. The absence of participatory structures does not, as is routinely assumed, rule out the possibility of community education. The conservative, liberal and radical perspective of community education can all operate without management systems in which local people can and do participate, although each model is orientated towards a fundamentally different type of participatory structure from the others.

A system of 'consultation' suits a conservative approach – an advisory group with whom the professionals must consult.

A pluralist system of 'partnership' can be applied to the liberal, reformist approach, with control vested in a governing body composed of professionals and non-professionals in strict proportion.

A system of 'community control' is more appropriate for the radical approach, in which the professionals form an advisory group to the controlling body of non-professionals.

While the concept of participation can easily be applied to each perspective in turn, it is *not* an essential characteristic of any of them. The fact is that community education may be practised from any one of these three perspectives by professionals who allow little or no formal community participation. The issue is considered relevant, but the essential question is: which forms of participation assist community education and which ones hinder it? Those who insist that 'real' community education is impossible without participatory structures are dictating a very different set of priorities for the student or practitioner and in the process devaluing a great deal of important work carried out by practitioners.

The current orthodoxy[7] discounts consultatory systems in favour of partnership structures for the management of community education, again promoting the 'reformist' or 'enrichment' ideology. But by recasting the debate as between 'more participation' and 'less participation', attention is again diverted from examination of the ideological base of the type of participation proposed.

Unchained melodies

The sixth assumption is that participants in community education are the masters of their own actions. Such a celebration of the power of the individual is, of course, paradoxical within a concept of community. While there is no agreement about ideology or ends – no common hub for the spokes of community education – the wheels of which they are parts are nevertheless there, as are the roads and the cycle frames. Community education is not entirely unpredictable, and certainly not haphazard.

Once we know the scale and nature of the resources available in human, material and cash terms, the nature of the base (primary school, college, community centre, detached etc.) and the surrounding environment and an idea of the problems locally, we will have a good idea of the sorts of community education activities or practices that are likely to emerge – or at least, we can be fairly sure what sorts of activities will *not* develop successfully. Midwinter and Lovett were unlikely to establish a substantial sports and leisure programme among the primary schools and pubs of Liverpool 8 for example. Neither were Cambridgeshire's commuter-belt colleges likely to develop radical Freirean projects aimed at awakening class consciousness.

The myth of individual practitioners as masters of their own – and the local community's – destiny, is a dangerous one. Its consequence is that setbacks and failures are taken to be the fault of the practitioner. Because the individual is to be held to account, the poor practitioner may well in turn blame other individuals – the powerless may be described as 'apathetic' and the dispossessed as 'greedy'.

Particular patterns of community education provision do have a structure which it is possible to analyse, and which make success and failure more comprehensible. This structure I have described elsewhere,[8] but it is too large a task to repeat here. Suffice it to say that the structure affects the balance of forces in determining the actual pattern of provision which emerges, and that understanding the structural forces at work enables the practitioner to work more effectively within the constraints.

Yet a belief in the powers of the individual (or a team of practitioners) is an important element of the reformist ideology, since to recognize the constraints of the social structure would lead to the questioning of the potential for reform without tackling the issues of unequal distribution of economic and political resources.

The machine in the ghost

Paradoxically, a common assumption, among educational administrators at least, effectively contradicts the last one. According to this, the practitioner is a mere functionary. Community centres and schools are stages and backdrops created by those at the top of the hierarchy, and all the practitioners merely players. As a practitioner in community schools, I have been only too aware of the self-deception characteristic of headteachers and chief education officers, for example, who fail to see, (or pretend not to see) the way that their policies are reinterpreted or resisted by the practitioners. Skrimshire provides a rare example of such a recognition among writers on the subject:[9]

> On the one hand there is a need for clear thinking about what is meant by a community school in any particular instance, what its objectives are, how far they are compatible with each other and with the existing structure. On the other, there is the need for flexibility in the field, for gradual evolution of new approaches to schooling which takes account of contemporaneous changes in its wider society The practitioners almost unconsciously keep redefining the concepts, to resolve the tensions inherent in their initial form. It is they in the end who know best, intuitively if not explicitly, what is the nature of community schooling when realized in practice, and what it can hope to achieve.

Community education as it is actually practised does not exist in the tidy accounts by heads and administrators, but in the actual social relationships of people in the thick of it. Moreover, while practitioners are not saints, neither are they neutral. Nor can they be, for the prosaic practice of community education reflects real political relationships in the community and the society as well as in the educational establishment. The practitioner is an active agent within those political relationships, whether s/he likes it or not.

This assumption of the practitioner as functionary, if accepted, acts as a restraint on the practitioner, and therefore promotes the ideology of the policy-maker or administrator. As we have seen, this is frequently far from clear-cut, since successful policy introduction may well require a degree of ideological fudging for a political coalition. Nevertheless, the broadly dominant ideology is a reformist one, and this particular assumption is likely to act as a deterrent to practitioners adhering strongly to more radical approaches.

Practice makes perfect

Against the myths of community education stands reality. The main purpose of this article is to expose some of the myths that have gained currency among policy-makers and practitioners, spurred by some of the widely-read texts in the field of community education. It may therefore appear negative. Space does not allow a positive exposition of the alternative ideologies of community education – conservative and radical – in full. This task I have attempted elsewhere.[10] In my case, the present critique has arisen out of the practice of community education, which leads the practitioner into almost daily dilemmas and conflicts, and in order to understand this process I have found it essential to re-examine many of the orthodox assumptions. It may be no accident that the orthodoxy springs largely from the pens of policy-makers and administrators rather than practitioners or recipients.

If these assumptions are in reality aspects of, or derivations from a particular, if orthodox, ideology, (although at the same time they purport not to be so, but rather to be general truths,) then by de-mystifying community education, I hope that practitioners can come to understand their own position and potential better, and hence participate more effectively in its successful development.

Notes

1   The 'standard texts' are here taken as:
Henry Morris, *The Village College: Being a Memorandum on the Provision of Educational and Social Facilities for the Countryside, with Special Reference to Cambridgeshire*, Cambridge University Press, 1925.
Cyril Poster, *The School and the Community*, Macmillan, 1971.
Eric Midwinter, *Priority Education: an Account of the Liverpool Project*, Penguin, 1972.
Eric Midwinter, *Patterns of Community Education*, Ward Lock, 1973.
Harry Rée, *Educator Extraordinary: the Life and Achievements of Henry Morris*, Longman, 1973.
Andrew Fairbairn, *The Leicestershire Community Colleges and Centres*, Nottingham University/N.I.A.E., 1979.
Reg Keeble, *Community and Education*, National Youth Bureau, Leicester, 1981.
Cyril Poster, *Community Education: its Development and Management*, Heinemann, 1982.

Contributions towards an alternative formulation include:

Pauline Jones, *Community Education in Practice: a Review*, Social Evaluation Unit, Oxford, 1978.
Keith Jackson, 'Some fallacies in community education and their consequences in working-class areas', in Colin Fletcher and Neil Thompson (eds), *Issues In Community Education*, Falmer, 1980, pp. 39–46.
Angela Skrimshire, 'Community schools and the education of the "Social Individual"', *Oxford Review Of Education*, vol. 7, no. 1, 1981.
Tom Lovett, Chris Clarke and Avila Kilmurray, *Adult Education and Community Action*, Croom Helm, 1983.

2   See for example J. Kelvyn Richards, 'A general theory of community
    education', *Community Education Network*, vol. 5, no. 5, May 1985, p.
    2.
3   See Brian Simon, *Studies in the History of Education 1780–1870*
    Lawrence & Wishart, 1965.
4   See Brian Simon, *Education and the Labour Movement 1870–1920*,
    Lawrence & Wishart, 1965; and Gerald Grace, *Teachers, Ideology and
    Control: a Study in Urban Education*, Routledge & Kegan Paul, 1978.
5   For a fuller exposition of the ideological base of community
    education, see the following:
    Ian Martin, 'From practice to theory and back: inter-professional in-
    service provision in higher education', in Community Education
    Development Centre, *Outlines 2*, Coventry, 1985.
    Bob O'Hagan, 'The struggle for community education: structure and
    process in the development of five community schools', Cranfield
    institute of Technology, unpublished thesis, 1985.
    There are differences between these two accounts, but broad
    agreement concerning the three community education ideologies.
6   Stuart Maclure, 'Background to the subject and the discussion' in
    Centre for Educational Research and Innovation, *Professional Education
    and Training for Community Education,* H.M.S.O., 1977, p. 18.
7   See Cyril Poster, *Community Education: Its Development and
    Management*, Heinemann, 1982; and The Taylor Report, *A Partnership
    For Our Schools*, H.M.S.O., 1978.
8   Bob O'Hagan, 'The struggle for community education: structure and
    process in the development of five community schools', Cranfield
    Institute of Technology, unpublished thesis, 1985, Chapter 9.
9   Angela Skrimshire, 'Community schools and the education of the
    "social individual"', *Oxford Review Of Education*, vol. 7, no. 1, 1981.
10 For an attempt at a fuller exposition, see Bob O'Hagan, (1985) op. cit.

A critical look at forms of practice

CHAPTER 5

Community education and school: a commentary

GORDON MITCHELL

This paper critically examines both the potential and problems of developing community education practice from the existing institutional base of the school. Mitchell suggests that community educators have not yet made the case for this convincingly. They need to actively engage in the practical business of reforming schools as they are in a much more systematic and self-critical way. Although this promises to be a slow and painful process, the general trend historically reflects a significant convergence between the aims of community education and the emergent reality of the neighbourhood school. In this sense, time is on the side of community education. Far from being a marginal or exotic enterprise, it can and should be an integral part of what goes on in all schools.

> Much of the literature is descriptive and uncritical. It tends to be somewhat anecdotal and bland.[1]

No one should be surprised that literature on community education has attracted such strictures. Almost every piece of writing on the theme begins by complaining about the extreme difficulty of accurate definition. As to the practice of community education, it would be a difficult task – even for a creatively gifted writer – to make coherent that which Jackson (1979) rather unkindly referred to as 'mindless ad hocery', namely that collection of policies, processes and practices typically agreed to represent 'community education'.[2]

Each one of these policies and practices attempts either to significantly improve what is conventionally available or to create programmes which will meet 'genuine' educational needs.

Together they represent a broad platform for the reshaping of the educational system, making it more accessible, more flexible, more democratically accountable and, potentially, more efficient. Indeed, the most radical interpretation of Community Education seeks to generate a kind of social renaissance through educational enlightenment.

Such lofty ideas may have inspired and underpinned the community education movement: they have tended to deflect debate from the key issues of (a) whether and (b) in what ways a 'reformed' education system can deliver what it promises.

To illustrate this fact, attention is drawn to Martin's analysis in this volume: 'Community education: towards a theoretical analysis', in which he describes attempts made at the annual conference of the Community Education Association (1983) to draw up a set of basic principles to which all community educators would subscribe. The key concept was identified as lifelong education and this was buttressed by six 'principles' which form 'a logical extension of the key concept'. As Martin pertinently observes:

> What really matters is how these general principles are interpreted, prioritized and implemented in practical situations.[3]

Yes, indeed, there is the rub! Opportunities for 'lifelong education' are no doubt an acceptable proposition for community educators (and many who have never heard of it) as a sensible albeit vague, response to the social, political and economic conditions in which we currently live. However, there is likely to be little agreement as to what form(s) lifelong education might take, still less as to how it should be financed and delivered to its consumers. Would post-school education be compulsory for everyone on a sabbatical leave basis? Would housewives qualify? What counts as 'valid' educational study? Could one opt out? Be sponsored by Sainsburys?

In short, however praiseworthy the attempt to clarify objectives, this community education manifesto provides us with little more than a simple set of slogans for those who firmly believe that our present system of education is neither fair nor enables the vast mass of people to develop fully those talents and abilities they possess. Furthermore, community educators have to face the fact that they cannot expect overwhelmingly enthusiastic support for their crusade! In the face of immediately pressing problems such as the underfunding of state education generally, or falling school rolls, community educators see their cherished beliefs often given only token support.

Nor is scepticism without good reason, for a decade and more ago Bernstein cogently argued that education *cannot* compensate for the shortcomings of the society of which it is a part. The contexts of formal schooling he declared, actively prevented the schools from promulgating a more just society. Since that time many other writers – labelled as functionalists, Marxists or Weberians – have come to similar conclusions. Indeed, Grace[4] reminds us in the opening chapters of *Teachers, Ideology and Control* that, from its inception, the formal system of schooling was narrowly conceived, rigidly regulated and has been concerned to transmit a particular culture. Similarly, the authors of *Unpopular Education,*[5] and *Education in Decline*[6] demonstrate how the formal education system provides remarkably little of real value for a substantial majority of the population. And it is a system which has remained stubbornly resistant to change despite the advent of secondary education for all, of comprehensive schooling, of child-centred learning, of computers in classrooms and the abolition of corporal punishment!

Assuming that the formal education system continues, approximately, in its present form, it is that system which community educators need to confront. Indeed 'community' education can have little meaning EXCEPT in the context of the prevailing political economy and current educational provision. Whilst community educators would certainly want to provide a 'better' service they can only hope to begin the task from the basis of existing institutions. The rest of this paper seeks to examine the potential and some of the difficulties and dilemmas in developing a community education service from schools.

In the light of this pessimistic prologue how is it that community education has managed to take root and has even flourished in some parts of the country? And what form does it take at the present time?

To answer the first question involves a brief recapitulation of the political context of state education.

In our parliamentary democracy, the elected representatives of the people shape the very nature of our existence through laws enacted in Parliament: executive responsibility is vested in 'local authorities' for the supply and administration of certain services in prescribed ways. Thus, while central government provides the legal framework for the national education system and regularly provides 'suggestions' and 'guidelines' in respect of 'desirable' policies, it is the local authorities who deliver the service. They undertake capital works programmes and recruit and deploy the various service personnel: teachers and advisers, bureaucrats and secretaries, caretakers and cleaners.

Theoretically, the system is rational. It has evolved over a century and appears to have achieved, on some reckonings, an acceptable balance between 'national interest' and 'local needs'. Theoretically, therefore, there should be consistent and equally fair provision throughout the country. However, the system of dual control (as the relationship between central and local government is usually described) has been subject to particular and quite severe political tensions. The net result has been quite marked variations in the quality and variety of the education service available in different localities. There are many reasons why this is so: three only are itemized here:

1 Whilst it is true that state education has, occasionally, been *the* central focus of consideration by central government (as for example in 1976 when Prime Minister Callaghan initiated the so called 'great debate'), more often than not it has been of minor concern. And so local authorities have been able to pursue policies *they* thought appropriate (subject, of course, to the impartial examination of Her Majesty's Inspectors of Schools). Some authorities have espoused allegedly 'progressive' policies: others have been content to sustain conventionally accepted practices.

2 Local authorities themselves have twice been 'restructured' in the last fifteen years – only recently (March 1986) seven 'metropolitan' authorities have been 'disbanded' and their functions transferred to other local authorities or non-elective' Boards. More importantly, however, central and local government have often been administered by political 'opposites'. Where Conservatives have formed the national government many local authorities have been 'controlled' by the Labour party and vice-versa.

3 The local management of individual schools and colleges has been gradually 'opened up' to broader representation from the neighbourhood. Now it is common to find parents, pupils, teachers, prominent citizens, representatives of local firms as members of school governing bodies. The interplay of these and other factors has given rise to the variations in local education provision.

Some authorities have seen the promotion of community education as a viable way to provide an 'expanded' education resource to meet local circumstances. These authorities, in particular, have been influenced by strong and diverse arguments for integration or, more accurately, the reintegration of schools with their local communities.

Rationale for school–community integration

The notion that the facilities of schools should be more available to all the members of the community in which they are situated is not new. As long ago as the 1920s, Morris, then Chief Education Officer for Cambridgeshire, sought to make schools into community assets in a bid to prevent the depopulation of the rural villages. This initiative to preserve or regenerate community in the face of rapid socio-economic change has continued. It was a feature of pre- and post-World War Two urban renewal programmes and it has remained so right up to the present, as for example, in the 'planned environment' of Milton Keynes.

Apart from what was seen as a 'general need' to provide community focal points, certain other factors have made it seem 'natural' that schools would be ideal for the purpose.

A large body of research into education in the 1950s and 1960s drew attention to the ways in which the child's educational performance was influenced by factors outside the schools. Especially important was the quality of support for the school by parents. It is now received wisdom that 'improvement' in home–school links has been instrumental in improving the academic attainment of many children in primary and secondary schools.

There have also been changes in the conception of a 'good' (i.e. appropriate) education. Successive national reports in the 1960s emphasized that schools should be as committed to the social, moral and emotional development of their pupils as they are to their academic progress. They also argued that schools should be more keenly aware of the potential afforded by their communities as environmental 'learning laboratories'. Such policies required broad patterns of local partnership between schools and social services and between schools and the world of work. Raising the school leaving age and changes to the school curriculum were reflected in the kind of accommodation provided in new schools. The broadening of the secondary school curriculum especially in respect of practical skills and the visual and creative subjects encouraged the growth of purpose-built accommodation: theatres, studios, sports halls.

Certain other facilities such as common-rooms, coffee bars and the like were reckoned more appropriate to the status needs of the many pupils who were virtually adults. The overall effect was to make 'real' adults feel less like intruders in that austere world of desks, blackboards and tables. These altered perceptions of the school's place in the social fabric have tended to develop a more 'active' relationship between school and community.

Further impetus to school–community integration derived from dramatic changes in the demands of the labour market. It has become increasingly clear that the traditional distinction between education and training is inappropriate. The provision of continuing education in some form by way of life skill 'packages' or for 'topping-up' academic attainments, came to be seen as an urgent and indispensable need of young adults.

At the same time, adult education, too, was moving away from the narrowly based programmes of evening institutes. Instead, as Morris had originally envisaged fifty years earlier, it became more widely concerned with at least some of the educational, social and recreational needs of the neighbourhood.

Some local authorities, Coventry, for example, in its policy document 'A comprehensive education for life' (1984),[7] assumed a flexible relationship of schools and colleges of further education to provide a 'seamless web' of educational, vocational and social provision for the neighbourhood.

In summary, then, the coincidence of many economic political and social factors has given impetus to developing uses of schools and colleges in ways other than that for which they were originally created. They have been seen as opportunities growth points – sites for supporting individuals and groups within a given local area. As the Director of Education for Clwyd has recently written (1985):

> ... the school on its own can never provide the full range of activities and experiences which young people will demand ... it will be necessary to mobilize the support of the F. E. sector, local employers, trade unionists leading figures in the community etc. etc. The role of the school will be central to all this but it will no longer be all things to all students, it will assume the function – partly at least – of a control tower/nerve centre/clearing house through which these many-faceted activities will be coordinated.[8]

Economic factors

Educationists tend to concentrate on educational factors in considering change at the expense of political and economic ones. This makes for unbalanced accounting: the influence of economic factors in accidentally bolstering the development of community education must not be underestimated.

Schools represent considerable public investment: some economists have believed the plant has been under-used for many years. Gradually schools have become, sometimes grudgingly, sites for adult education classes and youth activities especially in rural areas where the opportunity was taken to build schools incorporating facilities otherwise available only in the large towns. The commonest examples have been leisure facilities: often swimming pools provided by merging the capital investment cost of physical education space within the school building with financial support provided by the district council or grant from the Sports Council. It would be true to say that the driving force in developing coordinated facility projects have been the local authorities – there are few examples of cases where they have derived from popular local 'pressures'.

Coordinated facilities in primary schools

Some primary schools in rural areas have been built with youth service and/or adult education annexes attached. There is commonly, no operational relationship between the school and the other services – the additional accommodation makes easier dual (separate) use of the facilities. Local authorities like Leicestershire and Cambridgeshire have developed more comprehensive sets of arrangements. For example, in Leicestershire, Croft C of E Community Primary School provides, on its small campus, a base for a plurality of community needs service: educational, health and welfare and social/leisure. Other authorities e.g. Oldham, Rochdale and Cheshire have incorporated community centres into their newest building whilst some other authorities including those responsible for inner-city schools have focused upon informal programmes of parent education and have either provided purpose-built, or adapted existing spare capacity provision for this purpose.

Community schools

A relatively recent educational phenomenon has been the designation by some local authorities of schools as 'community' schools: some schools acquire the designation whether or not they have been officially so labelled. The labels themselves, are a source of much confusion. Secondary schools in Coventry, for example, are often described as community schools when their correct designation is 'school and community college' and such a title subsumes a rather different set of practices than that of a community school. More importantly, and deriving from circumstances discussed earlier, community schools are by no means homogeneous in nature. They differ in terms of resource allocation, in management structures and in the extent to which they interact with the local community.

At present, then, 'community school' is a generic term describing institutions which, although primarily designed for the education of children and young adults from 5 to 18, are expected to plan *for* and generate education in its broadest sense for the benefit of the local community.

In an attempt to summarize and simplify the range of practice, it might be useful to offer a modified version of Skrimshire's typology (1981) based on the following three broad categories:

1 The school makes conscious, but limited, attempts to relate to its community e.g. it seeks to develop home–school links, it encourages community use of school premises when the premises are not required for school purposes.
2 The links between school and community are broadened to include community contribution to school life itself e.g. parents and other adults taking the role of classroom auxiliaries. School facilities e.g. library and canteen are available to the community.
3 The totality of school-based enterprises are planned and coordinated so that the school can contribute in whatever ways possible to improve the quality of life in the community.

This categorization of community schools is constrained by the particular organizational methods used to manage them. Particularly important are:

1 *Form of management structure:* there are examples where all the activities on the premises are overseen by a 'school and

community association', in effect a school governing body together with members co-opted from 'school-user' groups. Sometimes the head of the school has responsibility for all provision; in other instances the head controls the educational programme, a manager taking responsibility for other community facilities. In other cases, e.g. that formerly employed in the Smallheath Community School in Birmingham, a management team is responsible for separate functions of the site – library, school, adult education, recreation and leisure etc.

2 *Operational funding*: finance may be via a 'block' grant – the school 'controls' the budget for all activities on the premises. Alternatively there may be separate estimates and allocations for each type of activity.

3 *Staffing*: school staff may work in different sectors (relatively common). In some instances staff with specialist knowledge, e.g. librarians, may serve as members of school staff. In some schools, e.g. Sutton Centre in Nottinghamshire, teachers recruited to the school staff 'contract' to work one-tenth of their timetable in or with the community. Where schools are combined with other community facilities, problems arise especially in terms of participation and accountability, responsibility and access. There is as yet, no unequivocally satisfactory way of managing coordinated facilities: some are administered under informal arrangements which depend heavily on the ability and willingness of the personnel concerned to work cooperatively.

Future trends

The provision of community education based upon school premises is likely to increase in the future. Some reasons have already been alluded to and it is not intended to repeat them here. One clear problem of a school-based education service is 'How can the needs of a community be identified?' For it is easier to state that the additional uses to which schools are put should contribute to the 'general well-being of the community' than it is to be precise about what the community needs are and, indeed, what the 'well-being of the community' means!

Few schools have the resources to carry out a detailed analysis of its community's needs. Even a sophisticated market research operation might not uncover them and there *are* dangers in the kinds of simplistic surveys that schools can promulgate. For example, people's expectations of what is possible may be governed by their preconceptions about schools and what they believe facilities can offer.

Whatever patterns of service provision becomes commonly accepted, and – as it becomes more general – in order to interrelate educational and other facilities, there will arise a corresponding need to reconsider many questions of controls and regulations. What are the legal liabilities of any school which uses the services, say, of a parent-helper on a school journey and where that parent is seriously injured? Similarly, different forms of public use will bring the buildings into different categories of regulations. Certain activities, for example the production and performance of plays and concerts and the sale and comsumption of alcohol can only be carried out under licence. However none of these issues is of such intractability as to provide serious hindrance to an evolutionary programme of school–community involvement.

A critical analysis of the school as the site of community education

The school as a facility base for various forms of community education and community use has one obvious advantage: its ubiquity. Even in quite small communities it can function at relatively little cost. Henry Morris endeavoured to convey his aims and ideals of an integrated socio-educational facility through the imagery of building design: especially (and symbolically) significant was his belief that the schools contained within the early Cambridgeshire community colleges were not so obstrusive as to emphasize the domain of the pedagogue and the caretaker! However, the tradition within which most school buildings have evolved puts them squarely in the category including monasteries, mansions and prisons: institutions designed to keep safely separate the dedicated, the priviliged or the vicious. Our latter-day primaries and comprehensives – catering for up to 1500 to 2000 pupils – were apparently designed to cater for all three! One fact is certain, relatively few have been built with broader community use in mind. The examples referred to earlier in the text truly represents a very small minority of schools.

Nor can it be claimed that community schools have as yet demonstrated conspicuous success as multi-purpose educational institutions. The findings of Wallis and Mee 'Community Sci. claims and performance' are not very encouraging. This is one the few published empirical investigations into the practice and performance of a small number of community secondary schools. Their work was limited to secondary schools, was restricted by a lack of resources and was specifically limited to an examination of the effectiveness of such institutions as providers of an adult education service. However, many of the comments quoted from their in-depth interviews have the ring of authenticity:

Inadequate funding

My quarrel with the local authority over community education is that it has been resourced on the old formula of the school plus a little bit more for community education. I believe that you've got to start afresh and devise a new formula when you're using a school over this great length of time … it's no good decorating the school once every seven years, it needs to be done much more frequently if you're going to have this multi-purpose use going on from 9 o'clock in the morning until 10 o'clock at night.

Shared facilities

You can quote the philosophy until you're blue in the face, that equipment is held in common between the school and the community but in the practical situation of very little money available the school quite naturally wants to keep what it's got.

Feeling for community education

We call ourselves a community school in the hope of pretending we're all one institution – we're not!

Staff haven't got it in their bones that this is one institution.

We have, of course, a responsibility for continuing education but there is not any coherent idea of what it means – we add as we go along.

Wallis and Mee[9] comment that their overall feeling is very strong that school staff have little understanding of the aims of community education and little sympathy for its practice. For example, adults on school premises were sometimes welcomed for such covert advantage the school might take from their presence.

Examples of manipulation

We have been using adult classes for extra 'O' level groups in language which are not catered for in the school timetable.

ool is an ideal place for adopting all kinds of ruses
ring the children back in an evening, give them a
ience lesson and call it adult education.

classes are a great bonus – you don't get the
problems and they get their homework in on time.

… we had two very difficult girls who caused a lot of trouble. Now
the mothers put up with this for one week and then, in the second
week they very quietly took those two girls aside, told them a few
facts of life, and we didn't have a spark of trouble for the rest of the
time.

Encouraging adults as students
It's a rare housewife who can fit in with our timetable.

I reserve the right to ask adults to leave if it doesn't work out.
It's a gesture of goodwill on the part of my staff.'

The authors' conclusions, then, appear to amount to an
indictment of community schools as purveyors of adult education
and, by extension, of community education. They find that there is
little cause for optimism: in terms of lifelong learning they say that
it seems unlikely that a future generation of independent learners is
being developed in community schools. They suggest that
community schools will have to overcome 'intractable obstacles' to
changes in curricula. They argue that the role needs of head
teachers, community educators and teaching staff in community
schools should be researched in order to identify areas of mismatch
between needs and previous training and experiences. Finally they
question whether or not community schools are the most effective
means of achieving many of the goals that they themselves identify.
Can the schools bridge the gaps between:

- School and adult students?
- The organizational and attitudinal differences involved in
  administering different kinds of service, the one compulsory
  and full time, the other voluntary and part-time?
- The tradition of centralized control of schooling and the
  necessary and flexible variable control required for local
  community usage?

The picture is probably one with which many community
educators, in school or out of it, are familiar – not least by this
writer who concedes the truth of their restrained and cautious
criticisms.

However, the fact that community schools have, as yet, only limited success in purveying 'community' education does not mean that they will never be able to do so.

There are a number of considerations which may allow schools to approach 'community' education more convincingly. First, the educational climate, like the English weather, never remains constant. The kind of community education of an all-persuasive kind which was at one time thought capable of developing communities, providing a socially relevant curricula and a base for local radical activists, cannot and will not be delivered through schools. Such goals were always *too* controversial, *too* speculative and simply inadequately thought through.

We need now to consider how and in what ways schools can effectively initiate some *clearly defined* forms of community education. Once such good practices have been identified, then, as Wallis and Mee suggest, they should be carefully monitored and made publicly available. *Community Primary Schools*, edited by John Rennie,[10] is one example of an attempt to make known to a wider audience examples of 'good' practice. Nor should the costs of good practice – financial and otherwise – be glossed over.

Organizational innovation of the kind involved in changing conventional schools to ones which offer close relationships with their communities requires careful planning and preparation. In 1953 Sealy and Wilkinson[11] made a major contribution to the development of community schools by identifying and classifying the difficulties to be encountered. It may be appropriate to recapitulate in abbreviated form, the three sets of issues to be resolved. Specifically, they referred to:

1 *School–community relationships:* e.g. difficulty in determining 'community' and 'community' needs, conflicts of values between school and community, misuse of 'community' surveys, democratic participation of community in school 'life'.
2 *Barriers involving policies and personnel*: e.g. ability of management to introduce policy, nature of experience and training of staff to implement policy, insufficient resources of people and equipment.
3 Problems involving premises: e.g. inadequate/inappropriate buildings and sites, recognition that multiple services, even though they use the same site, cannot be administered at the same cost as one of them.

Again, it is easy to provide lists separating out the individual difficulties and problems and even to suggest simple solutions. A major difficulty is that in 'real' situations the problems and difficulties appear simultaneously and impinge on each other. As a consequence, there has to take place a deal of messy compromise and horse-trading that is anathema to a 'natural' instinct for rationality in the conduct of human affairs, a desire for tidiness and clarity. And the whole balancing act is far more complex than is baldly presented. It involves motivation and reward, social psychology and group dynamics, what is euphemistically termed 'creative accounting' and the like. Teacher groups, social service agencies, various 'interested' groups, parent-bodies all have to be held in some sort of social equipoise. If any ideology of community education is to be effectively expressed from a school base then two factors need to be prominent – a realistic time-scale and a coherent planning process.

A realistic time-scale

It is quite common to hear criticism of community schools or schools with a community 'orientation' because it appears that they have little more to show for their work than 'traditional' schools. The labels are unfortunate and divisive. Is it that one type of school must strive to furnish evidence that it lives up to a predetermined status? Is it that schools which are 'traditional' need to take no account of parents or neighbourhood? Of course not. No school can avoid involvement with its community even if it chooses to do so minimally and reluctantly. Schools, have always varied in the collective will and ability of professional and other personnel to develop an education service for the community.

One straightforward way for schools to examine their current position would be to see how and in what ways their network of 'community' education practice matches with the kind of broad schemes produced by Coventry's Community Education Project. It is not suggested that any school – certainly not any primary school with its more limited resources – could and should attempt to establish the range of networks portrayed there. Nor could it be taken for granted that any school scoring highly in terms of the quantity of its links could automatically proclaim its pre-eminence as an 'advanced' base of community education. However it would enable schools to examine the present extent of their community commitment and identify for the future what was essential, desirable and/or practically possible. Consultative processes need to involve more personnel than school teachers, though it seems sensible that teachers – who, after all, have 'natural' avenues of contact via parents and other official voluntary agencies – should initiate developments.

It needs to be stressed again that many schools do involve themselves in so many ways with their communities. What few of them do is carry out any systematic recording and assessment of community education. One policy to be commended is that of the ex head of John Gulson Infant School – an inner city, multi-racial school in Coventry. Over a period of a decade or more she accounted the activities and dimensions of school–community involvement and analysed them.[12] Some initiatives were failures, some were seen to be effective as short-term projects; others needed modifying by using different personnel: others still were so successful that they became integral to the school's programme.

It would be idle to pretend that the programmes and planning involved in a college of further education bear much resemblance to that of an infant school. But the principles underlying the forms of community education remain markedly similar. Just as communities themselves are richly varied so will be the school or college organizations which provide for and with them. There seems good reason why this accounting of school and college stewardship could be valuable to both school or college and its community.

A coherent planning programme

It might be inferred from the preceding paragraphs that planning for community education is essential. Planning here refers mainly to local planning, but it also has implications at national levels too. If, for example, teachers enter the profession equipped *only* to work with young children, schools can hardly be expected to develop as community education bases. There are other skills essential to teachers as potential support systems for community education – and they involve the development and experience of social skills as well as intellectual ones: a commitment to practice, stamina in the face of difficulties, and an ability to think around contentious issues. Particularly desirable is the ability to relate to adults in a community confidently and sympathetically. In this respect teaching practice formally, informally or non-assessed ought to have some elements of experience for young teachers in training to work with parents and other adult members of the community. One way to circumnavigate the notorious insularity of school–college/university–school syndrome is to provide experiences for young people to work collaboratively or collectively in planning and implementing practice however small-scale or limited.

Planning for school-based community education ought to be an integral part of the school's on-going self-assessment and derive from its present practice(s). The very term 'school-based community education' used here may quite easily give a misleading notion. School-based community education does not automatically and exclusively imply 'on the school premises'.

There is no reason why – as indeed they do now – other locations than schools should not provide 'homes' for certain elements of 'community' education. A school and its personnel should seek to make whatever contribution they can. No school or college can provide a totality of 'community' education for it does not exist.

In summary, the neighbourhood school or college has enormous potential for benefiting its communities quite apart from its physical resources. It has unrivalled access to knowledge of people and places: it has a ready-made network through children's families for informal communication and, through its own position in the establishment, for formal contacts. Within its own precincts, it can–and should–be a frequent meeting place for many purposes by small community groups and even, for really large ones. Whilst it should not attempt manifestly what it cannot achieve, any school, by adopting a 'community education' approach has a unique opportunity to enhance the social and educational growth of individuals and groups. Schools themselves will benefit quite dramatically from the experience.

Notes

1   Jackson, K. (1987). 'Some fallacies in community education and their consequences in working-class areas', in Fletcher, C. and Thompson, N. (eds), *Issues in Community Education*, 1979, Falmer Press.
2   'Community education': towards a theoretical analysis' in Allen, G. *et al.* (eds) (1987), *Community Education*, Milton Keynes, Open University Press.
3   Ibid.
4   Grace, G. (1978). *Teachers, Ideology and Control*, London, Routledge & Kegan Paul.

5 Baron, S. Finn, D. *et al.* (1981). *Unpopular education,* London, Hutchinson & Co., in conjunction with C.C.C.S.

6 Bernbaum, G. (ed.) (1979). *Education in Decline,* London, Macmillan.

7 Coventry Education Committee. (1983). *Comprehensive Education for Life*, Coventry.

8 Outlines, vol. 2. (1985) Coventry: C.E.D.C.

9 Wallis, J. and Mee, G. (1983). *Community Schools: Claims and Performance*, Nottingham University, Dept. of Adult Education.

10 Rennie, J. (ed.) (1985). *Community Primary Schools*, London, Falmer Press.

11 Sealy, M. and Wilkinson, J. A. (1953). 'Overcoming barriers to the development of community schools', in Henry H. B. (ed.), *The 52nd Year Book of the National Society for the Study of Education, Pt. II, The Community School'*, University of Chicago Press.

12 Journal of Community Education, vol. 4, no. 3, 1985 December.

CHAPTER 6

Youth and community work and the community school

TONY JEFFS

In one of its crudest and most expedient forms community education may be about little more than bureaucratic rationalization. Both youth work and adult education have become the beneficiaries and/or victims of this version of the community school. Taking a youth work perspective, Jeffs reviews the arguments for and against such 'integration' and identifies some of the external, non-educational pressures which are accelerating the trend towards it. In terms of the aims, values and styles of youth work as social education, the case for school-based practice remains doubtful. In spite of this scepticism, however, Jeffs suggests that the trend is inevitable. It is therefore essential for community education to be understood as a commitment to develop new working relationships between teachers and youth workers which reflect the interests of young people and their communities.

With the possible exception of adult education it is doubtful if any other area of activity has been more affected by the expansion of community education and the community school than the youth and community service. As the momentum of the community education model has gathered pace and colonized LEA after LEA so, almost as a by-product, it has changed the very nature and structure of statutory and, to a lesser extent, voluntary youth and community work in those areas. Perhaps the most noteworthy thing about this change has been the extent to which it has taken place whilst creating little apparent interest amongst researchers and writers on youth and community work. As one researcher has noted when writing about school-based youth work 'The most astounding aspect of the literature is the dearth of it' (Sheils 1985, p. 1). The 'colonization' has inevitably been gradual but it has been unremitting and the pace has significantly quickened during the last decade. Estimates of what proportion of statutory youth workers is now school-based, and this usually means a community school setting, are difficult to ascertain. But informed assessments place the figure at between 20 to 40 per cent (Booton 1980); DES 1982; CETYCW 1985). Whatever confusion may exist regarding the size of the current proportions, all parties accept that the percentage will continue to rise and where it will plateau remains anyone's guess.

The origins and rise of school-based youth work

The increase in the volume of school-based youth and community work is not solely a consequence of the appearance of an expanding network of community schools, nor of the growing popularity of community education amongst policy-makers and educational administrators. Although it must be stressed that the appointment of school-based youth workers was, to a marked degree, pioneered by those LEAs that were in the very forefront of the community education movement, such as Cambridgeshire and Leicestershire, that is not the whole story. Other pressures and motivations have played a significant role since the appearance of the first youth tutors and school-based youth workers in the 1950s. It is important not to overlook those pressures and motivations.

The location of youth and community work within schools has a long and chequered history. School premises have always provided essential venues for youth work. The low level of funding for the service has meant that the bulk of youth work has of necessity taken place in non purpose-built settings. Church and village halls along with school premises have always been vital resources without which the youth service would be reduced to a barebones rump. In the case of the latter this can be illustrated by reference to recent DES research which shows that 55 per cent of secondary and 29 per cent of primary schools are used on a weekly basis by the youth service (DES 1985). However, allowing the scouts or guides access to a school hall or a village youth group the use of a classroom is, of course, substantially removed from the integration of the service into the managerial and organizational structure of a school or college. In both urban and rural localities the youth service has had a long-standing dependence upon access to premises rented or borrowed from schools. Such dependency, it should be stressed, has been a continual source of conflict and tension within the service. The style and tenor of much youth work with a traditional emphasis on activities and 'noisy' entertainment, linked with what many head teachers view as an overly laissez-faire attitude towards discipline within the youth service, has meant that the use of school premises has largely been viewed as a necessary but regrettable compromise.

Anyone who has run a youth club on school premises will know immediately the problems that are likely to be encountered. The 'morning after' phone calls from head teachers complaining of litter, damage to the toilets or the ripped pictures in the entrance hall display. They will also comprehend the annoyance of last-minute cancellations due to the precedence afforded the parents' evening, speech day or carol service. They will also know the chore of checking the building for damage or litter before you let the members in so you can legitimately deny any responsibility, and the late-night repair jobs designed to hide the damage before the cold light of the morning exposes it to the seemingly ever vigilant eye of a marauding caretaker. Only those who have never run a youth club would in normal circumstances choose to willingly locate one on school premises. Yet that is where they are increasingly to be found.

It would be simplistic and misleading to see the expansion of school-based youth work merely as an unfortunate consequence of a regrettable shortfall in the provision of purpose-built premises. Other factors have to be accommodated within any account of the shift towards school-based provision. For example, such a movement reflects the changing clientèle of the youth service. Historically, the users of the youth service were drawn from amongst those who had ceased full-time education. Insofar as the youth service was, and is, an educational rather than a purely leisure service, it was historically designed to offer social and remedial education to those who were no longer in daily contact with either a school or college. As a consequence, its strength derived in part from a clear physical separation from schooling. Where this was not wholly possible then at least the staffing was generally perceived as being a discrete entity, drawn overwhelmingly from outside the ranks of the teaching profession. That distance was, and to an extent still is, important, for it provided a fresh opportunity to make contact with the substantial majority of young people who had either rejected school or chosen to leave at the earliest possible opportunity. Thus the youth service during the nineteenth century and well into the present century consciously acquired a 'child saving' role, a function that led to its acting not merely as an educational but also a moral backstop for those young people who had severed their links with the educational system (Jeffs 1979). Over time that role has come to be predominately located elsewhere.

New welfare agencies both statutory and voluntary have emerged, whilst others, (not least the schools) have deliberately endeavoured to extend their role and function. For example, the latter have sought to create a presence beyond their traditional, narrow, academic remit reaching ever more energetically into the sphere of 'welfare'. In particular since their creation in 1970, the local authority personal social service departments, as well as more recently, specialist agencies concentrating on the treatment and diversion of young offenders and potential offenders, have become the key elements in this area of intervention. This restructuring and expansion of welfare provision has led to the youth service being delegated to the periphery within an area in which it once played a major role. The reasons for this shift in the terrain of responsibility are not difficult to ascertain.

Growing, if perhaps exaggerated, concern in relation to juvenile and adolescent delinquency has encouraged the creation of specialist agencies and departments staffed by trained professionals a relocation that has been perceived as essential both in the interests of the young person and community. This has been a long-term trend but since 1969 it has been graphically highlighted by the massive expansion of Intermediate Treatment(IT) designed both to divert young people from offending and as an alternative to custodial care. The meteoric rise of IT since the passing of the 1969 Children and Young Persons Act has been widely commented upon elsewhere (Adams 1987; Adams *et al* 1981; Holt 1985;) and does not need further elaboration here, but it should be acknowledged that the expansion of IT has amounted to the creation of a separate and distinct 'youth service'.

With its own staffing, national organizations and funding totally outside the control of the LEA, IT now has only the most minimal contact with the mainstream youth service that it was initially envisaged would oversee such work. The impact of the appearance of IT should not be measured solely in terms of funding and administrative structures. Paradoxically keeping the young offender in the community and out of care actually entails isolating the young person from the community, the neighbourhood and peer group to the maximum feasible degree. Treatment requires a 'sterile' environment and this is created within the IT unit or group. As a consequence, once the minority at greatest risk of offending and those who are most likely to infect their peers with a predilection towards anti-social behaviour are removed, it becomes more attractive, if not 'sensible', to locate the service for the residue that remains within the school. In other words, taking the service to the client, rather than engaging in the problematic exercise of drawing the client to the service, becomes a preferable option.

Other factors have also been influential in encouraging an emphasis upon school-based youth work. Not least amongst these has been the staggered raising of the school-leaving age which, coupled with the growth in voluntary staying-on, has meant that the proportion of those in the client age range not in full-time education has sharply declined. An inevitable side-effect of the current unprecedented levels of youth unemployment has been the de facto continuation of this trend with both higher rates of staying-on and lengthening of the affiliation with school. When nationally over half of 16-year-old leavers in 1985 failed to secure a 'real job' as opposed to a place on an MSC programme it is hardly surprising that a growing number opt to remain at school if they stand the faintest chance of securing a negotiable qualification. Of those who do leave at 16 the majority remain outside the traditional labour market in the initial period with 380,000 out of 580,000 entering the now two-year YTS. Thus a clear majority of those aged 16 to 19 are now outside the traditional labour market, being located on training schemes, within schools or FE and HE. With that shift in terms of the location of the majority of young people, much of the earlier raison d'être for the traditional youth service has, arguably, evaporated. For if, and it is a big if, social education or training is needed, if counselling is required, if non-academic and non-vocational education is called for then the gap can be filled not by calling into play an outside agency, the youth service, but by the expansion of the curriculum of those agencies already involved.

The school, the MSC or the FE college with their respective life and social skills packages, TVEI and remedial programmes not only seek the right to control the social education of the young adult but promise to do so in a more direct and less hit-or-miss fashion than the youth service, which after all could only ever work with those who choose to affliate themselves to it. It has not only been the MSC that has been the 'great colonizer' but the schools, FE, HE and other welfare agencies. Partly they have operated in this fashion out of a desire for organizational self-preservation but in this context the motives are of less significance than the impact. This has been to largely weaken the mainstream youth service. Direct funding has been reduced (Davies 1981: Smith 1986: Smith and Jeffs 1987) and although this has been partially offset by the wholesale use within the youth service of MSC-funded community programme staff, the last decade has seen the continued erosion of the service in terms of staffing levels, training provision and capital and current expenditure.

Not only has the youth service been squeezed by the growth of full-time education in its many guises but also by the irresistible rise of commercial leisure provision. Clearly under the impact of increasing levels of youth unemployment, the expansion in the scale of commercial provision has to an extent been curtailed, nevertheless this has not put the clock back to the 1940s or beyond. The commercial disco or club, the theme pub, the students' union, the snooker hall or the music concert, amongst others, all remain the bench-mark against which other forms of leisure activity for the majority of young people are assessed. The youth centre or club is a badly placed also-ran as far as most young people are concerned (Hendry 1983; Gibbon *et al* 1984). The youth service may offer a pale imitation for those too poor, too immobile or too young to gain access to the 'real world of youth culture' but that is all. It can never offer an authentic style or élan since it lacks the resources, flexibility and probably the will to do so.

Reduced to offering a second-class leisure provision it has also to provide or become a bolt-hole for those excluded or nervous of entering the 'commercial world' due to a real or an imagined fear of encountering discrimination, violence or abuse as a consequence of their gender, disability, ethnic origin or sex. It may be a crucial and vital role to provide an alternative to the 'commercial' fare but it is not necessarily one that the youth service and youth workers would have opted for or are equipped to engage in. Certainly the cynical might well suggest that much of the latter-day conversion amongst youth workers to girls' work, anti-racist work and the provision of, for example specialist counselling inputs has a great deal more to do with a need for the youth service to justify its existence – having lost much of the mantle of being a mass provider – than to any real commitment or assessment of need and demand. Be that as it may, much traditional youth work feels itself both exposed and threatened and under increasing pressure to map out a clearly defined role. This is, of course, nothing new but it does damagingly weaken the ability of the Service to secure resources. The school, community or otherwise, with its much more clearly recognized role and function is thus advantaged and offers for an increasing number of LEAs a more attractive site for investment, be it in terms of leisure facilities or of resources allocated for that most nebulous of enterprises-the 'social education' of the adolescent.

Trapped between the decline in employment of young people and the growth of commercial provision targeted at the client group, as well as the squeezing of the youth service budget by a government determined to reduce public expenditure, the increasing location of the service within the school or college setting becomes the 'rational' administrative solution to a number of problems. The school or college seems to be the 'natural' home for a service which is already primarily catering for young people of school-age or thereabouts. The community education movement has therefore probably been as much a beneficiary of structural change as an innovator in the arena of provision for young people. It seems certain that even if the community schools had not wished to have drawn the youth service into their orbit they would have almost certainly have had it imposed upon them. Either on grounds of economic rationality or educational efficiency or both. The rhetoric of the community education movement with its desire 'to promote educational, recreational and social development of the community through all the age and ability ranges' (Boulter 1980) may have aided the smooth passage of both the youth service and adult education into the schools but in a very real sense it was probably pushing at an open door.

The case for school-based youth provision

A substantive case for the integration of youth and community work within the community school structure has been consistently argued for in recent years. This case is based upon a number of assertions and claims and it is important to set these out before proceeding. These benefits need to be considered for they function as a powerful justification for school-based youth work and for the inclusion of youth work within the community education package. It is important to stress that they should not be viewed as automatically advocating a monolithic structure. Although some advocates of community schools, notably Fairbairn (1969), have questioned the need for any separate youth and community provision, this is almost certainly within the contemporary context a minority stance. Few I suspect would, at least publicly, echo his view 'that the youth service as such has outworn its usefulness and ought to be allowed to wither away quietly.

Therefore, the case for school-based provision can best be interpreted as an argument for one form of provision within a pluralistic model. The trouble with pluralistic models is that within the context of a period of severe economic restraint they rarely survive beyond the planning stage. The weakest almost invariably go to the monetarist wall with the pluralist model remaining just a model with the strongest surviving and small, innovative and usually already under-resourced tending to lose what funding, staff or premises they already possess.

So what constitute the advantages and strengths of school-based youth and community provision? Firstly it is often claimed that the location of youth work within schools in general and purpose-built community schools in particular has given young people access to resources that are in the main a major improvement on those normally encountered within youth clubs. The sports' halls, theatres, libraries, specialist rooms for arts and crafts and the abundance of small rooms available for group work are light years removed from the church hall or even the purpose-built youth centre. As a consequence, community schools that have given youth work a high priority have opened up new vistas for youth work. They offer the potential for the curriculum of youth work to be extended beyond the predictable diet of table tennis, discos and football. The access to specialist facilities and staff has the potential to enable that curriculum to more rapidly shed more of its in-built masculinity and cultural chauvinism. At present there is little evidence of this occurring on any scale but it is crucial that this potential is recognized and exploited.

Secondly, the integration of youth and community provision within the community school has, according to the advocates of school-based youth work, gone some distance towards breaking down much of the traditional isolation of both the youth service and youth workers from the mainstream of education which is inevitably dominated by the school sector. The enforced contact flowing from the shared use of facilities may, as noted earlier, be fraught with danger. However the integration of youth work within a community school structure is designed to overcome those problems which are rooted in the segmentation of provision. This unification within one institution can according to Webley (1971) be beneficial to all parties; not least the teaching staff of the school many of whom he argues may 'thrive in the youth centre environment' which can open for them 'considerable areas for experiment, essentially for teachers with an informal approach, skilled in relating topics to the personal needs and experience of young people' (pp. 145–6).

It is not merely the school that benefits according to this line of argument. For example, it is stressed that as a result of this closer association with the school and the community education team, the possibility emerges that the long-standing ambiguity over management that bedevils so many youth projects can be removed, once and for all. Once the youth worker or tutor becomes a member of the community school staff they are no longer trapped in a void between management committees, local authority officers and other agencies. Instead, they acquire an unambiguous location and place within the clearly defined management structure of the community school. Certainly the Secondary Headteachers Association believe that such integration will offer youth workers 'strength, security and career structure ... that is to the mutual benefit of these involved' (1979, p. 177). Similarly the youth worker in becoming a member of staff with the same claim over resources as any other also gains an entrée to the decision-making processes of the school. They are no longer a threatening interloper but an integrated part of the school community. As such, they can be protected to an unprecedented extent from the vagaries of local authority decision-making, particularly in terms of resource allocation. In the current climate size does offer a dubious safety in numbers that youth workers may understandably find attractive.

Thirdly, other discernible pay-offs may flow from integration. For example, the widespread ignorance amongst teachers concerning the role and function of the youth worker may be reduced by daily contact in staffrooms and meetings. As the youth worker or tutor is usually allotted a designated teaching commitment, contacts are not only formalized but encouraged in a way that can simultaneously lift the status of the youth worker in an institution which will invariably lay considerable emphasis upon academic criteria. This teaching commitment and presence within the school also offers the youth worker a valuable opportunity to recruit well-qualified and potentially useful part-time youth workers from amongst the teaching and ancillary staff. The potential for conflict over resources will remain. However, by the construction of youth wings attached to, but recognizably separate from, the main school building, it may be possible to achieve the best of all possible worlds: all the advantages of the free-standing youth centre including an absence of restrictions over noise, independence of action and the like, plus access to the facilities of the well equipped community school.

Fourthly, a crucial by-product of this integration is the opportunity it provides for the youth worker to make contact with the actual and potential clientèle. Through the school, particularly a community school, which by definition cannot be operating in an area where selection is retained, will pass virtually all the young people living within the catchment area. The youth worker will consequently have an unrivalled opportunity to make contact with those young people, to discover their needs and wants and, where feasible, respond in a positive fashion. In particular via the school setting it is possible to unearth the requirements of those young people who would be reluctant to enter the 'average' neighbourhood youth club. For just as the community school setting offers the potential to expand the curriculum of youth work so it also offers a means to broaden the base of the patronage of the youth service.

Finally, it is important not to overlook the ways in which the community school is the beneficiary from the integration of youth work within its remit. It is far from being a one-way traffic. The youth service has long displayed an ability to work with and to 'contain' many of those young people who pose for the school the severest problems with regard to their behaviour and attendance. The style of intervention, the expertise of the youth workers and ambience of the youth centre or group have often graphically highlighted the failings of the school. Youth workers in clubs and IT groups have often succeeded where countless teachers have failed. The presence of the youth worker within the community school will therefore often introduce an alternative approach to pedagogy and the maintenance of discipline, thus hopefully discouraging the use of such practices as corporal punishment, which are totally incompatible with the philosophy of a community school.

The less formal setting of the youth group or club also offers the class room teacher a unique opportunity to form, in a relaxed atmosphere, creative relationships with the students, a chance to break down many of the barriers to learning and to acquire a better understanding of their needs and aspirations. Both parties are given a chance to escape from the pre-ordained roles of pupil and teacher, as they are also provided with a means of maintaining on an informal basis a relationship after the cessation of full-time education – a link that can ease the transition from school to work or, as is more often the case in the current climate, provide a much-needed source of support during a prolonged period of unemployment. As Thompson notes the young person leaving such a school:

> is well acquainted with the building, the staff and the range of resources on offer and the transition is, therefore, smooth and unimpeded ... familiarity ... built up over a number of years, is more likely to lead to opportunities being grasped in other contexts. The theatre, leisure centre and community education classes are all examples of areas of life at Abraham Moss made more accessible to adults as a result of an understanding generated in earlier years (1983, p. 60).

Certainly there is some evidence that school-based youth provision has been much more successful in catering for the young unemployed than free-standing units (Linell 1983). For the precise reason that they have the facilities to offer a wide-range of activities and that they give the young person the chance to retain an identity.

The integration of youth and community work within the community school clearly has the potential to offer immense benefits to the school. Having said that, it is crucial to recognize that there are many dangers and pitfalls and that the integration of youth work within a community education setting has not always been effectively achieved. Indeed the evidence that does exist tends to indicate that a great deal of caution is required when assessing the claims put forward regarding the benefits of integration.

Doubts and reservations

The problems that appear to flow from the integration of youth provision within the community school in particular and in a more general sense from its annexation to the community education structure have to be recognized. In part they are located within the structural weaknesses of the community school itself. In these instances, the problems are to a considerable extent similar to those encountered by adult education which like youth work, has overwhelmingly been assimilated within the community school where LEAs have adopted that model (see for example Wallis and Mee 1983; Fletcher 1980; Lawson 1977). Suffice it to stress that much of the critique is inter-changeable. However that is not true in totality and the integration of youth work provision within community schools has produced its own limited literature as well as an identifiably separate debate – not least because integration has produced its own clash of traditions and professional ideologies, and exposed certain structural weaknesses within the 'community school' model.

Advocates of the community school, from Henry Morris onwards, have always laid considerable emphasis upon the links between the institution and its host community. At times much of this thinking has been somewhat simplistic. It has often been founded upon a false assumption that if a school serves a community then it will by some strange process of osmosis become a part of that community. This is of course rarely the reality, especially in the case of the community school based upon a secondary unit. Size for such schools is an important strength and not merely an unfortunate by-product. Parents and pupils, responding to the changing social technological environment, rightly demand a broad curriculum along with the necessary specialist staff and facilities. The too-often overlooked but undeniable advances that have been achieved in the quality of education offered to young people during the last two decades have in part flowed from this development.

Morris certainly recognized the need for larger units to enable the breadth of experience presented to the pupil and community alike to be extended. He also justified his experiment – it should never be forgotten – by stressing the potential economies of scale that could be secured from the amalgamation of scattered and poorly resourced schools. Efficiency was not, of course, the only justification for larger units. Supporters of comprehensive and community schools in particular have always seen them as a means of achieving a social mix, of breaking down class and ethnic barriers. For example the working party set up in 1965 to advise the government on comprehensive reorganization laid down three objectives for a comprehensive school which were:

1   To gather pupils of the whole ability range in one school.
2   To collect pupils representing a cross-section of society in one school.
3   To concentrate teachers and facilities to use scarce resources economically.

(NFER 1968 p. xi)

Those objectives may have been embellished but they have never been jettisoned. The second of them is of course a laudable aim but given the growing ghettoization of British society along the lines of class and income, not least as a result of housing policies enacted since the early 1950s, it is an objective that can only be achieved by the creation of artificial catchment areas of recourse to 'bussing'. Especially in the urban setting, any catchment area designed 'to collect a cross-section of society' must seek recourse to the linking of 'communities' and the division of others. By this means the LEA can, they hope, prevent the creation of 'sink schools', whilst also endeavouring to satisfy the demand of teachers for their 'fair share' of the academic achievers.

   What they cannot do, if we are honest, is satisfy all parties. In many areas and localities, whatever the rhetoric, the introduction of the community school has been a cop-out for a weak LEA – an easy option that is founded on a policy that deliberately sets its face against the uncomfortable decisions that are entailed for an LEA that opts to break down ethnic and class barriers. Middle-class and white parents, often with the connivance of teachers, councillors and even community workers, may enthuse about a community school precisely because it isolates their children from working-class and black children or because it 'makes the job easier'. There is, whatever the more naive advocates may say, no longer anything profoundly radical or progressive about the community school, or for that matter, school-based youth work. Both are, in a sense, the new orthodoxy and as such posses little cachet. Indeed as Nash (1980) notes in the case of the village colleges of Cambridgeshire, a number even by the late 1950s had 'without a positive commitment to community education and without a distinguishing curriculum … become an unremarkable secondary school' (p. 24).

This needs to be stressed for it means that support for community schools and their expansion should always be conditional and based upon a critical assessment of their potential impact and designated function. For youth workers such critical support for community schools and school-based youth provision can only be conditional and must always be based upon an engagement with questions of access and the relationship of catchment areas to need.

In rural localities policies linked with both the establishment of community schools and comprehensives have meant that whilst one village or small town may gain a major resource in the shape of a new or enlarged community school, others will lose their often cherished local school. It also means invariably that an increasing number of pupils will have to travel longer distances to school. Similarly, if less dramatically, in the urban and suburban context such policies have resulted in schools drawing their pupils from a wider catchment area. The distances travelled in terms of mileage may be less but with regards the community boundaries traversed they can be both more traumatic for the school student and inhibiting for the adult or young person seeking access to adult education or youth facilities. Fewer and fewer schools are likely in the future to serve a single or clearly defined community as new and as yet often uncharted pressures come into play.

Firstly the amalgamation of existing schools will increase in the coming months and years as a result of the need for LEAs to achieve substantial economies of scale in order to eke out their shrinking budgets and survive the impact of declining school rolls. The pressure on LEAs to close and amalgamate units has now become virtually irresistible following the report of the Government's Audit Commission (1986) which called for the closure of over 1,000 secondary schools in the interests of greater efficiency. Secondly, especially in urban areas, but not exclusively so, as the rights granted parents and young people under the 1980 Education Act become more widely known these will seriously erode the ability of LEAs to create for schools, even community schools, a clearly defined catchment area and therefore determine the shape of their admissions. All this must of course be set against the backcloth of a steady but continuous reduction in the quality and availability of public transport. Already many community schools are isolated from a sizeable proportion of their potential clients by an absence of public transport. The potential clients of the youth provision are amongst those most likely to lack access to private transport. As a result many youth wings attached to community schools cater for a tiny minority of those for whom the facility was ostensibly established. As a consequence these facilities despite the best intentions of the workers involved become the 'property' of a small segment of the potential client group.

Youth workers have long accepted that young people are divided, sometimes dramatically so, not only by class and race but also by allegiance to a sub-cultural grouping and to a neighbourhood. This leads to a complex interrelationship between young people. Membership of one group is of course not exclusive and links and cross-fertilization do take place on a significant scale, but such divisions do create a tendency for a measure of homogeneity amongst the clientèle. Clubs, projects and units tend to become the property of one segment of the potential client group. Those who come to control its character may be simply those who happen to live in the immediate neighbourhood, or the young people from a single ethnic grouping, or those with a particular sub-cultural affiliation, or a group of young people who are not only the pupils attending a particular school but who, in addition, have a shared identity. As Whiteside found (1984; see also Tann *et al* 1983) in the community schools he researched this shared identity may relate to the location of the young person within the hierarchy of academic achievement with those 'from the top and bottom ends of the performance range under-represented'.

It is hardly surprising that the evidence further indicates that those young people who reject schooling will also tend to turn their backs on any youth provision linked to the community school (Holland 1976). Potentially, that element within the school population may embrace not simply those who truant, but also pupils under suspension and the generally disaffected. Self-evidently, the size of that grouping will vary from school to school, reflecting not only the nature of the catchment area, but also more importantly, the internal structure and policies of the school (Reynolds 1976, 1980: Smith 1986). Irrespective of the particular conditions appertaining to an individual school, it is important to acknowledge that the number who may, to one degree or another reject the school, are not significant. Certainly, after all the research, the Thompson Report found that only 61 per cent of young people were positive in their attitude towards school (DES 1983), whilst Pratt and Grimshaw (1984) found that by the last year of schooling over 5 per cent missed half the lessons. It is therefore naïve to imagine that a youth service integrated within a community school structure will be capable of meeting the social education needs of these young people who choose to reject the school itself. For such young people, alternative non school-based provision will remain an essential prerequisite for any sustained intervention. Insofar as the community school and school-based provision syphons resources from such forms of youth work, it needs to be restrained.

School-based youth provision, irrespective of whether or not the institution concerned is a community school, has a number of severe limitations. These have to be recognized from the outset. However, the flaws are not necessarily endemic and should not be allowed to obscure the potential strengths of such forms of provision. Community schools have a valuable role to play in the future development of the youth service and it may well be the case that over the coming years they will emerge as the dominant mode within the statutory sector. The absence of any sustained capital investment in the youth service means that as the youth clubs which were built in the years following the Albemarle report (1960) come to the end of their useful life and grow evermore dilapidated, then the service will have to be located within school settings. The widespread use of redundant school buildings which LEAs are currently transferring to the youth service is nothing more than a short-term solution to a chronic lack of facilities.

Firstly, a high proportion of those schools are redundant precisely because they are located in areas of declining population and therefore cannot serve the needs of more than a tiny proportion of young people. As always, facilities, if they are to be of any use, must be accessible to young people who will normally lack independent transport. Secondly those buildings are overwhelmingly unsuitable for the needs of the youth service. They were designed for a totally different function and cannot be adapted without massive investment which simply is not available and if it was could probably be more effectively spent elsewhere. Finally, redundant school-buildings are extremely expensive to maintain in terms of running costs. Such costs can rarely be pared down for the absence of adequate daily maintenance means that those costs inevitably rise steeply over time. Within a few years, LEAs will have no alternative but to bulldoze many, if not the majority, of those buildings to the ground. At that point the youth service will either have to shift into existing school units or engage in a building programme on an unprecedented scale. Given the economic climate it is unlikely that the latter course of action is a realistic policy option. Therefore growth of the school-based youth service has an air of inevitability about it. As has already been noted, this could be a retrograde move but this need not inevitably be the case.

Youth work within the community school

The community school will have to acknowledge that the traditional limitations of school-based youth work must be overcome whilst building upon its undoubted strengths. This means that as far as youth work is concerned the community school will have to adopt a model of intervention that lays much greater emphasis upon outreach work. The existing school-based youth work overwhelmingly fails to meet the needs of the wider community. This failure is not the fault of individuals or even necessarily a reflection of the shortcomings of particular styles of work but is the inevitable by-product of the structural divisions within our society. The community school must learn that it is not feasible to expect more than a small proportion of the client group of the youth service to be catered for within one building, however lavishly endowed that building might be. The community school must therefore, as a matter of course ensure that resources are set aside for detached work on the streets, for small groups meeting in alternative venues off-site and for project work that takes place away from the youth wing or unit.

They need also to listen to the young people themselves who often have a clear perception of the manifest gaps in current provision. This requires, as the Wolverhampton survey showed, that youth provision must provide more skill training, offer more advice and counselling services, stay open later and not confine itself to school terms, lay on more educational courses and a wider diet of activities (Willis 1985). It must also be prepared to fund and staff units that may duplicate its own provision but which are targetted towards groups of young people unable or reluctant to use the facilities located on the campus. If it does not, then significant groups of young people, (for reasons already discussed,) will be disenfranchised as far as access to youth work facilities are concerned.

A few community schools are already beginning to operate according to a model that recognizes the self-evident limitations of what can be achieved with and by even the best of workers operating within a school-based setting. At present such community schools tend to be the exception rather than the norm. In the vast majority youth work is, not surprisingly, given a low priority and off-site youth provision even more so. The probability that the majority will in the immediate future shift their orientation to any significant degree is not high. Success still tends to be measured in terms of the number through the door, whether it be with regard to adult education or youth work. Indeed 'budget-financing' and other schemes to encourage the financial 'autonomy' of the community school are putting even greater pressure on them to operate the numbers game with a predictable concentration of resources upon the profitable and the popular. The belief in increased financial autonomy for community schools on the part of LEAs has unfortunately less to do with a conversion to de-centralization and a great deal more to do with the trimming of budgets and the transference of responsibility for the taking and implemenation of uncomfortable decisions relating to resource allocation down the line to middle-management, such as head teachers and community staff.

Whatever the rhetoric, and however great the hypocrisy, the end product of such policies is not difficult to predict. Overwhelmingly it leads to the gradual but marked erosion of resources made available to those groups who are expensive to cater for and who possess low incomes. Young people unfortunately have an unhappy knack of being both – simultaneously.

The ability of community schools to cater for those who do not, or cannot, come to them is not in doubt. What is, though, is whether they have the will or desire to do so. Wallis and Mee found in the context of adult education 'little evidence of positive outreach' and noted the insularity of the community schools reflected in the inflexibility of their opening hours and in the absence of 'sensitive networking' with community groups and other agencies in the field. The same writers also found that they 'tended to use fewer outside premises than other types of adult education institutions'.

In relation to youth work, the literature makes for equally dismal reading. The consensual view that emerges is that community school structures can create for the youth workers and tutors operating within them almost insurmountable problems (Dunlop 1985; Kirby 1985; Jeffs 1979). These workers find themselves to be operating in an environment in which their colleagues have little clear idea as to their role and function or in which they found virtually no understanding of either the aims or objectives of youth work. The result is so often that the school staff, rather than gaining sympathy and insight from the proximity to youth work practice, merely have their prejudices confirmed. Even worse, the youth tutor may come to be seen as a source of disruption and discontent, an enemy within, to be isolated and anatomized.

Youth work is about many things, but it has a crucial function to perform as an agency offering support and advice to young people. For many young people their 'problems' flow not from their own inadequacy but from the manifest failings of the education system. A dynamic and supportive youth worker must, as a consequence, inevitably clash at times with the school system if s/he is to serve the real as opposed to the artificial needs of young people. Unless youth tutors are to deliberately opt out of working with young people who truant, are disruptive or are victimized in some way by the school, then they will themselves inevitably be placed at the very vortex of the conflict between the young person/client and the institution of the school. Also, unless they choose to reject or modify key elements of youth work practice, such as the right to voluntary attendance, the right to participation within decision-making process for the clients and the sustaining of non-directive relationship with the young people, then they will find themselves working within a tradition that is at odds with that of the school system.

Youth work within a school setting is not an easy option and the history of failure and conflict that has been highlighted by so many writers cannot lightly be dismissed as flowing from clashes of personality and bad management. The structural causes of that conflict have to be understood and addressed by all parties, but especially by those who within the current structures control the institutions. Is it any wonder then, given a combination of the nature of their work and the pattern of their working day, that school-based youth workers find themselves both marginalized and given a relatively lowly status? This can occur to the extent that, according to one study, 'there was only limited contact between school staffs and community education workers' (Nisbet *et al* 1980).

Head teachers and other senior management within all schools are drawn overwhelmingly from backgrounds that give them little understanding of the realities of youth work or the pressures that the worker is likely to experience. As a consequence, those in overall charge appeared to perceive youth work overwhelmingly in terms of activities and judge the ability of the youth worker according to their success or failure in sustaining what are perceived as 'constructive activities' (Jeffs 1979)

This lack of clarity and understanding has serious consequences not ony in terms of job satisfaction, but also in the nature of the tasks performed. As Dunlop (1985) notes, as a consequence school-based youth workers all too easily find themselves in a position where the tasks and responsibilities allotted them may bear only a passing relationship to creative or constructive youth work. In another example Stone (1986) provides a graphic description of the experience of one worker which shows how they were expected by an unsympathetic management to function primarily as a caretaker. The inappropriate use of youth tutors partly flows from the fact that those who come to hold the senior positions and particularly the headships of community schools are rarely trained or prepared for that role. They are chosen from the ranks of the teaching profession, in much the same way and according to much the same criteria as any other head teacher and few, if any, have prior experience of adult education, youth or community work. The gaps in their background can be partly overcome by sensitive training programmes and more careful selection, but it is likely that such a solution will lead to more than a marginal improvement. The root causes of the problems encountered both by adult educators and youth and community workers operating with community schools lie deep within the structures of those institutions.

The specific difficulties facing youth workers may flow from the reality that community schools are a great idea grafted onto a bad institution. A major problem is that the concept of the 'community school' is based upon a vision of what the school might become. Indeed its most vociferous advocates often sustain it as an idea on the grounds that it will reform the school system by stealth. The motives are excellent but it is misguided to imagine that the youth and the adult education services can be used in some way as a fifth column to reform and liberalize our schools from the inside. Given the unequal size of the combatants, the outcome of the conflict is predetermined. It will not be the youth and adult tutor who will change the school but the school that will change, marginalize, burn or drive *them* out.

As long as our schools remain the undemocratic institutions they are at the present, run on a managerial model that Captain Bligh would find attractive and in which the main consumers, the students, are accorded no basic rights, then youth work and community work will find itself uncomfortable in such a setting. The lack of a real say in school affairs for teachers, students, parents and other consumers makes a mockery of concepts such as involvement and participation within the youth work setting. The disillusionment of so many youth tutors with schools is rooted in a clear conflict over styles of work, professional ethos and training. Such conflict cannot be lightly wished away for it is a manifestation of a fundamental clash which relates to how the worker should treat and engage with young people. Good youth work practice is to be found within community schools and the community school without an active commitment to youth work is a misnomer. Having said that, the resistance of many youth workers to a closer involvement with community schools and community educators will not be easily overcome. They rightly distrust the imperialistic nature of the school system and the concentration of administrative and managerial power within it in the hands of one barely accountable individual. They also need to be convinced that the growing integration of youth work within schools has more to recommend it than short-term economic and administrative expediency. When they have been shown that community schools will change internally and are beginning to adopt styles of teaching, curriculum practices and administrative structures that give their students and the wider community a role to play beyond that of the passive consumer then, and only then, will the barriers begin to dissolve.

References

Adams, R. (1987). 'Youth workers and juvenile justice', in Jeffs, T. and Smith, M. (eds), *Welfare and Youth Work Practice*, Macmillan.

Adams, R., Allard, S., Baldwin., J. and Thomas, J. (1981). *A Measure of Diversion?* National Youth Bureau.

Albemarle Report. (1960). *The Youth Service In England and Wales*. HMSO.

Audit Commission. (1986). *Towards Better Management of Secondary Education*. HMSO.

Booton, P. (1980). 'De-schooling youth service', in Booton, F. and Dearling, A. (eds), *The 1980s and Beyond*, National Youth Bureau.

Boulter, P. (1980). 'Size, site and systems', in Fletcher, C. and Thompson, N. (eds), *Issues In Community Education,* Falmer Press.

CETYCW (Council for the Education & Training of Youth and Community Workers). (1985). *The Supplying of Training*. CETYCW.

Davies, B. (1981). *The State We're In*. National Youth Bureau.

DES. (1982). *Experience and Participation.* (Thompson Report), HMSO, Cmnd 8686.

DES. (1983). *Young People in the 80s: a Survey.* HMSO.

DES. (1985). *Statistical Bulletin 2/85.*

Dunlop, S. (1985). 'The role of the youth tutor', *Youth & Policy* (12).

Fairbairn, A. (1969). 'Youth service in community colleges', *Adult Education*, vol. 41.

Fletcher, C. (1980). 'The theory of community education and its relation to adult education', in Thompson, J. (ed.), *Adult Education For a Change*, Hutchinson.

Gibbon, R. and Waters, S. (1984). *Young People in Gwent*, The People and Work Unit, Newport, Gwent.

Hendry, L. (1983). *Growing Up and Going Out.* Aberdeen University Press.

Holland, J. (1976). Parental involvement in an evolving community school', unpublished B. Phil, University of York.

Holt, J. (1985). *No Holiday Camps.* Association of Juvenile Justice.

Jeffs, A. (1979). *Young People and the Youth Service.* Routledge and Kegan Paul.

Kirby, R. (1985–6). 'Democracy and control in community education', *Youth Policy* (15).

Lawson, K. (1977). 'Community education: a critical assessment', *Adult Education* vol. 50, no. 1.

Linell, J. (1983). 'Looking after the early leavers', *Youth In Society*, no. 80.

National Foundation for Education Research. (1968). *Comprehensive Education in England and Wales.* NFER.

Nisbet, J., Hendry, L., Stewart, C. and Watt, J. (1980). *Towards Community Education.* Aberdeen University Press.

Pratt, J. and Grimshaw, R. (1984). 'School absenteeism and the education crisis', *Youth and Policy*, (10).

Reynolds, D. (1976). 'The delinquent school', in Hammersley, M. and Woods, P. (eds), *The Process of Schooling*, Routledge & Kegan Paul.

Reynolds, D. (1980). 'School factors and truancy', in Hersou, L. and Berg, I. (eds), *Out of School*, Wiley.

Sheils, F. (1985). 'School-based youth work, unpublished report, National Youth Bureau, Leicester.

Secondary Headteachers Association. (1979). 'Report no. 3 (June 1979) of Community Schools Working Party', *SHA Review*, no. 234.

Smith, David R. (1984). *Great Today: Gone Tommorrow?* National Council For Voluntary Youth Servies.

Smith, D. (1986). School suspensions, *Youth and Policy*, 18.

Smith, M. and Jeffs, T. (1987). 'The political economy of youth work', in Smith, M. and Jeffs, T. (eds), *Welfare and Youth Work Practice*, Macmillan.

Stone, C. (1987). 'Youth Workers and Caretakers', in Jeffs, T. and Smith, M. (eds), Youth Work, Macmillan.

Tann, S., Gann, N. and Whiteside, T. (1983). 'Youth and the new Leicestershire community colleges', *Journal of Community Education*, vol. 2, no. 2.

Thompson, N. (1983). Abraham Moss Centre: the experience of continuing education', in Moon, B. (ed.) *Comprehensive Schools: Challenge and Change*. NFER, Nelson.

Wallis, J. and Mee, G. (1983). *Community Schools: Claims and Performance*, Dept. of Adult Education, University of Nottingham.

Webley, I. (1971). 'The youth wing', in Rogers, T. (ed.), *School For the Community*, Routledge & Kegan Paul.

Whiteside, T. (1984). 'Youth and community education', unpublished mimeo.

Willis, P. (1985). *The Social Condition of Young People in Wolverhampton in 1984*. Wolverhampton Borough Council.

CHAPTER 7

Neighbourhood centres, not community schools

KELVYN RICHARDS

This proposal challenges the basic assumption, built into the organization of most community schools and colleges, that the professional management of formal education is compatible with community access to and control over campus resources. Richards argues the case for segregation rather than integration (based on dual as distinct from unified management) as the guiding principle for institutionally-based developments. This is, in effect, a radical proposal to literally 'deschool' community education. As such, it raises fundamental questions about the rationale of community education and, in particular, the balance between its educational, social and political components.

The Community Education debate has involved discussions about:

- The nature of education.
- Access to, and control of, the education service.
- Participation in the education process.
- The use of educational facilities.
- The relationships between professionals and clients, and the institution and the users.
- Accountability and responsibility.
- Hierarchy and democracy in educational institutions.

The community education movement has been concerned to evaluate and criticize current practices in schools, colleges and other educational centres, (Midwinter 1975; Fletcher and Thompson 1980; Fletcher 1984). For the development of community education in this country has been school focused. The assumption has been that if it is to do with education, then it must be to do with schools.

If it is to do with schools, then it must be paid for and controlled by the local education authority. (Midwinter 1973; Poster 1982; Fairbairn 1978).

The dilemmas of community education

Community education in debate is a reappraisal and critique of the current practices of educational institutions, but in practice is based in those institutions. Schools and colleges may be seen as bureaucracies, operated by hierarchies of professionals. (Wallis and Mee 1983; Easthope 1975.) Given that community education in theory is based on a set of propositions that are to do with:

- Access to any educational opportunity for all at any time.
- Greater participation by more people in the decisions about the use of educational premises and the kinds of curricula that are offered by them.
- Informal learning in the family, in clubs, community centres and on street corners.

It becomes clear that community education in practice should not be subject to schools and colleges. What is more, one ought to ask what we thought we were doing creating community schools or community colleges. They are not run by local communities, but by groups of professionals who may have very little in common with them. Such enterprises may be seen as being much more to do with the aggrandizement of the professionals of the education service than with the education of the local communities.

A matter of resources and facilities

Having come to such a conclusion does not actually help. It simply confronts us with yet another dilemma. Local communities cannot afford to ignore the facilities, equipment, buildings, resources, and staffing that are invested in their local schools and colleges. If you asked the people living in a given neighbourhood what sort of provision they required, it would certainly include meeting rooms for clubs and societies, rehearsal rooms for drama, opera and musicals, a hall for dances, for public meetings, and for performances, for weddings and receptions, facilities for sports and training; local branches of the local library, social services, employment, and police; centres for the unemployed, for skill training, for drugs; clinics for guidance and counselling; youth clubs; facilities for organizing pre-school playgroups, adult literacy groups, luncheon clubs, women's groups.

The limited resources available to any area necessitate the most careful scrutiny of the use of available facilities. This means that schools and colleges as buildings cannot be ignored, because they contain an abundance of amenities essential to all these activities. If such campuses were available for seven days a week, 52 weeks of the year, many of the demands of the neighbourhood could be satisfied (Midwinter 1975; Poster 1982; Fairbairn 1978; Fletcher 1984). You may wish to protest at this point that the question of the use of facilities is marginal to the theory, debate, and practice of community education. It is being suggested that this question leads directly to issues about access, ownership, accountability, and responsibility for education, all of which are at the centre of community education.

Local neighbourhoods would be foolish if they did not avail themselves of the facilities in educational institutions. This conclusion may help to find a way around our several dilemmas. In the first place, it may be useful to think of a 'school' or 'college' as a facility – as a set of buildings, as a campus, which is occupied for part of the week, and for part of the year, by teachers and pupils/students. Unfortunately, we are well conditioned to regard such schools and colleges as the properties of the teachers in general, and the head teachers in particular. We do not normally regard them as a facility, as a local amenity for the neighbourhood, the town, or the district. Therefore, in the second place, if we begin to see the teachers and pupils as tenants, and no longer view the head teacher as the landlord, then it is possible to conclude that other groups have a right to be tenants of these facilities. Local residents have access to these campuses. In the past the principal tenant, the school or the college, has been allowed totally to determine how the campus was used, and to control access and availability. This has happened in spite of the fact that this tenant has occupied the premises for only seven hours out of any 24, and 40 weeks out of 52. These campuses are the property of the rate payers, however. The local communities may be regarded as collective landlords, and need to exert their responsibilities for the use and development of such places. (Easthope 1975; Wallis and Mee 1983.)

Local government

This is all easier said than done. We do not live in a participatory democracy in which our rights to be involved in decision-making processes would be protected; we do live in a representative democracy, where we depend upon the understanding and support of others in order to bring about change. Therefore, it is necessary to consider any proposals for change within the present structure of local government. It is possible within the confines of local government to establish a pattern of what may be described as neighbourhood campuses? Is it possible to operate a system of local control within the requirements of centralized budgetary controls? Is it possible to run a neighbourhood campus without it becoming dominated by the school?

Education is a service provided either by county councils or by metropolitan district councils; it is not one of the services provided at a local level. If community education is part of this existing pattern of school provision, then the involvement of local communities in the planning and organization of these 'community schools' is highly unlikely. In order to promote the local development of community education in the form of neighbourhood campuses, then it is necessary to render them subject to local control as a legitimate part of local government (Midwinter 1975; Byrne 1981; Poster 1982).

Under the 1972 Local Government Act, local authorities were reorganized into larger units of local government so as to ensure that sufficient resources were available to provide the required services. Most, if not all, of the borough and rural councils, as well as the smaller county councils, were abolished.

County councils

Forty-seven county councils were created, with populations varying from 100,000 to almost 1.5 million, responsible for most of the planning, protective, (fire, police, consumer protection, disease of animals, licensing), and personal services (education, careers, and social work).

District councils

Within these counties 333 district councils were formed, with populations ranging from 18,000 to 422,000, responsible for such services as housing, environmental health, and amenities. Six metropolitan counties were also created – but these were abolished from April 1986. Within these, there were 36 metropolitan districts, which are now responsible for planning, transport, and highways; as well as housing, education, welfare and environmental health; and the planning and provision of amenities (Byrne, 1981).

Local councils

The Redcliffe-Maud report which formed the basis of this Local Government Act made it clear that the committee was worried by the fact that their recommendations were instrumental in placing the reins of power a long way from local communities. They were most concerned therefore to promote the formation of local councils.

In England, a third tier of local government was retained – the parish council. There are at present 7,200 parish councils in England. In Wales, there are community councils. In urban areas, there are still town councils. Collectively, these are known as local councils. These local councils are subject to the district councils. Their functions are four-fold:

1 The provision of local amenities such as allotments, community halls, parks and playing fields, swimming baths, bus shelters, parking facilities, cemeteries, footpaths, public conveniences, control of litter, and the encouragement of arts and crafts, and tourism.
2 They have the power to precept and spend a 2p rate, and spend it on particular interests if necessary.
3 They must be consulted about the appointment of managers to primary schools, and notified about local planning applications and changes in the bye-laws.
4 They act as a forum for the discussion of local affairs and represent the interests of the local communities to the district and county councils.

While it is true to say that such local councils do not have any responsibility for educational services, it could be argued that their concern for local amenities could be used as a basis for influencing the decisions of the other tiers of local government. It is this possible development of the role and function of the local council that should be of greatest concern to anyone interested in the promotion of community education in local neighbourhoods.

Neighbourhood councils

Since 1972 successive governments have also encouraged the formation of 'neighbourhood' councils. This has been most significant in urban areas (for we must acknowledge that parish councils function predominantly in rural areas). At the present time, such neighbourhood councils are non-statutory, and are based on populations ranging from 3,000 to 20,000. They are often the product of local community issues and local action groups.

There is an Association for Neighbourhood Councils, which is determined to establish neighbourhood councils on a statutory basis, with the right to provide services and to precept on the rating authorities.

The objectives of a neighbourhood council may be:

1 To represent to other organizations such as the county council, the district council, the central government, or industrial or commercial companies the needs and wishes of the local communities; to act as the 'ears, eyes and mouth' of the neighbourhood on all aspects of community development; to campaign for local amenities such as sports facilities, shopping areas, play space, or a community hall; to protect the local environment by questioning development plans, the derelict land and the empty properties in the area.
2 To organize self-help in local areas in order to improve the quality of life for the residents, for example, play schemes, or good neighbour projects.
3 To help those in need of special facilities by providing services and amenities, and providing advisory services.
4 To foster and preserve a concern for the neighbourhood amongst the residents. (q.v. Byrne 1981).

It would seem that there is the scope to create local councils, which could provide the support within local government to develop neighbourhood centres. (Midwinter, 1975). Indeed some local authorities are actively pursuing such a policy. For example, the City of Birmingham over the last two years has set up a comprehensive network of local neighbourhood councils in order to promote local consultation. Derbyshire, in its most recent policy document on community education is beginning to talk about community education councils, which would control educational provision within prescribed areas.

Neighbourhood centres

Educational services are the responsibility of county councils or metropolitan district councils, but local amenities are the responsibility of the local council, in collaboration with the district council. If the buildings and facilities of a 'local school or college' are regarded as a local amenity, a neighbourhood centre, in which the formal education of young people takes place for part of the day, then it is possible to see that the use of that campus for the rest of the time can become the responsibility of the local council, and not of the head of the school/college, nor of the county council.

In reality, of course, the situation cannot be as clear cut as it is stated here. In order to make clear the point of the argument, it is necessary to polarize the relationships between the local council, the school/college, and the county council. The creation of a neighbourhood centre would require considerable negotiation and cooperation. Although the local council may administer the neighbourhood centre in the interests of the local communities, it could never afford to run it out of its own resources. The whole operation would still need to be funded by the county and the district councils. The local council would act as the organizing agent for the local residents on the one side, and the county/district councils on the other. This arrangement may also result in the education department, and the education committee negotiating with the local councils as to the design, organization, and use of such campuses (Fairbairn 1978).

A plan for neighbourhood centres

The statutory local councils are intended to represent populations of up to 20,000 in number. This seems to be rather a large number for effective consultation and participation in local matters. It is suggested therefore that the statutory local councils could establish neighbourhood councils designed to represent up to 4,000 people. For example, a town with a population of 12,000 will have a town council; but it could also establish a number of neighbourhood

councils, say four, each representing 3,000. Each neighbourhood
council could represent community groups, action groups, tenants'
association, cultural groups, leisure groups, social services,
educational services, special interest groups.

A town council, with four neighbourhood councils, decides that
it wishes to develop a plan of neighbourhood centres, based upon
the existing school campuses in the town. There happen to be four
secondary, and six primary (junior-infant) schools in the town, on
four campuses. There is one campus in each neighbourhood.

Clearly the discussions and planning relating to the
implementation of such a plan would take a long time, involving
many people from the local communities, the local schools, as well
as local and central government. However, the basis of the
negotiations needs to be that the 'school' is owned by the county
council for the use and benefit of the local residents; that although
one of the principal users of the neighbourhood centre will be the
young people and their teachers, 'the school', the responsibility for
how it is used, and by whom, is that of the town council and the
neighbourhood council.

The centre and the school

Who should be in charge of such a neighbourhood centre? This is a
most difficult question. Given that the principal user is the school,
then it would seem to make a lot of sense to make the head of the
school the head of the centre. At this point the implications of the
previous analysis – that schools, by definition, are to do with a
single client group, children, and limited access, and not to do with
the whole community, participation, and open access.
Headteachers are more concerned with running a closed system,
than they are an open system. It is thus a very bad idea to put the
head of the school in charge of the neighbourhood centre. These are
not the only reasons for coming to this conclusion. Those of you
who have worked in schools or colleges that are designated
'community' will know only too well that the school system comes
to dominate all other considerations. The school has a mandatory
obligation to educate the children. This means that every initiative
is subordinated to this obligation. Any activity that does not
involve children is secondary to those that do. Over a period of
time this had the effect of diverting resources to the school away
from the 'community'. For example, if you are involved in a

'community' activity, and there are not enough members of staff to cover the school classes, then you are required to fulfil the mandatory obligation. If monies are left unspent at the end of the year, then they will be spent on school, rather than community. In timetabling the work of the 'community school', it is common practice to timetable all the school activities as top priority, and then to allocate staff time for the community activities as a secondary priority. The services offered by such institutions tend to reflect the skills of the staff rather than the requirements of the local communities – 'service-delivery'. The local residents are expected to accept what is on offer, what services are being delivered. In these ways the 'community schools' or 'community colleges' operate as educational institutions, rather than as neighbourhood centres. The head of the school/college inevitably runs the institution on those terms. As was observed earlier, the principal tenant functions as the landlord (Fairbairn 1978; Poster 1982; Fletcher 1984).

There is another set of reasons for keeping the school/college separate from the overall organization of the neighbourhood centre. In those local authorities where schools/colleges have been developed as community campuses, there has been a constant concern that the school is not being sacrificed to the interests of the community. Actual experience has shown that such fears have been totally unfounded, and that the reverse has been the case. Nevertheless, local residents and parents and local councillors have been worried by this possibility. Indeed, this worry has been so entrenched that boards of governors have appointed people to be heads of these 'community schools/colleges' that they are certain will look after the interests of the school/colleges (Willis and Mee 1983; Fletcher 1984) to the exclusion of all other interests.

The concept of the neighbourhood centre that is being developed here may avoid such concerns simply because the use of the centre by the school need not have any curriculum nor organizational implications for the school. The organization of the campus will change, but the school can operate as before during the school day. This option may be regarded by some as an advantage. One of the most serious reservations held by parents about 'community schools' is that they will interfere with the education of their children.

Management and governance

There will be a management committee. This will represent the interests of the county council, and the local councils, the users of the centre, the local residents, and the various special interest groups in the neighbourhood. The school will be represented on this committee as one of the principal users. It will be a federal system, not a warden system.

The function of the management committee will be to identify the principles and priorities according to which the centre will be run; to develop policies concerning the future development of the centre, to arbitrate in major disagreements concerning the use of the centre, and to represent the interests of the centre at the local and county councils.

Hopefully this management committee would relate to, and work with the board of governors of the school. But it is not essential; their functions are fairly distinct. The management committee would be responsible for the use of the whole centre, while the governors would be concerned with the school – only one aspect of the work of the whole centre. One would expect that the governors would be members of the management committee of the centre. Indeed, it may be acceptable for the local councillors and county/district councillors to be members of both bodies.

General administrator

The management committee would not run the day-to-day affairs of the neighbourhood centre. This should be done by a general administrator, with the assistance of an administrative secretariat. The general administrator would be directly responsible to the committee. S/he would implement policy and monitor the use and the condition of the premises. The secretariat would be responsible for bookings, fees, terms and conditions of use, the coordination of cleaning and caretaking. An important part of the work of the general administrator would be the marketing of the centre to the local neighbourhood, making it clear that it is available for their use at all times, that it is a facility for them and their families. S/he would constantly liaise with the school, the further education tutors, the sports and leisure organizations, as they would probably be the principal users of the centre. S/he would also need to meet frequently with the management committee in order to monitor that the centre was being run according to the accepted principles and priorities, as well as make plans for the future.

The general administrator would need to be a negotiator, as well as an administrator, in order to run the centre efficiently. S/he should be actively aware of the needs of schools, and the perspectives and priorities of teachers. It would be essential for the administrative secretariat to work cooperatively with the school staff so as to promote maximum access to various facilities during the year. For example, the secretariat would need to understand the vagaries of school timetables sufficiently to know that a room or equipment that is ostensibly timetabled for use throughout the year may actually not be used for up to half the year, or only in six week cycles, or not in the month of December. Or, in the secondary school, that during examinations many rooms and facilities are unused. This may mean that actual use of facilities and equipment by the school may not match timetabled use, and therefore it may be necessary to monitor actual use week by week.

The model that is emerging is similar to that of an arts or sports centre, both of which comprise specialist equipment and rooms for hire. No one group owns the centre. Everybody does. Inevitably, those who use it the most come to consider that it is theirs and that they – possess it. But they do not and may need to be reminded of that fact now and again. One of the major roles of the general administrator will be to supervise the different demands of the various users. If the centre is to be accessible to all potential users, this may cause some friction. For example, the use of the facilities by the youth club may not be compatible with the expectations of the school, or sports groups, or adult evening classes. If the centre was to host a drug therapy unit, there may be many raised eyebrows by the old age pensioners, or the play group leaders, or the nursery class. The development of training sessions for unemployed youngsters may encourage them to hang around the centre and be perceived as a threat by others. Open access does not mean unsupervised access. The centre would have to be run so that all users feel at ease for most of the time. Negotiations would need to take place concerning the use of the premises and the location of the various activities.

Financial implications

What are the financial implications of these proposals? Even though they are based upon existing provision, the proposals will attract additional costs. But the most significant feature of the concept of a neighbourhood centre is that it may only involve the redistribution of finances, rather than the raising of new revenues. Obviously, the whole idea depends upon the county council continuing to provide the buildings, staffing, and equipment for the schools on the campus. Other services, such as the youth service, social services, community health, adult education, libraries, careers, leisure and recreation, could be involved in the resourcing of such a centre. This would not be in addition to what already exists, but instead of what is currently provided. The creation of such a neighbourhood centre would mean the centralizing of services and facilities on one site. The county and the district councils would no longer be involved in duplicating premises for the different services, they would all be found on the same neighbourhood site.

The neighbourhood centre could include a youth club, a library, a sports hall and gymnasium, classrooms, interview rooms, offices, a swimming pool, a meeting hall or theatre, and so on. Each different service would provide its own staffing, and would be in a position to share the capital costs for buildings (Ball 1974; Fletcher 1984). Two of the best examples of such campus provision are to be found in Nottinghamshire: the Sutton Centre in Sutton in Ashfield, and the Dukeries Centre in Ollerton.

The operation of the neighbourhood centre would raise income. The clubs, societies, and groups would pay fees for the hire of the premises. It may be that the different services may pay rental charges for the use of the centre in order to cover the costs of the cleaning and maintenance of the buildings, and the purchasing of equipment. The income of the centre could be paid entirely to the county council, or it could be used to pay for the additional maintenance and cleaning costs that would be incurred as a result of the more intensive use of the premises. It could also be used by the administrator and management committee for development work in the neighbourhood, or for sponsoring various activities at the centre. On the other hand, once the neighbourhood centre had been set up, it could be made totally responsible for the finances. This does not mean that it would not receive any income from the county council, only that the centre is allocated an annual budget, and is made responsible for spending it in the interests of the centre and the neighbourhood. If more money is required, then the administrative secretariat is responsible for raising the additional funds.

It is worth remembering that the local council is entitled to charge a 2p rate. This could mean that additional resources could be raised in order to finance particular local initiatives (Fairbairn 1978).

The appointment of a general administrator, and the formation of an administrative secretariat, would be an additional cost. This need not be a charge on any one department of the county council, but could be paid for jointly. The level of pay is a major problem. Should the administrator be paid a salary greater than the head teachers of the schools? If s/he was supervising their work and organizing the curriculum of the schools, then the answer would be 'yes'. Under these proposals, however, the administrator may not, need not, have anything to do with the running of the schools on the campus. Therefore, the salary does not have to be related to theirs. The management committee may feel that as a matter of status and seniority, their salaries should be comparable. In the final analysis, only local circumstances will resolve the position. For example, if money is limited, and there are limited opportunities for development in the first place, it may be decided to make the secretary of the local management committee the general administrator of the neighbourhood centre. Such an idea has quite a lot to recommend it other than financial considerations – for it would make sure that the organization of the centre is retained in the hands of local interests. One of the main drawbacks of making the general administrator a professional on a high salary is that s/he may become more concerned with professional standing in relation to the schools, than with providing an efficient service to the local neighbourhood. Another example may be that the resources available may not justify the creation of separate administrative secretariats. This may mean that in our town of 12,000 with the four neighbourhood councils, and four neighbourhood centres, there may be four administrators but one town secretariat.

Consultation, participation, accountability

However these matters are resolved it is most important to maintain the principles of local neighbourhood consultation, participation, and accountability, and not to get bogged down by arguments over status and bureaucratic efficiency. For example, such developments could not happen overnight. There would have to be extensive discussions not only between county, district, and local councillors, but also teachers, adult education tutors, youth workers, parent's groups, and community groups in the neighbourhood. Each party would have to see the neighbourhood centre as a local amenity for the benefit of all in the neighbourhood. It must not be seen as, and operated as, some department's or some group's empire. Systems of management and organization would have to be negotiated which would preserve rights of access and use for everyone.

At the same time, lines of accountability and responsibility would have to be drawn. Who is responsible for breakages, for replacements, for new equipment? What will be the lines of communication between user groups? Who arbitrates in matters of dispute? Who checks up on the bookings and the provision of equipment? One does not want to set in train a complicated system of bureaucracy in order to run these centres, but there must be agreement amongst all the users as to what the rules, regulations, and procedures are to be, along with a determination to abide by them. An inevitable consequence of these requirements is that decisions must be made in committee, not in a corner by a special interest group. Obviously such groups will attempt to further their own particular interests, but this must always be done in public, in committee. If any group contravenes the decisions of the neighbourhood centre committees, then there must be some means of redress – the payments of fines, or a ban from using the centre.

There must be agreements about the kind of use of the centre. It is to be 'educational, leisure, recreational' only, or available to any group for whatever purpose. What about 'strip shows' on a Saturday evening? Is the bar to be open normal opening hours? Could the premises be used for political meetings by any political party or organization? These matters need to be decided at the outset by everyone as a matter of policy. As all policies would be decided in committee, they can be changed too. Inevitably, practice and experience will lead people to see that some policies cannot be made to work, or have unfortunate side effects. For example, any decision to have the bar open normal licensing hours may mean that drunken adults are wandering around the school premises, threatening young people. It may be decided to close the bar, or to move it to a different location, or to base the local police station on the campus. Whatever is decided, decisions are to be taken by the neighbourhood centre committees, not unilaterally by one of the users of the centre. The creation of neighbourhood centres depends upon cooperation and communication between groups of local residents, local councillors, and officers of the county, district, and local councils.

General conclusions

Whatever notion of community education one has, if it is to become a reality then it has to be tailored to the actual systems and procedures of resource allocation and local government. The concept of neighbourhood centres is an attempt to match the ideas of local consultation, participation, and accountability, and access to education with what is possible within the constraints of local government and county council provision. While it is true that schools are not the best institutions in which to pursue community education, they do occupy buildings and use facilities that are ideal for the development of community education policies. The ownership of these resources is crucial to how they are used. For too long we have preteded that by simply calling a school, 'a community school', it automatically becomes the property of the local communities, and accessible to them. This is not the case. A 'community education campus', or a 'neighbourhood centre' does not need a school as an institution. It may need the facilities. A neighbourhood centre may have a school as part of it, but it is not the school.

Often we assume that there should be a policy of community education first, whereas all that is required initially may be the possibility of gaining access to resources and facilities that have hitherto been locked away behind closed doors. Once the doors arc unlocked, and the local residents get used to having access to them, then they will develop their own policies as to how they want them to be used. One way of securing access is to alter the system of management and governance of educational campuses. This alteration does not involve revolutionary changes. It does involve developing the roles of the local councils, and creating that of the neighbourhood council (Fletcher 1984).

Whether we like it or not, revised systems still require committees. All the proposals presented in this chapter will lead to more committees. This seems to be unavoidable. If the object of the exercise is to extend participation, consultation, negotiation, and administration to as many people as possible, then a necesary corollary of that is a more comprehensive network of committees. This statement is not intended to suggest that there is a complicated network of formal and boring committees. It may be better to think in terms of meetings to discuss policy and priorities. In the centre, each user group will be responsible for its own internal management and organization. But as regards the use and development of the centre, each interested party should be part of the decision-making procedure. In order to facilitate this, not only will each group be represented on the centre management committee, but each representative will be required to represent the views of the group, not merely their own personal views. This means that these representatives will have to develop procedures of consultation with their members. It is in this way that more people will be involved in more meetings. In the long run it may be necessary to make them formal committee meetings in order to record the proceedings, or at least to record the proposals agreed by the group. Only by recording what has been decided, can those decisions be transmitted to others. It also means that professionals working with these committees may have to become used to consulting and negotiating, rather than making arbitrary decisions.

If more people are expected to become part of the 'meeting' structures of the neighbourhood centres, then this may inhibit a number of people from becoming involved simply because they are intimidated by the very rigmaroles of serving on committees. To combat this, it may be advisable to implement not only training programmes on how to serve on a committee for all those who are interested, but also to develop means of meeting and consulting with people and recording their decisions without having to go through any of the rigmaroles.

The neighbourhood centre could not only become the arena for greater local participation and control over public amenities, it could also foster considerable inter-professional cooperation. The intention of the centre would be to establish as many of the public services as possible on one site. Each group of professionals would need to negotiate with the general administrator, and through the management committee for the use of resources. The resolution of these negotiations will often lead to their carrying out discussions with each other beforehand. This could of course lead to, at best, greater interprofessional cooperation, or, at worst, increased collusion and ganging up against the local residents. In order to avoid this it is most important that all decisions of policy and priority are made by the centre management committee, and not by any individual, or group. If the professional groups wish to establish priorities for the use of the centre, then they will have to consult and negotiate with the other interested parties. It would be naïve to believe that these professional groups will enjoy such consultation. Teachers, for example, are used to being consulted by parents. They are not used to consulting with parents, and even less with other residents.

The development of the neighbourhood centre will certainly lead to the more efficient use of premises. As we noted at the beginning, any public amenity that remains closed and inaccessible for so much of the time ought to be opened up. If we can think of those educational campuses that we call 'schools' as public amenities rather than the property of the head teacher, then they automatically become more accessible.

In future, when we think of community education, perhaps we should first ensure the use of educational facilities by the communities in the neighbourhood, before we consider whether or not the community is being educated.

References

Ball, C. (1974).'Hypermarket of corporate life', *Times Educational Supplement*.

Byrne, T. (1981). *Local Government In Britain*. Penguin Books.

Easthope, G. (1975). *Community, Hierarchy and Open Education*. Routledge & Kegan Paul.

Fairbairn, A. (1978). *The Leicestershire Community Colleges and Centres*. Dept. of Adult Education, University of Nottingham.

Fletcher, C. (1984). *The Challenges of Community Education*. Dept. of Adult Education, University of Nottingham.

Fletcher, C. and Thompson, N. (1980). *Issues In Community Education*. Falmer.

Midwinter, E. (1973). *Patterns of Community Education*. Ward Lock.

Midwinter, E. (1975). *Education and the Community*. Allen and Unwin.

Poster, C. (1982). *Community Education*. Heinemann.

Wallis, J. and Mee, G. (1983). *Community Schools: Claims and Performance*. Dept. of Adult Education, University of Nottingham.

CHAPTER 8

Community education: Third World perspectives

JOHN SAMUEL

Most community educators in the industrialized countries of the West remain remarkably ignorant of initiatives in community education and community development in the so-called 'Third World'. And yet, in many ways education systems in developing countries have more experience of responding to structural change in communities, and the expectations it stimulates and the social costs it creates. In this paper Samuel introduces the useful distinction between formal, nonformal and informal education and relates this to some of the concerns of community education. He goes on to examine key issues in the development of educational policy and practice in Tanzania, Kenya and Cuba and to indicate their relevance to contemporary community education in the West.

Much has been written about community education but very little is of immediate practical value to policy-makers and practitioners as the bulk of the literature is centred around conceptual abstraction or restricted to mere descriptions of a limited range of case studies. No one has ever had a glimpse of the total picture, that is, the global picture, simply because such a picture does not yet exist. The existing community education literature tends in the main to reflect Western European and North American traditions to the virtual exclusion of 'Third World' perspectives. The use of the terms 'First World' and 'Third World' is problematic. The terms themselves are value-laden and can generate notions of superiority and inferiority on the one hand and domination and subservience on the other. No such understandings are intended here. The terms 'First World' and 'Third World' are used in the popular sense, the former referring to those advanced, industralized nations in such areas as Western Europe, North America and the Far East which are characterized by high standards of living and high per capita incomes. The latter term principally refers to those countries commonly described as 'developing' or 'less developed' with comparatively low per capita incomes and standards of living, with mainly agriculture-based economies and which tend to have gained their political independence comparatively recently. These countries are mainly in Latin America, the Caribbean, Asia and Africa.

This chapter is essentially a comparative, qualititve account of community education in a number of randomly selected developing countries. In particular, it seeks to identify and analyse the competing and often conflicting, ideologies underpinning policy and practice and to explain the nature of policy and practice in their various historical, political, social and economic contexts.

Community education in most Third World countries has emerged from attempts at education reform but why were such reforms necessary at all? There begins the community education story:

Defining the context

Most of the Third World has at some point in history been European colonies and consequently, the education systems have in the main mirrored European counterparts. However, since independence, and even during the colonial period there have been changes in political orientation ranging from 'maintenance of the status quo' to formation of totalitarian regimes. What has sadly continued is the growing economic dependence on the West to an extent which has led to massive problems of unemployment, poverty, illiteracy, nil growth, disease, and population explosion in huge areas of the Third World. It is quite clear therefore that educational systems in the Third World have had to face up to quite different challenges from those experienced by educational systems in the 'First World' countries.

It is therefore not surprising that community education in the Third World has correspondingly taken different forms. These tend to be called *formal, informal* and *non-formal* education. They are defined thus:

Formal education: the hierarchically structured, chronologically graded 'educational system' running from primary school through the university and including, in addition to general academic studies, a variety of specialized programmes and institutions for full-time technical and professional training.

Informal education: the truly life-long process whereby every individual acquires attitudes, values, skills and knowledge from daily experience and the educative influences and resources in his or her environment – from family and neighbours, from work and play, from the marketplace, the library and the mass media.

Non-formal education: any organized educational activity outside the established formal system – whether operating separately or as an important feature of some broader activity – that is intended to serve identifiable learning clientèles and learning objectives.

(Simkins 1977:7)

Community education in the Third World at a practical level takes many forms but at a conceptual level, it is, according to A. R. Thompson (1981), largely concerned with 'ways in which we may meet the whole range of educational needs of all members of the community, irrespective of age, sex, ethnic origin or social status'. (Thompson, ibid: 4). Community education in its *informal* variety provides instruction in values, traditions, relationships and technologies sufficient for the needs of relatively small-scale, largely self-sufficient, and often insecure, societies in which the emphasis is on continuity and stability. In short, *informal education* in the emerging nations of the Third World is concerned with learning through everyday living and doing and with providing a basis for socializing new members into the norms, customs and values of traditional societies.

However, the advent of colonialism, and later independence, and other large-scale social, political and economic changes in many Third World countries created a demand for forms of education and training which could not be provided through traditional socialization and informal education. Several Third World governments in the immediate post-independence period, introduced administrative structures which affected everyday life within communities more regularly and purposively than had previously been the case and, in Thompson's view, have become increasingly concerned with bringing about change deliberately, and with promoting the development of more complex, large-scale, progress-seeking societies involving far-reaching changes not merely in the techniques and technologies of the various communities they embrace but in their social structures and the value systems in which they are embedded.

Since these techniques, structures and values desired in new emerging nations of the Third World were not necessarily present in the old societies and could not therefore be communicated by traditional means, new educational patterns were superimposed on the old, gradually taking over many of the functions of the old but introducing new functions also.

Education was formerly an instrument for promoting social stability and continuity, for communicating the values and skills of existing members of the society, for generating a consensus of beliefs and values and for socializing individuals and preparing them for their roles in life. These tasks were performed adequately by informal educational networks in traditional societies for centuries. The contemporary scene, however, is very different. The education system today has to serve as an instrument for promoting, managing and directing change. It has to transmit new national values and provide opportunities for acquiring new technical and social skills. It has, above all, to prepare individuals for life in a highly fluid and rapidly changing national and international community with pluralistic patterns of beliefs, values, customs and traditions and with multiple problems, injustices and inequalities.

The result of these new demands and needs in Third World nations is a distinct shift away from informal patterns of education towards more *formal* and *non-formal* forms of education. Thompson argues that these formal educational processes were derived largely from the schooling tradition of the colonial powers and were not dissimilar in many ways to the kinds of formal processes which some of the large and more centralized state systems in the developing countries had themselves been forced to develop prior to the advent of colonialism.

The emergence of community education

The above was typical of the situation prevailing in many British colonies in Africa, the Caribbean and Asia both in colonial times and for some time after independence. In short, school was (and in many cases still is) a place which breeds inequality and élitism. Many of its activities are focused beyond and outside the local community and this tends to divorce the child from his community and culture – an aspect of schooling much deplored in educational circles for well over

a century! This undesirable alienating influence is sometimes reinforced by other factors such as the building of schools apart from the
community, paradoxically often in order to have available land for
farming activities designed to reintegrate the child with his
community.

Given these tensions in formal education systems, particularly in
schooling, there has been a long tradition of efforts to enable the
school to serve 'local' in addition to 'modern sector' interests and to
ameliorate the divisive impact of the school, mainly through
curricular reforms directed at what were perceived as being the needs,
if not the desires, of the local community.

Developing countries, particularly former British colonies in
Africa, have responded boldly to the challenge of educational reforms
by developing in parallel with and also within formal education, a
type of 'community education' called 'non-formal education' which
exhibits features of both formal education and community education
as they are popularly understood in Britain today.

Much of the kind of activities commonly referred to as community
education in advanced Western countries is subsumed under such
headings as informal education, formal education, non-formal
education and community development in the Third World.

The East African experience

One area of the Third World currently undergoing rapid economic,
political, social and educational change is East Africa; but it is with
educational change that we are here concerned. In the 'abstract' of an
illuminating article on 'The School as a Force for Community Change
in Tanzania', Maliyamkono (1980) observes:

> In newly independent countries where traditional theories of education
> policy have continued to be followed, education has persisted as little
> more than a sophisticated mechanism for the recruitment of elites, and
> there has been an increased dependence on the advanced industrial
> nations for aid, experts and educational models.

Tanzania is today, however, one of the growing number of
developing countries that are seeking a development strategy based
on independence, self-reliance and socialism. It has, over the years,

initiated a number of educational reforms, including:

- The integration of schools and the planning of uniform curricula.
- Education for manpower requirements.
- Education for self-reliance.
- Decentralization of education.

(ibid: 337)

In Tanzania, unlike the situation in most advanced countries, community education is not set apart from the rest of education nor apart from community self-help. They are all part of one and the same process. For example, President Nyerere in 1967 enunciated the objectives for education for self-reliance as relating education to rural life, correcting the élitist bias of education, and changing attitudes among students towards agriculture and rural life. Five major programmes of reform covering primary and secondary education, teacher and higher education, and examinations were to be pursued, ensuring a closer integration of schools with local communities, e.g. through school farms and cooperative shops, and making curricula directly relevant to local needs. Therefore, community education in Tanzania in the form of education for self-reliance is a major step towards achieving the desired goal of integrating the school with the local community and represents not a separate, but an integral part of schooling and the rest of the education system. Schools are not merely to be made into productive units but are also supposed to be complementary to the learning process. The real criteria for evaluation are meant to be the changing attitudes and behaviour of the students, teachers and educational administrators towards manual labour.

Education in Tanzania, then, is much more than selfish academic pursuit. It is to do with the inculcation of new attitudes towards the importance of manual labour and a heightened awareness of, and commitment to, civic duties not only in relation to one's own community but to the nation as a whole. This philosophy of education is common to a growing number of emerging socialist Third World Countries. Caribbean countries like present-day Cuba and Grenada (just prior to American invasion of October 1983) are part of that tradition.

Education for self-reliance is not the only example of educational reform of note in Tanzania. Its policy on decentralization of education is another extremely significant development because it allows for a much greater participation at community level in decision making.

How then does community education feature in all this? Specific mention of the term 'community education' is seldom made in the educational literature of developing countries. Tanzania is no exception. This is because all education is 'for the community' (and the nation). Community education as a label becomes superfluous. Like so many developing countries nowadays, Tanzania has expounded a distinct philosophy of development. Under President Julius Nyerere, it has generated its own socialist ideology of development which is firmly based on giving priority to rural areas. Education, and in particular adult education, has a central role to play in the pursuit and attainment of national goals.

There is an underlying emphasis on the 'functional' aspects of education, that is, the aspects of education related to day-to-day experience of living. This is borne out by the fact that Tanzania has sought to achieve its educational objectives not through formal education but through what it calls 'mass education campaigns'. The earlier campaigns between 1969 to 1971 involved the Institute of Adult Studies at the University of Dar es Salaam and the Cooperative Education Centre and focused mainly on literacy and, from this experience, a health education mass campaign was planned for 1973, which was 'designed to reach one million adults, 750,000 in Ujamaa villages and a further 250,000 in districts which had undergone a literacy drive in 1971' (Simkins, ibid: 45). It is noticeable from the foregoing that adult education in Tanzania brings together different kinds of institutions in the search for solutions to the nation's problems. Further, adult education is not for a select few as it tends to be in many advanced countries but involves whole neighbourhoods and localities and has an unmistakeable political focus in line with national goals, targets and objectives.

Mass education campaigns are seldom seen in developed countries on anything like the scale witnessed in developing countries. Advanced communication techniques have seen to that. In Tanzania, however, mass education campaigns involve the integration of three media: radio, the printed word and face-to-face discussion. Printed materials consist of a cheap text with study guide and also a manual for group leaders. These materials are central to the campaign concept and groups often conduct their meetings from these alone if for any reason the radio programme is not received. Nevertheless, the radio programmes are important in providing additional information in a very immediate way and in stimulating discussion.

The mass education campaigns in Tanzania are as much valued for their process as for their content. Because they involve large numbers of people, unit costs are very low and so are remarkably cheap. They are demonstrably flexible having been utilized for such diverse purposes as literacy, education in basic economics, politics and functional health. However, difficulties are not unknown in these types of educational programmes. Shortages of relevant textbooks and other printed materials are among the commonest problems. However, these mass education campaigns clearly represent a kind of non-formal education as defined earlier. They also bear some resemblance to the more radical forms of adult and community education found in parts of Britain and the West.

Such differences in educational programmes are not only evident between developing countries and advanced, industrial Western nations. There are significant differences between developing countries themselves. For example, neighbouring capitalist Kenya has developed educational programmes markedly different from socialist Tanzania. One such programme is its network of Village Polytechnics which is a way of addressing itself to the vocational needs of its school-leavers (Anderson 1973, Court 1974).

But what were the special internal problems in Kenya that gave rise to the Village Polytechnics? Simkins mentions a few: one is the very rapid, but uneven, economic growth in Kenya since independence in 1963, with manufacturing and tourism taking the lead over agriculture. This is quite unexpected given the fact that over 90 per cent of Kenya's population still live in rural areas with four-fifths of these mainly engaged in subsistence farming. However, this situation is typical of a growing number of developing countries which have chosen to model their economic development on that of Western Europe, often without heed of the inappropriateness of the industrial model of economic development to their local circumstances, needs and traditions. This has led, in Kenya, to growing inequalities between individuals and communities, rising rural-urban migration and increasing urban unemployment.

The other problem to note has been the phenomenal expansion of the school system in Kenya. Enrolment in the primary sector had almost doubled in the decade 1963 to 1973 while in the secondary sector, it had quadrupled and this already intolerable situation was aggravated by high wastage rates through repetition and drop-out. Additionally, schools's curricula were largely irrelevant to local needs. They were essentially academic in that they were largely orientated towards formal examinations which control entry to higher levels of the system.

Similar conditions in Western Europe and North America in the 1920s and 1930s sowed the beginnings of what is not variously referred to as adult/community education, continuing education, lifelong education, etc. These conditions occurred much later in developing countries like Kenya and provoked different educational responses. Kenya developed a system of village polytechnics, the first of which was established in 1966 and the movement has expanded steadily since. According to Simkins, by 1973 the Kenyan government was funding 67 village polytechnics with almost 4,000 trainees with the target for 1977–8 being 250 such institutions with 22,000 trainees.

It was not too long before the Kenyan government also realized that despite its economic prosperity overall, the majority of its population lived in impoverished rural areas and that its modern urban sector had only limited capacity to absorb new workers. Progress, the government felt, must be based on widespread rural development of agriculture and of small-scale industries related to rural needs. Such development too, must occur on a local basis with an emphasis on self-reliance. Educational institutions were to have a crucial role to play in this development: they were to develop as an integral part of, and to service, their own local communities and so help to stem the tide of migration of primary school-leavers to the towns. Educational institutions were also assigned the task of helping to motivate and so enable these school-leavers to contribute directly to the development of their own communities. This was because hitherto formal schools showed no inclination to face this gigantic challenge, and it was therefore their failure that village polytechnics were designed to remedy and that accelerated the pace of their development.

But how different are village polytechnics in Kenya from, say, community schools in Britain? The 'village polytechnic' attempts to link education to economic development at both local and national levels.

> (It) is a low-cost training centre in a rural area. It aims at giving primary school-leavers from that area skills, understanding and

values which will make them able to look for money-making opportunities where they live, and to contribute to rural development by building up the economic strength of their own community.

(Simkins, op. cit: 40)

The 'village polytechnic' type of non-formal education, therefore, supersedes the types of community education that exist in advanced Western countries, in that the former is not 'education in isolation' but is closely related to agriculture production, rural development, employment and local contribution to the national economy. In this sense, it is part of the same continuum as community development which in the Third World, is underpinned by three 'bedrock' principles – *felt need, self-help* and (mass) *participation*.

Surprisingly, very little 'concrete' information is available about the village polytechnics in Kenya. What is certain is that they have been set up in response to a peculiar set of internal economic and social conditions with very specific educational objectives. However, there have been very few evaluative studies that purport to shed light on the effectiveness of Village Polytechnics and on the extent to which they have achieved or are achieving their objectives. This is regrettable but hardly surprising for it is notoriously difficult to evaluate educational innovations of this type. The same is true of the varied types of community education programmes in Western Europe and North America. The enormous complexities and diversities in philosophies, ideologies, policies and practices exhibited by those innovations mean that they do not readily lend themselves to any systematic evaluation.

Although village polytechnics represent a major educational innovation aimed at changes in individuals' attitudes and expectations through corresponding changes in the content and process of formal education itself, there still remain a number of unanswered questions. How far have the practices of existing village polytechnics deviated from the ideal models and what factors have contributed or are responsible for such deviation? To what extent have village polytechnics embraced the characteristics of formal schooling itself? How successful have the village polytechnics been in motivating their students to stay in the rural areas and in providing them with the knowledge and skills to do so productively. How much of the success of particular village polytechnics is due to the degree of non-formality in their structure?

Perhaps the village polytechnic movement is too young to be able to answer these searching questions, but already there are very encouraging signs: from the scant and sketchy information available, Simkins concludes that between half to two-thirds of village polytechnics leavers have found some kind of paid work or self-employment and this compares favourably with the experience of other young people with a corresponding level of education and that two-thirds of these remained in the rural areas. Furthermore, employers seem to be valuing the vocational skills obtained at village polytechnics over more general qualifications, which must be registered as one of the successes of the movement.

The Caribbean experience

Perhaps the most compelling example of attempts to link the education system to the production process, local needs and the national economy is that being pursued in the Caribbean island of Cuba through the socialist policies of Fidel Castro. Prior to the revolution in 1959, Cuba had a per capita income higher than most other countries in Latin America and, like other capitalist states, exhibited marked social inequalities, in particular a great gulf between the urban middle and upper classes on the one hand and the rural peasants on the other.

Castro, on seizing power in 1959, immediately enunciated the major objectives of his new revolutionary government. They were:

- To expand and utilize fully the society's productive capacities and to transform the Cuban economy ... into a rapidly growing system capable of ensuring increasing abundance for all.
- To eliminate economic, political and cultural dependence on the United States.
- To replace the rigid class structure of capitalist Cuba with a classless and egalitarian society; ... to end the city's economic, cultural and political domination over the countryside.
- To transform work into a challenging and creative activity for a new socialist man, motivated by social consciousness and the desire for self-expression.

Castro promulgated right at the very outset, that education had a crucial role to play in achieving the objectives of his new socialist Cuba. It is not surprising that explicit objectives were set for the education system itself that would complement those of the nation as a whole.

The specific educational objectives were:

- The democratization of access through providing education on a mass basis.
- The establishment of an education system geared to the imperatives of economic development.
- The overcoming of individual and collective alienation through the creation of the new socialist man.

(Simkins, op. cit: 50)

As in Tanzania, and in Kenya in particular, 'community education' is not distinct from the rest of the education system. All education is geared towards the nation's economic development with heavy emphasis on rural development. This, however, is where the resemblance ends. Educational developments in Cuba under Castro took a direction which is so far not witnessed in any other developing country. The attention given to the creation of 'the new man' with a particular set of attributes is also unique to Cuba. During the first ten years of the revolution, the first two educational objectives predominated with massive expansion of educational provision for children and adults. It was during this period that Cuba experienced a reorientation of the whole education system away from its earlier humanistic bias towards a much greater emphasis on scientific and technical subjects (which were more in line with the demands of nation's economy). The basics, however, were not forgotten: the famous literacy campaign of 1961, for example, saw the country's illiteracy rate fall from 25 per cent to just under 4 per cent in the space of only a year!

However, since the mid-1960s, Cuba had been grappling with operationalizing the concept of 'the new man'. The concept was originally conceived by Ché Guevera, a Cuban-born revolutionary and friend and contemporary of Castro, as having three main characteristics.

First he ('the new man') has a sense of personal and collective identity in belonging and contributing to an authentic Cuban process of development. Secondly, he understands and is therefore able to shape his own destiny. And third (he) has a radically different relationship with his work.

(Simkins, op. cit: 50)

Central to the Cuban concept of education and development, therefore, is the integration of work and study and it is this philosophy that has guided the reorganization of the Cuban education system from 1959 to the present day. Education in Cuba is unlike that in advanced Western Countries and its neighbouring Caribbean nations. 'Education for the community' is not separate from, or an appendage to, 'formal' education. No such sharp distinctions exist. Work–study relationships are at the core of the country's education system which itself is geared to local and national development. Although the emphasis on forging links between education and work is laudable, it has regrettably not emerged or evolved through any systematic consultation or discussion with local communities, but as was also the case in Tanzania and Kenya, was decreed by politicians and planners from on high.

Socio-economic inequalities led to the replacement in 1959 of a capitalist system in Cuba by one based on a socialist/communist social order under Fidel Castro. But, what was so objectionable about the education system at the time that provoked Castro into such drastic reorganization? Has the integration of work and study really succeeded?

At the time of the revolution in 1959, Cuba unlike many developing countries did not have an education system expanding at an explosive rate. Primary enrolments, for a number of reasons, were well below the Latin American average. Castro saw education as a birthright and a foundation for his new society. The first priority of the revolution, therefore, was for the expansion of the education system through mass participation in literacy and other programmes to a level equivalent to primary school graduation.

Prior to the revolution, education in Cuba was essentially a preserve of the urban élite so expansion through mass education was very specifically expansion of rural education. Attention was correspondingly paid to teacher education/training by improving teachers' courses and establishing new teacher training institutes, the basic aim of the government being to destroy the dualism of pre-revolutionary Cuba. The 'commitment' which the teacher training institutions sought to induce, was, for example, very much a commitment to work in rural areas. However, it was in the application of the Cuban concept of the 'new man' to secondary education that emphasis on work/study became more pronounced. This development is significant for the emphasis given to, and the new role designated for, the community and environment in education. Nowhere in the Third World is there a stronger community focus in formal education as the developments in secondary education.

The value of such a system is immediately obvious: a deeper mutual understanding of the education system, industry, etc., and opportunities for the acquisition of relevant basic skills as well as for increasing one's own knowledge are among possible spin-offs. If this system were adopted in Britain, say, it would mean at a local level, the LEA, industry, the health service, social services and voluntary agencies working in complete, harmony with one another. What a rare occurrence that would be!

The system is not without its critics. Simkins himself comments that these activities are essentially marginal 'to the schools' prime activities, and furthermore most secondary schools are in urban areas despite the fact that just under half of Cuba's population is still rural' (Simkins, op. cit: 50).

These and other criticisms led to the introduction of a more radical programme which began in 1966, called 'schools to the countryside' movement (*escuela al campo*). This involved junior high school students (grades 7 to 10) spending 45 days each year in rural camps undertaking:

> a minimum of class work and a maximum of working with state farms, private farmers, and the military in the production of such products as sugar cane, coffee, tobacco, citrus fruits, vegetables and other ...
>
> (Paulston, 1973: 247)

The organization of these rural camps is specifically designed to achieve changes in attitudes and expectations of students while at the same time making a contribution to production and fulfilling wider social, political economic aims. The 'schools to the countryside' programme was aimed primarily at people whose schooling took place mainly in urban areas and so provide an opportunity for them, too, to contribute to rural development. The programme also represented an attack on the élitism and inequality in Cuban education at the time. Although many observers have commented favourably on the programme, there have also been criticisms, not least from Cubans themselves. Simkins hints at some of these criticisms when he comments:

It has been suggested that goals are often not clear, that productivity
in the camps is often low and leadership lacking, that the time lost in
the countryside has serious effects on students preparing for higher
education, and that urban students in fact make few meaningful
contacts with peasants and often maintain attitudes of superiority in
relation to them.

(Simkins, op. cit: 51)

Faced with these criticisms, the revolutionary government in 1971,
launched a new programme called 'schools in the countryside
(*escuela en el campo*). Under this programme, it was hoped that by
1980, there would be 1000 such institutions each accommodating
about 500 students so that all junior high school education would
take place in countryside schools. The students in each of them
alternate on a half-daily basis between the classroom and the fields
with the intention being that the production from each school will
be sufficient to cover costs.

As expected, no evaluative studies of any of these bold and novel
programmes are available. However, they represent the most
serious attempt yet to achieve fusion between work and study at
secondary level – an innovation which is the envy of many
developing countries. The 'deformalization' of schooling and the
emphasis on work embodied in the 'schools in the countryside'
programme has:

important outcomes with respect to instilling knowledge and skills
of vocational relevance, and a feeling of participation in the
development process, but also helps invert the traditional schooling
value system whereby academic abilities are best rewarded.
Furthermore, student leadership and participation in the brigades,
togeher with the fact that teachers and students work together
towards common goals should break down the authoritarian relations
of the classroom and contribute to a collective consciousness.

(Simkins, op. cit: 53)

Many observers argue that despite these innovations in education in
Cuba and their potential benefits to the local community and the
nation at large, the Cuban school is still heavily influenced by
examinations and competition for grade promotion. Progress has
been further hampered by teacher shortages and shortcoming in the
quality of instruction consequent upon rapid educational
expansion.

While recognizing that the 'new man' in Cuba is yet to be born,
the large-scale education reforms through integration of work and
study which the special programmes have introduced are making a

significant contribution to mass education, rural development and economic development. Involvement of the masses in education and development in Cuba is being achieved to some degree due largely to political commitment – a feature which is in stark contrast to the situation in most advanced Western countries. While Cuba might be scorned by the major capitalist nations of America and Western Europe, its model of education and economic development was copied by at least one of her Caribbean neighbours.

A revolutionary government came to power in the island nation of Grenada in March 1979 after a bloodless coup d'état, allegedly with active military assistance from Cuba. Economic assistance, however, was openly provided by Cuba in the building of an international airport in Grenada which opened towards the end of 1984. Many of the educational reforms that were introduced by the revolution for a time permeated Grenada's entire education system. For example, there was a similar emphasis on the linking of education to the production process and this was reflected in the three major educational projects/programmes launched by the People's Revolutionary Government of Grenada. These programmes were:

- The National In-Service Teacher Education Programme (NISTEP).
- The community School Day Programme (CSDP).
- The Centre for Popular Educaton (CPE).

These programmes, however, came to an end with the invasion of the island by combined American and Caribbean forces in October 1983 in response to an internal armed struggle which resulted in the death of the Prime Minister, some of his Cabinet colleagues and scores of innocent Grenadian citizens.

The examples of community education chosen from different countries were all very different and complex educational programmes. So what have we learnt? There is one common element in community education across the First and Third World and that is in all cases, there was a heavy emphasis on the *programmes* (i.e. the actual activities themselves) to the exclusion of the *process* of community education (i.e. engaging the local community in management, organization, decision making, etc.). The paternalistic and exploitative relationships between 'providers' and 'consumers' of community education continue though there have been some notable exceptions. This means that the gaps

John Samuel

between institutions' intentions and communities' expectations are as wide as they ever were. This writer believes that with the new emerging emphasis on 'process' rather than 'programmes' in community education, there will inevitably be a vast improvement in the patterns of relationships between institutions and their local communities. Much of the inequality and imbalance in the relationship is due in large measure to the reflection by community education and educational systems generally of a middle-class ethos and value system. Community education literature is devoid of a class critique or meaningful discussion on 'values'.

Despite its many shortcomings there is something refreshing about community education the world over that stems from innovation and change. A few examples of community education practice have been discussed and analysed, both in First and Third Worlds. Tremendous tensions exist between formal and non-formal education systems. Yet the potential for learning through genuine community participation and involvement is considerable. The relative success of programmes such as mass education, literacy, and extension services in Kenya, Tanzania, Mali, Zambia, Senegal and Malawi; animation rurale in Morocco; the Brigades in Botswana; village polytechnics in Kenya; young pioneers in Malawi and Ghana; the national youth services in Kenya and Tanzania bear witness to the potential of non-formal education in the Third World in achieving change.

References

1 Simkins, T. (1977). *Non-formal education and development, Manchester Monograph 8*, Department of Adult and Higher Education, University of Manchester.

2 Thompson, A.R. (1981). 'Community Education in the 1980s: what can we learn from experience? in *International Journal of Educational Development,* Volume 3, no. 1, pp. 3–17.

3 Maliyamkono, T.L. (1980). 'The School as a force for community change in Tanzania', in *International Review of Education*, volume 26, no. 1, pp. 335–346.

4 Hall, B. and Dodds, A. (1974). *Voices for Development. Tanzania Radio Study Group Campaigns*, International Extension College (cited in Simkins, T. op. cit.).

5 Anderson, J. (1973). 'The formalization of non-formal education: village polytechnics and pre-vocational training in Kenya', in Foster, P.

and Sheffield, J., *World Yearbook of Education 1974: Rural Education*, Evans Brothers, London, (cited in Simkins, T., 1977, op. cit.).

6 Court, D. (1974), 'Dilemmas of development: the village polytechnic movement as a shadow system of education in Kenya', in Court, D. and Ghai, D. (eds), *Education, Society and Development; New Perspectives from Kenya,* Oxford University Press, (cited in Simkins, T., 1977, op. cit).

7 Jungnitz, P.G. (1983). 'Mature students in the sixth form of a community school'. M.A. Thesis, Department of Education, University of York.

8 Paulston, R.G. (1973). 'Cuban rural education: a strategy for revolutionary development, in Foster, P. and Sheffield, J. (eds), *World Yearbook of Education*, Evans Brothers, London, (cited in Simkins, T., 1977, op. cit.).

CHAPTER 9

Education, training and the rise of the MSC: which side are you on?

DAVE GORBUTT

Community educators have often been accused of being coy about their professional and political values. The massive intervention of MSC, both as the prime agent of the educational management of unemployment and an extensive colonizer of community education practice, is a stark reminder of this important critique. Gorbutt reviews the exponential growth of MSC, recognizing both the efficiency and the expediency which help to explain its ubiquitous influence. In contrast, community education (in all or any of its guises) has singularly failed to construct a viable alternative agenda for education and training. MSC represents the latest and most urgent challenge to community educators to come clean about what they stand for – and against.

During the decade 1976 to 1986 the pace of change quickened in British society to an unprecendented degree against a background of poor economic performance and growing mass unemployment. Changes in education have been uncertain and piecemeal, often lurching from one reaction to another. But with the publication of the government White Paper 'Working Together: Education and Training' (1986) it is possible to trace important patterns of development in education and training which have far-reaching implications for community education, not only through schools, but beyond in the world of continuing education.

In this paper I want to trace major policy responses to unemployment in the field of education and training and look particularly at the rise of the Manpower Services Commission as a major instrument of government policy in this field. Finally, I want to examine the implications for community education and pose the question for community educators 'Which side are you on?'.

For some community educators the letters MSC are a signal to avoid all contact ('Must Stay Clear'), whilst others reluctantly and conditionally engage, hoping to reform from within by exploiting the space between the rules ('Maybe Some Cash'). There are further those who believe MSC to be a major instrument of modernization and reform in our social and economic life ('Most Sensible Course'). There are of course parallels here with Ian Martin's typology of community education practice.[1] I will return to this later.

The Manpower Services Commission was created in 1974 following the Employment and Training Act (1973), placed on the statute book by the Heath Government. Its subsequent development, as a quango responsible to the Secretary of State for Employment, has frequently been controversial and its importance as an instrument of economic and social policy of successive governments has increased against the rising tide of unemployment.[2]

After twelve years MSC is substantially centre stage in government policy in tackling training and unemployment. Its influence as a national body is unlikely to diminish and, under a Conservative administration, is extending its interventionist role. In administrative terms it has constantly shown its capacity, unfettered by direct departmental supervision, to be an effective and efficient delivery system. It has also proved invaluable in being a vehicle for the development of EEC policies and is backed by EEC funding. In that sense it is a net contributor to the UK exchequer. Calls for the replacement of the MSC frequently fail to recognize that it has been shaped to maximize the inflow of EEC funds into the British economy.

The MSC is a quasi-autonomous, non-governmental organization (i.e. a quango) which is controlled by a board of ten members who represent the interests of employees, trade unions and the education service. Separate boards exist for Wales and Scotland and are responsible to the appropriate minister. There are also regional boards which exist to coordinate activities on a regional basis, and at a more local or sub-regional level the MSC is advised by area manpower boards which are made up of the nominees of local industry, trade unions and education authorities. Area manpower boards give approval to applications to run YTS and CP schemes. The whole operation is coordinated by commissioners at national level, working through a Civil Service bureaucracy centred on Moorfoot, Sheffield.

The MSC has also split into divisions, currently the Employment and the Training Division, although these are presently under review against a bewildering background of complexity of funding arrangements. Frequently officials at local level may be unable to answer direct questions and have to refer queries 'to Moorfoot' for answer.

Under the 1973 Employment and Training Act, the MSC took over specific responsibilities for industrial training (e.g. oversight of 29 Industrial Training Boards) but these have diminished as budgets and policies have switched from being employer-led and market-directed, to being MSC led and manpower planning orientated. It is this process which has led the MSC into an increasingly interventionist role and brought it up against vested interest in education and training. But what began to bring the MSC into the limelight in the second half of the 1970s was rising youth unemployment. The recession might be said to have begun in 1973 when an outcome of the Yom Kippur War was the trebling of Arab oil prices. By 1976 unemployment in Britain had grown to over one million people. Of particular concern within the overall statistic was the increasing number of the young unemployed, principally amongst young school leavers.[3]

By 1976 the MSC was well established and already beginning to find itself within a controversial limelight: the spending of millions of pounds in a headquarters in Sheffield for an organization which, at that time, few believed could have more than marginal significance in the social and economic problem of the nation.

1976 was, of course, the year of the Ruskin Speech in which Prime Minister James Callaghan set out a new agenda for the world of education. His most significant achievement was to transform the criticisms of education as leading cultural and moral decline into the need to change education so that it could more closely link with the needs of industry and the economy. But the MSC took no part in this debate and busied itself in reacting to the rising growth of unemployment amongst school leavers.

The Holland Report (1977) chaired by MSC commissioner Geoffrey Holland, led to the establishment of the Special

Programme Division and through it the Youth Opportunities Scheme (YOP). YOP provided mainly work experience on employer's premises with the government paying an allowance, and with no cost to employers.

The scheme chimed in well with the tenor of the post-Ruskin education debate. The inability of school leavers to get jobs was being directly linked to the quality of schooling which they had received and the 'wrong attitudes' acquired through it. YOP could provide an opportunity for youngsters to come into contact with employers and come to a realization of what was preventing them from gaining employment. The underlying explanation of youth unemployment was that it was voluntary and could be overcome by a programme of personal reform. At the same time the unattractiveness of youth to employers had its roots in the structure, nature and content of state schooling. Most people wished to see unemployment as voluntary and cyclical, (and therefore temporary). The underlying structural changes in the economy were largely not perceived.

One of the arguments in the post-Ruskin situation was whether the major criterion to tackle unemployment directly should be taken by the Department of Education and Science through the LEAs and FE colleges, or through the Department of Employment and the MSC. Significantly, the DES lost the battle and the MSC have proved to be the leaders in staking out new forms of vocational education, particularly in the development of the Youth Training Scheme (YTS) and the Technical and Vocational Education Initiative, (TVEI). Four issues of criticism arose, particularly out of the YOP scheme, and these have lived on to haunt YOP's successor, the Youth Training Scheme, introduced in 1983.[4]

Firstly, there was the issue of job displacement. Many trade unionists believed that unemployed youngsters on government subsidised wages were being introduced into the work situation to enable employers to sack more costly adults. The criticism was that YOP was simply cheap labour.

Secondly, the level of allowance given to the youngsters was lower than their wages would have been on the open market. The net effect of YOP, the argument ran, was to depress youth wages and help them to 'price themselves back into the labour market'.

Thirdly, for all the talk of need for youngsters to obtain training in order to be more attractive to prospective employers, the training provided in YOP was patchy and of unreliable quality.

Certainly, so the argument ran, it was no substitute for a traditional apprenticeship.

Fourthly, the issue was whether YOP would lead to jobs for the youngsters. Although at some levels there has been a playing down of the ideas of a success rate for YOP and subsequently YTS, ministers and managing agents (who organize the schemes for MSC) are quick to establish and publicize the rates at which young people go on to secure a permanent job.

Many community educators, of course, particularly those involved in youth work, were in a good position to observe the personal impact of unemployment on young people and the effectiveness or otherwise of YOP.

The idea of community education in all its guises seems to sit uneasily with vocational education. In can be argued that community education has its roots firmly in the liberal education movement which sees the prime purpose of education to be concerned with values and the whole person. Certainly the liberal view has been to downgrade the practical and vocational and to focus on personal liberation as a goal. One response to the narrowing tendency of vocational education has been to insist that there is a place for general or liberal education in parallel with it. This view has strong expression in the Crowther Report (1959) and in the whole liberal studies movement which grew in further education during the 1960s and 1970s.

This movement found its expression in YOPs and later in early YTS through elements usually called social and life skills courses. These became the centre of controversy in that they were seen as becoming 'too political'. This arose out of the commitment of social and life skills' tutors to work with trainees, not only to encourage a better understanding of how they could improve their employment chances, but also to set this against the realism of the nature and causes of unemployment within a capitalist economy. Above all, many tutors saw it as bad faith not to point out to youngsters that they were being trained for non-existent jobs. Within YTS as it has developed there is little or no trace of social and life skills courses. Such 'political' elements are officially discouraged by MSC.[5]

As YTS has developed, it has also become more institutionalized and subject to endless bureaucracy and central control. The earlier days when managing agents could be readily found from amongst community organizations, as well as local employers, has given way to schemes upon which MSC is determined to stamp a hallmark of quality. Standards of training now required to achieve approved training organization status are exacting and could not be achieved in informal education settings. The involvement of community education in YTS has diminished and in many areas had become non-existent.

In developing YOP and YTS the MSC has studiously stayed clear of the world of secondary education (11 to 16 years). Youth training has been seen as taking place in the world of post-compulsory education. Schools have responded to growing youth unemployment in a number of ways by providing RSA, City and Guilds and other vocationally orientated courses for the 14 to 16 age group – especially those lacking in motivation or apparent ability to collect the standard bag full of 'O' levels. More recently, schools have also become involved in the Certificate of Pre-Vocational Education (CPVE) – a DES-inspired development which is not smiled on by MSC and may fail to achieve the stamp of approval from the National Council for Vocational Qualifications.

However, in November 1982, the government announced the Technical and Vocational Education Initiative which allowed the MSC to extend its influence across the 16-plus by proposing four-year pilot schemes to run from 14 to 18 years.[6] The scheme proposed a mixture of technical and vocational education, interspersed with periods of work experience. The scheme would begin in the last two years of compulsory schooling and continue in parallel with both YTS and more traditional sixth-form education, but at the same time providing real work experience. In fact, although it was never admitted at the time, what was being launched was a transition education programme, designed to facilitate the transition from school to work. Moreover, this programme was part of an EEC initiative and hence qualified for EEC funding.[7]

Although many educationalists and administrators questioned the wisdom of allowing the MSC through the school gates, (asserting a traditional boundary line between liberal education and training), the TVEI scheme had been decreed by the Prime Minister, thus neatly overriding potential inter-departmental rivalries between the Departments of Employment (MSC) and Education and Science. As the details of the unheralded scheme were worked out, it also became clear that enterprising LEAs could bid for pilot schemes, thereby boosting the education budgets, flagging under the pressure of public expenditure cuts.

In the event, ten LEAs made successful bids for pilot projects involving age cohorts of approximately 250 children and begun in September 1983. In Exeter, for example, the scheme involves five High Schools working in close collaboration with Exeter College, a tertiary institution. However, the MSC allowed LEAs to make submissions with broad guidelines and positively encouraged experimentation. The TVEI scheme has been subsequently expanded to involve many more local authorities, although some are still refusing to be involved. However, it should be remembered that even if each of the 104 LEAs in England and Wales was operating a pilot scheme, it would only involve about 4 per cent of the age cohort of secondary school children. The 1986 White Paper 'Working Together: Education and Training' announced a decision to extend TVEI from pilot projects into a national scheme. Although doubts have been expressed about the adequacy of the funding, what is being strongly signalled is a fundamental change in the orientation of education and training 14 to 18.

Criticism of TVEI has largely come from the liberal education corner which has always viewed vocationalism as narrowly instrumental and incapable of promoting the development of the whole person. On the other hand, TVEI has dimensions which are radical and challenge traditional tenets of schooling. Assessment, for example, is student-centred, (e.g. profiles, records of achievement). The curriculum content is process-orientated rather than knowledge-centred and contact with the world outside of school is encouraged, both with the community and the world of business.

These features would appear to be attractive to community educators who believe that their mission is to open up schools to more outside contact which is 'reality based'. It is for this reason that voluntary service with old people, for example, has been justified on educational grounds. Could the value of the same experience be denied if it is organized for vocational reasons? The deep split between education and training is revealed. In fact, the grounds of objection might be said to lie in the finance and intentions of the paymaster, rather than the experimental value and learning outcomes of young people. Or is it, as T. S. Eliot suggests in *Murder in the Cathedral* the 'greatest treason is to do the right thing for the wrong reason'? In broad terms this raises a question for community educators who seek to bring educational change through the reform of schooling: can vocational education as defined by MSC be a legitimate part of community education? Or do community educators share with liberal educationalists a distaste for vocationalism?[8]

Further dilemmas and contradictions are raised by the development and extension of the Community Programme. The Community Programme (CP), which began in October 1982, is the principal way in which the MSC seeks to provide help for long-term unemployed people. It is the successor to a number of programmes (e.g. Job Creation Scheme) which have run since 1976. Basically CP is designed to promote temporary part-time employment on projects which are of benefit to the community, which would not be otherwise done (e.g. are the responsibility of the local authority). Early schemes were predominantly orientated towards projects for cleaning up the environment, leading, in some areas, as one wag put it, to 'making the bramble an endangered species'. Early provision was made for over 100,000 places in CP. By October 1983 106,000 places had been filled and by progressive expansion, the target will be 270,000 by Autumn 1986. The CP has been delivered through agents and there has been a growth of more adventurous projects, many of them established through the cooperation of community education workers.

The dilemmas posed by MSC schemes for community educators are brought sharply into focus by the policies adopted by the Community and Youth Workers Union (CYWU). In March 1985 the CYWU carried a motion at its AGM to absolutely reject 'the Community Programme as a vehicle for youth and community work'.

The main points which led to the rejection were based on objections to salary and conditions of service under CP (e.g. low pay, twelve-month contracts, eligibility rules which discriminate against women) and the need for only full-time, permanent and properly trained personnel to be involved in developing youth and community work.[9]

In October 1985 a Special General Meeting of CYWU was called to consider a motion by the Gateshead branch. The motion attempted to devolve the final approval for proposed projects to branches in the light of local circumstances. It also called for a campaign to improve CP by pressing for non-discriminatory eligibility rules, raising the average wage and properly funded training. The Gateshead branch pleaded that within the current economic climate and government policies, it was unrealistic to expect LEAs to expand the Youth and Community Service. The decision of CYWU, it was agreed, would actually lead to the loss of jobs in the north east, some of them amongst CYWU members. Finally, Gateshead argued that it was better to effect change, improve quality and set standards of the Community Programme. In the event, the Special General Meeting voted 211 against the Gateshead resolution and the CYWU is not actively campaigning against the Community Programme by witholding Union approvals which are vital for support for MSC Area Manpower Boards.

The arguments within the debate are interesting. On the one hand the dominant group in CYWU is arguing a traditional professional line in which the interests of members supersede those of clients or groups in need. On the other is the position which, whilst wishing to protect its members' interests, wishes to make a wider identification with the need of unemployed people to have jobs. The unions' refusal to countenance association with CP could be seen to be acting within their self-interest, whereas the opposition group takes a more pragmatic reform-from-within position. Meanwhile unemployment in Gateshead is over 25 per cent.

MSC is now having a major influence on further education and tertiary colleges, many of which have served as strong bases for community education. For example the nature of funding for YTS programmes bought shorter contracts and different conditions of service in many colleges. Since 1984 colleges have had to live with the reality of MSC providing 25 per cent of funding for non-advanced further education courses and thereby require LEAs to coordinate and submit academic plans. FE colleges which have been adaptable in a free market situation against a background of growing public expenditure are finding it hard to adjust to MSC requirements to tailor courses to employer's projected, (rather than actual,) needs, and the uncertainties of local manpower planning.

1986 saw the publication of the 'Review of Vocational Qualifications' – a unit established by the MSC to reform the area. The government agreed proposals for a National Vocational Qualifications Boards which will hallmark appropriate qualifications in the national interest. This could have far-reaching implications for the development of the CPVE in colleges.

The MSC is also deeply involved in various schemes under the Adult Training Initiative. It is the principal body by which the government gives its expression to the idea that the economy can draw out of recession through investment and modernization of the training system. It is as well to note the achievements of MSC as an

organization. An achievement checklist for MSC (1973 to 1986) might read:
'The MSC had demonstrated that it can:

- Sucessfully establish schemes of training in the public and private sector at relatively short notice.
- Shape policies and programmes to qualify for EEC funding, thus relieving pressure on national expenditure programmes.
- Maintain the confidence of trade unions and employers at national level.'

On the other hand, the MSC shows the sinister growth of the corporate state in its attempts to shore up an ailing capitalist economy. Its ideology of training serves to individualize the justification for the means of control for large numbers of unemployed. It is also the instrument of a supranational bureaucracy, (the EEC,) which is dedicated to promote the free market economy, regardless of social cost.

At the end of the decade the MSC is clearly here to stay. None of the major political parties is proposing to abolish it the other side of a general election. The policies, the political personalities and the rhetoric may change, but the outcomes of the MSC are impressive in administration. If, for example, one considers the 1981 White Paper 'The New Training Initiative' and chart the progress over five years, remembering that this has been supported by the CBI and TUC, then it would be difficult to find a parallel in modern times.

By contrast, it could be argued that community education has failed to put its mission on the agenda, has suffered marginalization in the public sector, plagued by retrenchment and financial cutbacks. Above all it has failed to bring forward major proposals for dealing with unemployment amongst youth or adults. It has been forced into a defensive position.

Faced with the rise of the MSC in the world of education and training and its impingement on youth and community work through the Community Programme, it is pertinent to ask the question 'Which side are you on?'. Of course it is clear there will be a different answer according to the personal, political and professional ideological commitments of community educators. It is important to recognize that those involved in community education are not simply community educators, but also employees, who may or may not see themselves as professionals, and persons who have strong political and personal interests which may not find a ready expression in their work situation. Finally, it is clear that community education is a contested concept for there are competing definitions around which people debate. These groups find organizational expression for example through CYWU or the Community Education Association.

If 'community education' is to have credence as a concept, then it ought to be possible for its adherents to tackle the question as to whether it can face, reject or absorb vocationalism, whether it is for young people or adults. To answer the question 'Which side are you on?' one needs to resolve dilemmas and contradictions relating to four interacting elements. These relate to being a professional, the needs of clients, social challenge and social control. Finally these have to be linked to conceptions of community education. This can be spelt out in examining the relationship between the MSC Community Programme and community education. At one level CP looks like a £1 bn gift to develop community education beyond schooling, a cheque to 'do something' practical and tangible about unemployment. Why cannot community educators simply embrace it and sport car stickers which state boldly 'Thank God for the MSC?'

The first dilemma relates to being an employee who also aspires to achieve the status of professional. Professional groups have common characteristics: they seek to control their work situation, restrict entry by insisting on appropriate forms of training, collectively claim the right to define clients' needs against employers' definitions of their role. The dilemmas are deepened since community educators are either local authority employees and must act as servants of the authority, or employees of voluntary organizations typically bound by charitable status. The contradictions and tensions in the situation have been well charted by sociologists.[10] It has been argued, of course, that professions are inherently conservative in that they seek to perpetuate narrow definitions of members' self-interest to secure continuing employment. They are also held to breed dependence and subjugation of their clients. Illich and Freire, heroes of radical community educators, might well be scathing about the rhetoric of professionalism cloaking economic self-interest. Professionals are part of the deep structure of contemporary society and therefore essentially agents of social control, the sum of whose actions is to perpetuate the status quo.

Radical definitions of community education which see it as an agent of social change characteristically fail to perceive the conservative nature of what the MSC would call the delivery system.

Finally, there remains the dilemma of personal and political commitments. It would be easy to characterize community educators as radicals, but community education seems to harbour its fair share of conservatives, liberals and anarchists as well as different shades of the radical left. Ian Martin's typology is useful in helping us to sort out some of the different perspectives as ideologies.[1] But as I have pointed out, there are also contradictions between professional and political ideologies. One way of working at it is through a simple typology on strong and weak dimensions (figure 9.1).

Figure 9.1   Political commitment

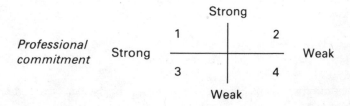

The four positions can be described and clearly the letters MSC mean different things for each position:

1 Purist radical   – (MSC = Must Stay Clear)
2 Pragmatic radical   – (MSC = Maybe Some Cash)
3 Calculated involvement – (MSC = Most Sensible Course)
4 Migrants   – (MSC = My Second Choice)

In the end withdrawal from the MSC is a luxury that many cannot afford. In refusing to participate CYWU is adopting an essentially conservative position which is unlikely to bring about social change. In the end the union will be isolated and ignored by MSC and the government. No government is going to bow to 1,000 community workers and add a quarter of a million people to the dole queue overnight. The pragmatic radical response, the Gateshead position, seems more reasonable. Bertolt Brecht was asked to account for specific lines in his plays by the House Committee on UnAmerican activities. He replied that his work was misunderstood and badly translated.

To leave the field to the careerists is to miss an opportunity to challenge orthodoxy from the position of an informed and critical participant. I use the term migrants to describe those whose current position is to be working within CP, having been recruited from dole or redundancy queues. Anybody who has worked in CP cannot but be struck by the way in which it draws in such a rich variety and diversity of professional and former employment experience. Like birds of passage, they move on from temporary resting places.

Finally the four million unemployed people and their families need to come into view. The personal benefits of work are well-known to those of us lucky enough to have it. Where is our mandate to deny a piece of it to others? They are the victims, the innocent bystanders in a crisis in capitalism which is not of their making. Why has the community education movement failed to place this in the centre of the debate about community and education?

References

1　Ian Martin. (1985). 'Ideology and practice in community education', *Community Education Network*, February.
2　For a background to the growth of MSC see A. Thompson and H. Rosenberg. (1986). *'A User's Guide to the Manpower Service Commission'*, and C. St John Brooks. (1985). 'Who controls training? The rise of the Manpower Services Commission', Fabian Tract 506.
3　M. Casson. (1979). *'Youth Unemployment'*. Macmillan.
　　J. Payne. (1985). 'Changes in the youth labour market 1974–1981', *Oxford Review of Education*, vol. 11, no. 2.

　　The following is a selection of the growing literature which is critical of YOP and YTS.
4　Fiddy, R. (ed.). (1983). *In place of Work*. Falmer Press
　　Gleeson, D. (ed.). (1984). 'On the politics of youth training', *Education Review*, vol. 36, no. 2.
　　Bates, I. *et al.* (1984). *Schooling for the Dole? The New Vocationalism*. Macmillan.
　　Gleeson, D. (1983). *Youth Training and the Search for Work*. Routledge & Kegan Paul.
　　Schofield, P. *et al.* (1983). *Youth Training: the Tories Poisoned Apple*. ILP Publications.
　　Rees, T. and Atkinson, P. (1982). *Youth Unemployment and State Intervention*. Routledge & Kegan Paul.

5   An early indication of the dilemmas and contradictions facing youth workers can be found in B. Davies. (1979). *In Whose Interests? From Social Education to Social and Life Skills Training*, National Youth Bureau.

6   For an account of the emergence of TVEI see Gorbutt, D. (1984). 'The new vocationalism: a critical note' in *Perspectives* 14, University of Exeter. See also McCulloch, G. (1986). 'Policy, politics and education: the Technical and Vocational Education Initiative', *Journal of Education Policy*, January–March, vol. 1, no. 1.

7   'Policies for transition', in *Education* 6 July 1984. 'Education for transition: the curriculum challenge', *IFAPLAN*, Brussels (1984).
    White, R. Pring, R. and Brockington, D. (1985). *The 14–18 Curriculum: Integrating CPVE, YTS, TVEI?*, Youth Education Service, 1985.

8   See for example the following for a defence of liberal education against the onslaught of TVEI.
    Holt, M. (1983). 'Vocationalism: the threat to universal education', *Forum*, Summer 1983.
    Golby, M. (1985). 'The new educational consensus', *Curriculum*, vol. 6, no. 2.
    Johnathan, R. (1983). 'The manpower service model of education', *Cambridge Journal of Education*, vol. 13, no. 2.
    Dearden R.F. (1984). 'Education and training', *Westminister Studies in Education*, vol. 7, pp. 57–66).
    Norton Grubb. (1984). 'The bandwagon once more: vocational preparation for high tech occupations', *Harvard Education Review*, vol. 54, no. 4.

9   See Rapport (Journal of CYWU) for August and November 1985.

10 e.g. K. Prandy. (1965). *Professional Employees*. Faber.

Acknowledgements

I would like to thank Garth Allen for criticism and encouragement in writing this paper. I am indebted to Dave Thorpe and Paul Grosch for their helpful suggestions on earlier drafts. Thanks are also due to Diana Whitefoord for her patience and word processing.

The personal and political in practice

CHAPTER 10

Professional ideology versus lay experience

JOHN BASTIANI

The literature of community education is full of rhetoric about 'participation' and 'partnership'. This paper focuses on the relationships between professionals and lay people and demonstrates the gap between much of this rhetoric and the reality of their encounters. It is important to note that the problem is to do not only with form and content but also with professional presumptions about what counts as valid knowledge. Bastiani grounds his account in specific examples recounted in the words of people who have been at the receiving end of such 'professionalism'. Having developed a careful analysis and critique from this material, he goes on to propose an alternative model and to consider its implications for policy and training.

> I asked Karen's teacher the last time I went in, I says, 'Is there any way I could help Karen with her maths?' She says, 'Just don't bother', she says 'You would never understand the first thing!'
>
> (Parent)

> Parents can be effective partners only if professionals take notice of what they say and how they express their needs, and treat their contributions as intrinsically important.
>
> (Warnock Report, 1978)

Accounts of the place of the professions in contemporary society have become both an established ingredient of social science courses and texts, and a feature in the training programmes of many professions. But, with few honourable exceptions, they share a number of chronic limitations of perspective and treatment.

Such accounts are written from a 'macro' perspective and in the grand manner. They are theoretical in orientation and speculative in style, virtually ignoring issues that derive from the formulation of policy and the development of practice. They tell us little or nothing about the everyday dealings of professionals with their clients. As they have no roots in collected evidence, they often embody the powerful lore and mythologies that are a part of the work of social agencies and which have such a strong influence upon the ways they are both studied and understood. Above all, they are written by professionals for each other, with all that that implies.

In the present account, by contrast, an attempt is made to tap the experience of parents in their regular dealings with professionals, *from the parental point of view* and *in their own words*. In order to do this, material has been drawn from a number of more or less contemporaneous studies carried out in Nottingham in recent years, which examine contact with a number of agencies concerned with the education, health and welfare of children. The emphasis here is upon *educational* processes, (in the broadest sense,) and the subjects have a common experience of parenting, (although they are often otherwise referred to as 'clients', 'patients' and 'consumers' – and even 'punters' by the agencies with whom they come into contact.)

Reference is also made to other arenas of professional activity, as a further source of illustration and comparison. For examples from fields such as medicine, social work and the law lend support to a developing conviction that professional authority and relationships with clients are reproduced in similar ways across a wide spectrum of social life.

The data on which the present account is based, are drawn from two main sources. For the most part, parental viewpoints and reported experience are drawn from studies which rely heavily upon relatively open parent interviews, carried out in their own homes. The process of listening hard to what parents and other client groups are saying, produces accounts which are both detailed and vivid, but also thoughtful and revelatory.

Sources of parent data

- *Mainstream Schooling: Parents' Dealings With Their Children's Schools*, Goode (1982); Bastiani (1983); Atkin (1985).
- *Special Education: The Diagnosis and Assessment of Special Educational Needs*, Hanson (1985).
- *Health Education: The Management of Illness by Parents of Small Children,* Spencer (1979); O'Neill (1985).

Interview material is also supplemented by a small but significant number of studies which are based upon the detailed analysis of actual encounters between professionals and their 'clients' (Byrne and Long, 1976; Mayer and Timms, 1970; Bastiani, 1985.) Here, too, there is a relatively untested assumption that there are a number of common features between for example, teacher/parent interviews, diagnostic and casework interviews and doctor/patient consultations. The present analysis certainly suggests the emergence of common themes and processes such as the reporting of normal progress or the effects of remediation, the identification of special concerns, diagnosis and assessment, referral and placement.

Finally, the relative scarcity of such rich and potentially rewarding material can be explained in terms of the so-called professional ethic of 'confidentiality', which can also be interpreted as a somewhat spurious kind of secrecy, which is invested in most professional/client encounters and which makes raw data difficult both to obtain and interpret.

Parents' experience of contact with professionals

One of the most deeply embedded features of encounters between professionals in many fields and their clients, is a sense of 'taken-for-grantedness' about the way things are. Such implicit acceptance makes it very difficult to mount a sustained critique, or to examine existing practice in a fresh way. From such a viewpoint, the encounters between professionals and their clients are staged within a model of social relationships in which a knowledgeable and powerful expert dispenses wisdom and judgement to an ignorant client, who has sought help, or been referred, for a variety of reasons.

Within this ideology of professional/lay relationships, widely accepted as being legitimate, there is a general assumption (usually shared by parents and professionals alike,) that problems relating to education, health and welfare, are matters of *professional* judgement and concern. From this, it follows that professionals are 'only doing their job' in taking the initiative, in defining the nature and terms of the relationship, the agenda for communicating and contact, and, above all, in taking responsibility for decision making and subsequent action.

Dealings with professionals will be on *their* terms and this is

usually accepted as quite proper, unless there are special problems
or the system patently is not working.

> We went and asked to see a copy of his records, which we saw, and
> no matter what we'd said in the past that part that said 'Is this school
> suitable for this child?' it always said 'Yes'. There was no mention of
> us saying he wasn't happy, and that was when we started arguing it
> out. No one at the school actually came out and said to us, 'No,
> you're wrong, he can't do it', but they seemed to give us smug little
> smiles as if to say 'You carry on trying to convince yourselves, we
> know better'. In the end we'd had enough, we didn't want any more
> to do with experts.
>
> (Hanson 1985)

Parents may be assigned a role but it is secondary and supportive.
In their dealings with their children's schools, for example, parents
are often encouraged, even expected to *help* the school in
fund-raising and social events, to *support* school policies and
decisions but, at the same time, not to interfere in the central
processes of teaching and learning.

> ... at this particular school, they like you to be involved in the things
> they do at school, but as far as your child's work and things like that
> are concerned, I think they like you to leave that to them. They like
> you to join in with things, you know, erm, anything that's going off
> at school – sport and all that – you're involved in all that, but the
> actual work that the child does, I think they just prefer to tell you
> their bit, and er, you know ...
>
> (Goode 1982)

Further illustration of the widespread acceptance of professional
authority, as it is generally practised, comes from a study of
teachers' dealings with their own children's schools. It is quite
salutary to discover that many teachers experience the kind of
obstacles to effective contact with *their own* children's teachers, that
are identified by parents generally.

> T: I felt the whole approach was not as I would prefer it to be.
> I: So what did you do about that, as a parent?
> T: Nothing really, except moan at home I didn't feel that I could,
>   er, challenge the teacher at all, I felt I had to accept it, but I was
>   put out.
>
> (Atkin 1985)

Let's say I think such a situation (an open day with 5 minute
appointment) is of very limited value, erm, in spite of that,
nevertheless to me it is their professional decision – and therefore I,
inasmuch as I have no standing in the school other than that of a

parent, erm, I try, I would tend to restrict anything I have to say to
the school, erm, to my own child. I think it would be wrong of me
to suggest how they should run their school, which would include,
erm, parents' evenings.

(Atkin 1985)

Although studies of parents' contact with a variety of professionals
are characterized by a widespread acceptance of the way things are,
even a tolerant good humour, there are clear limits. Much of the
critical nature of parental comment stems from the *manner* in which
decisions are made and advice given. Whilst many parents would
accept the right of professionals to play the dominant part, it is the
way in which this is done that can give offence.

But it is in the detailed arrangements for communication and
contact that the one-sidedness of professional/parent relationships
can be seen most sharply, in the ways in which parents can be
excluded from the making of important decisions that concern their
children, in which individual personalities can become distorted
through the use of impersonal, bureaucratic records, or bad news
clumsily communicated without prior warning.

They invited us to a case conference at the school – at least from the
letter we thought that was going to happen. When we arrived
everyone else ... all the professionals were just leaving. They'd
invited us to *tell* us what they'd decided!

(Hanson 1985)

Mrs Bailey, a foster parent, also found that decisions were being
made based not on accurate assessment, but on reputation:

When William came to us he had a hearing problem which has never
been sorted out so he had no speech at all and he was very disturbed
... he came with a reputation and a place at the ESN(S) school. We
hadn't had him very long when it was obvious that there was a lot
more to him, he wasn't really this extremely disturbed little boy
everybody thought. On paper he looked dreadful, whenever anyone
had a report done about him it was that he was virtually
non-educable so we had a lot of problems getting people to assess
him.

(Hanson 1985)

The teacher sort of looked round and thought 'Perhaps *you* were
next. Or you were next.' And you'd sit around saying 'After you',
and getting more and more furious. And if you had three children,
you were there most of the night! ... By the time you get to your
third teacher at nine thirty, you were worn to a frazzle.

(Bastiani 1983)

M: Well no, not before the open night, we wasn't notified that she was being awkward or anything. Not at all.

I: So it was a bit of a shock?

M: It was a *terrible* shock, in fact, we didn't go home, me 'usband had to go for a drink first, he says otherwise he would 'ave probably done her some harm. So he calmed himself down and we discussed it over a quiet drink and then, I must admit it's good now. 'Cos it's the first bad report we've ever had and it was quite upsetting, to be honest.

(Bastiani 1983)

Meetings with professionals can seem intimidating or inappropriate; professionals can appear to be offhand and arrogant – or even disinterested!

We go and I never quite know if Mr X is taking in what I'm saying. There is never any reaction from him. I often wonder if I went in there and stripped off in front of him, if I would get a reaction then. He's completely passive and he nods and says 'Good' and 'Yes' and that's about the stretch. So it's good in that the child's seen regularly and Mr X has got an excellent reputation, but not so good in that you go wanting to know how he's getting on and you come out with a vague feeling that you never went.

(Richardson, quoted by McConkey 1985)

So, too, they can appear to be ill-informed, to act in ways that contradict parental knowledge and experience, or even to fly in the face of common sense and reason itself.

F: The thing that always annoyed me, and I always, ever since she was at school – was the fact that they kept saying she was good at spelling, and we kept saying that she wasn't good at spelling and this year, in her fourth year, they've eventually admitted ... you know, after all this time ...
And we've asked – why? 'Oh yes', they say – what was it? – they aren't actually looking at it for its spelling or something.

M: Red marks give them an inferiority complex or something ridiculous.

F: [reports are] useful to some extent. We tend to contradict half of what's in them, i.e. the spelling. They've consistently said 'It's bloody awful', and the last time we went to the school, we said to the teacher 'She's not a good speller' and he said 'Well, I might have to agree with you.'

(Goode 1982)

Parental interviews and accounts frequently contain direct and indirect references to the *inequality of relationship* in their dealings with teachers, health service professionals, social workers and others encountered in the 'caring professions'. An important insight into this experience is provided by the frequent figurative use of images of the small, helpless child attempting to deal with large, uncomprehending and insensitive adults, particularly parent and teacher figures.

> I'm sure that teachers do talk down to a lot of the parents. I've noticed at these social do's, the way they talk to some of them. It's virtually as if ... particularly the ones who are helping them ... admittedly they've got to organize them and sort something out, but *it's almost as if, you know, they're just bigger kids.*
>
> (Goode 1982)

> He ... made me feel *really small.*
>
> (Bastiani 1983)

> Let us do the teaching, you do the parenting sort of thing ... We felt metaphorically we'd had our hands smacked.
>
> (Goode 1982)

Such a metaphor provides a rich illustration of the feelings of inequality, social distance and powerlessness that many parents would otherwise find it difficult to put into words – and which parents' evenings in children's schools, for instance, so richly illustrate with their queuing in corridors, sitting at teachers' desks on infant-sized stools and the common experience both literally and figuratively of being talked down at from a great height!

Professionals know best! This is an attitude that is engendered in training and which is hardened by experience. And, if this is so, listening to their clients is seen as largely irrelevant or, at worst, as a waste of valuable time. Apart from assumptions of lay ignorance, professionals working in the area of health, education and welfare also tend, despite the mythologies generated by the media, to underplay the effects of social circumstances upon the issues under consideration.

Where this is true, it appears that much professional activity is characterized by an insensitivity towards the lives of those they work with, together with a failure to listen and to pick up important information and knowledge of value in dealing with particular cases and circumstances.

> M: I can't sort of understand why a baby is better brought up on breast feeding than what it is on a bottle *you* can eat anything and *do* anything but when you breast feed you've got to watch what you eat because of the baby – I've had it drummed into

me that much that it put me right off it – you know I had no
feeling to do it and I think if *you* don't feel like doing it it's no
good to the baby anyway cos you're not going to be interested
while you're doing it.

(Spencer 1979)

Often professionals and those they work with appear to be living
in different worlds! Here, close analysis of actual examples is
helpful in pinpointing some of the reasons for this. In general,
being on different wavelengths can be seen in terms of the sharp
difference between the *formal knowledge of professions*, acquired
during extended training and developed during the years that
follow, and the *everyday knowledge and common sense of clients, derived
from their lived experience*. As a consequence, much professional
help, however well-intentioned, is often wide of the mark. At
worst, professionals and parents continue to inhabit different
worlds, with little or no real contact.

Such fundamental and intractable problems are intensified in two
areas. Firstly, they are heightened by differences of age, sex and
social background. The raw, young, middle-class social worker
offering totally inappropriate advice to hard-pressed parents is a
firmly established stereotype in situation comedy, but it does have
some substance in the real world too!

Mandy went to ... to each person down there. She saw the speech
therapist ... I mean, to how we talk they speak a lot more correct ... I
mean, they say 'barth' where we say 'bath'. The first time we took
her down it was Alison Wood, I don't know if you know her. We
didn't like her at first, we thought she was a bit, you know, nose in
the air, but she was ever so nice when you got to know her.
Anyway, it was quite funny, Alison had got this doll's with this bath
as we call it [laughs]. So she says to Mandy [puts on 'posh' voice]:
'Can you put the baby in the barth?' and Mandy, she didn't know
what she was talking about [laughs]. So I said: 'put the baby in the
bath' and she did it. So I says to Alison: 'We say 'bath', we don't say
'barth'. So she says 'Oh', and after that she said 'bath' to Mandy.
After that she tried to talk a bit more like us. [laughs]

(Hanson 1985)

I mean, some of these people ... they should be people what's had
children, what's been through some of these experiences not these
bloody la-di-da flirty women with skirts up to their arses and fancy
perfume, or these young blokes that's just preaching to you what
they've learned in a bloody book, that's no good to anybody.

(Hanson 1985)

The second illustration concerns the work of agencies in family-related areas where the work principally derives from problems which stem from the experience of parenting and running a family. This is particularly true for agencies that are concerned with acute social and educational disadvantage, where family problems are often bound up with chronic poverty and unemployment. These differences are often deeply felt and vividly described!

> She comes in here with her Marks and Spenders pleated skirt and her leather gloves – what does she know about bringing up two mucky kids.
>
> (O'Neill 1985)

Professionals often have little or no lived experience in areas that are close to the centre of the work of the caring professions themselves. These are often concerned with deeply entrenched problems of health and poverty, of social and educational disadvantage in general, or the more specific themes on which this account draws, such as:

- The repeated experience of educational failure.
- The problems of raising recalcitrant and alienated children of school age.
- The health problems associated with early childhood.
- The daily experience of coping with severe handicap in a family setting.

Professional/client activity is frequently characterized by a tension between professional, theoretically-derived *knowledge* derived from study, and the *experience* of clients derived from everyday life. The former, derived from academic study (often tellingly referred to by parents as 'going by the book'.) consists of the application of theories, rules and procedures, generally applied; parental experience uses as *its* point of reference the knowledge of what is normal for individual children, derived from a cumulative picture of behaviour in a wide range of settings. Professionals are often ignorant of how individuals characteristically behave in out-of-school or non–clinical settings. This, of course, is just what parents are good at!

> *M*: Yeah. Now that's the way you have to deal with Yvonne. You have to get mad with her for her to do something. David's completely opposite ...

F: They're miles apart, yeah. They're er mirrors of our own
      personalities, actually ...
M: Oh, yeah. Yvonne's like me ...
F: 'Chip off the old block' sums it up perfectly ... David talks
      about what he's doing. He'll show us what he's done –
      homework. I came in last night. He was sitting there and he'd
      done a graph for ... various water flows or something. I didn't
      catch what it was. But as soon as I walked in, I hadn't even got
      my coat off ... and he's showing me.
        'I've done my homework, Dad!'
        'Oh, Christ! What is it?' I was with him then and we sat and
      had a look at it.
        Yvonne doesn't say anything. David'll come in and say,
      'We've been doing so-and-so and *I* did it. Now Yvonne won't.
      We have to find that out when we have an Open Night ...
                                                        (Goode 1982)

Another feature of professional ideology and practice is its
reliance upon *talk*. This is exemplified in the actual *form* of the
contact itself – the teacher/parent interview, the doctor/patient
consultation, the case-work interview etc. For many professionals,
language is the major element in the task of analysing and
diagnosing problems, making decisions and taking remedial action.
It is also a powerful tool in the management and control of
awkward clients.

For many parents, the opposite is true! There are many for
whom discussion is a prelude to action, a substitute for it or a form
of procrastination. To talk with professionals is to expose yourself
to the 'flannel' of 'word merchants', who can 'pull the wool over
your eyes'.

When we came out of there the fourth time, my husband said, 'What
do you think of it?' and I said, 'I don't know what to think of it.'
Then my husband said, 'He just don't give you any idea what he's
going to do or anything. He just keeps on saying come back and
have some more talks'. Well, while he's doing that, we're not
getting anywhere.
                                              (Mayer and Timms 1970)

F: I think the most effective thing they do at the comprehensive is
      the work experience ... the kids learn more in a fortnight's work
      experience than from all the talking and whatever earlier on.
                                                     (Bastiani 1983)

Finally, parental accounts of contact with a range of agencies
concerned with the health, education and welfare of young people,

testify to deep-seated tensions and conflicts in the work of professionals, however well-intentioned. Such conflicts can be characterized as a tension between the demands of helping, caring and enabling, (so much at the forefront of professional ideology and deeply embedded in its rhetoric,) with the problems that relate to the management and control of clients in relation to:

- The allocation and use of scarce resources (especially the time and energy of professionals themselves).
- The limitations of their knowledge and expertise.

For parents, such tensions are experienced as early or inappropriate attempts to pin down or 'label' problems, (or, paradoxically, a refusal to do so,) the pursuit of contradictory policies or objectives with different agencies or personnel, or an attempt to convince parents that nothing more can be done.

> *M*: My eldest boy is dyslexic. Now you know that causes me a lot of problems throughout education. We moved around the London area quite a bit and their idea was they put him into a class of, a *remedial* class, which wasn't good for him because he's got a fairly high IQ, uh, and that wasn't good for him.
>
> Then they thought of sending him to a special school because he wasn't settling in at the remedial and they couldn't understand why. Uh, we stopped that, we wasn't having that … Uh, then we went to Bournemouth and they just gave him pencil and paper and let him draw his way through sums. So I stopped him going to school … so I had the kind of performance … Er he came out with three 'O' levels and he's now just finished his apprenticeship as a toolmaker. And he really was quite bad.
>
> (Bastiani 1983)

So an examination of parental accounts in these areas is highly suggestive of a general pattern of professional/client relationships and of the ways in which these are created and sustained. A key feature of such relationships is their social and ideological distance, which derives from attitudes and assumptions, but which is reinforced by the actual arrangements for communication and contact themselves.

Meetings between parents and professionals can often be seen, then, to be characterized by:

- Institutionalized insensitivity.

- Tensions between professional knowledge and training and the lived experience of clients.
- The consequences of deep conflict within the role of professionals and the nature of the services they offer.

Taken together, such characteristics serve to prevent professionals from recognizing the limitations of their expertise and, at the same time, from acknowledging the value of their client's knowledge and experience. For this reason it is very useful to examine the potential of situations where, for a variety of reasons, normal circumstances do not apply, where alternative arrangements exist or, as readers of this book will recognize, very different assumptions about the role of the professional in the community operate.

A parent–centred rationale*

In the previous section a critique of the established relationships between professionals and those with whom they work was briefly developed. It was rooted in studies of parental experience of a range of health, education and welfare agencies.

In this section an alternative model, based upon very different values and practices is outlined. This is followed by a brief look at several of the implications of such an approach for policy, training and practice, of likely interest to those with a broad interest in the relationship between families, communities and education.

Whilst it cannot be easily defined, a "parent–centred" philosophy can be seen as having a number of distinct, though overlapping, purposes, which have rather different implications for thinking and practice:

1. The careful and systematic consideration of the experience of parents, and other groups, should be a crucial ingredient in the appraisal and evaluation of public services, particularly in the fields of health, education and welfare. Such consideration needs to go beyond matters of provision and access, to consider both the needs

---

*Note: In this account as a whole, the professional/client dichotomy has been used as a critical focus. In the following section, however, the term 'client' has been deliberately avoided both because it implies an unequal distribution of authority and knowledge and is regarded as inappropriate and because such a term, however, liberally interpreted, seems incompatible with the idea of partnership.

of parents, as *they* perceive them and their assessment of the quality of their current experience. (How to identify and respond to the needs of communities has been a long-standing and problematic issue in community education.)

2. As consumers of public services, parents (and others, including children and young people themselves,) have important rights and obligations. In recent years, supported by a series of reports sponsored by successive governments, (Plowden; Court; Taylor; Warnock), it has become increasingly accepted that parents should be consulted about, and involved with, processes that deeply affect both the shorter and longer-term development of their children.

In the last decade, the rights of parents have become more overtly politicized. This has led, amongst other things, to the creation of new legislation, particularly in the spheres of schooling and the education of children with special needs, in the 1980, 1981 and 1986 Education Acts respectively.

3. There is growing acceptance of, and support for, the view that when professionals and parents share some of the same goals and work together in an active partnership, things can really begin to happen! A most striking contemporary example, which can draw upon powerful evidence from Haringey, Coventry, Rochdale, Sheffield and elsewhere, concerns the involvement of parents in their children's reading. For the evidence shows conclusively that where parents and teachers work together, the gains that children make are both dramatic and sustainable, even when those children have started from a position of serious under-achievement.

Such encouraging experience, based upon new kinds of teacher/parent partnerships is becoming more widespread in other areas and can be found in the pre-school world, elsewhere in the education system, in social work, youth and community work and in the work of the health and welfare services. It also appears likely to survive the influence of contrary forces, of accelerating centralism and inimical government policies and resource allocation.

4. Parents, (although the same is true of other lay groups such as claimants, patients, etc.) possess crucially important knowledge and experience, which not only complements that of professionals, but is valuable in its own right. In educational terms, parents are an essential resource and also have unique opportunities as educators – a powerful combination.

Whilst such an argument has long had a place in the rhetoric of home/school relationships and in the field of community education, it has not yet acquired a clear place in the everyday assumptions that are made about teaching and learning. Nevertheless, the recognition of the educative elements in communities is an area where progress is being made, in a steady but unspectacular way.

5. Finally, there is an important element in a parent-centred rationale which is nevertheless very difficult to pin down. It is centrally concerned with respect for the everyday lives of ordinary people, both as individuals and in groups, *for its own sake*, and is strongly invested with philosophical, political and moral significance.

Such a value, described variously as 'autonomy' or 'respect for persons' in education, or 'client self-determination' in social work, is deeply embedded in the rhetoric of the caring professions. It is particularly audible during training, though it is more difficult to find in subsequent practice!

These values, and the actions they give rise to, constitute the outline of a rationale that offers a very different model of professional/parent relationships. It also suggests, at least in outline, a number of areas for development and practice.

Some areas for development

> The first daydream is this: that all teachers and therapists will come to regard work with parents as an integral part of their job and not as an extra. The second is that all parents, no matter in what part of the country they live, will have the opportunity of being involved in furthering their child's development through working alongside professionals. The third is that our service administrators and civil servants will provide the resources and systems whereby parental participation can become a reality and that they will treat this as an obligation, not an option.
>
> (McConkey 1985)

> ... while the bandwagon of parental involvement may be moving quite fast, we are still a very long way from achieving a more equal relationship between parents and professionals.
>
> (Pugh 1984)

This article has attempted to develop, in outline, a critical analysis of professional/lay relationships. It has roots in the careful consideration of accounts by parents, in their own words, of their dealings with a number of agencies concerned with the education and welfare of their children.

Such an examination challenges widespread, but often hidden, assumptions and attitudes that characterize such dealings and shape their form and outcomes. Taken further, such an analysis offers potential for the development of new ways of thinking and working, of new roles and relationships, which has implications both for professionals and parents alike.

But the scale and complexity of such a task cannot be under-estimated. Just as professionals exhibit a wide range of beliefs and attitudes about their work, so do those they work with! When a parent says, 'Being friendly with a teacher is like doing business with a relative!', he is operating a clearly demarcated view of the role of teachers and parents, which is in every way a counterpart to the teacher who claims that, 'I'm a teacher, not a bloody social worker!' Such attitudes, which are still widespread, serve to strengthen the resistance of the old order, and give it legitimacy. Although it is beyond the scope of this article, similar problems stem from the petty jealousies and territorial disputes that often characterize *inter-professional* activity and cooperation; particularly in areas such as pre-school provision, working with disaffected teenagers and the diagnosis of special educational needs.

The development of an active and genuine partnership between professionals and those they work with involves, then, the formulation of new attitudes and purposes, as well as the introduction of new ways of working, if real change is to take place, as this challenging statement by Barbara Tizard suggests:

> To attain the (Plowden) goal of partnership, the teachers would have to sell parents the view that the child's nursery experiences were educational, and persuade parents to reinforce them in appropriate ways at home. Alternatively, they would need to consider with the parents what they would like their children to learn and how the curriculum might be modified to meet these wishes.
>
> The first course involves trying to change parents, the second trying to change teachers. Neither is easy and both involve extensive changes in the teachers' way of working.
>
> (Tizard 1977)

Two areas for development

Much of both the theory and the practice of community education give emphasis to the development of appropriate *institutional* forms and patterns of provision. The present account seeks to redress the balance somewhat by giving more emphasis to professional/client *relationships*, from the perspective of those who have dealings with the educational and welfare services.

From a wide range of possibilities, two areas have been chosen for comment:

THE DEVELOPMENT OF MORE EFFECTIVE WAYS OF WORKING THAT ARE CONSISTENT WITH A CLIENT–CENTRED PHILOSOPHY.

- A number of studies, (most of which are referred to at the end of this article) suggest that we should pay much more attention to the circumstances in which communication and contact take place. This should take both form and process into account. The careful examination of one's own practice in this way can be both salutary and far-reaching.
- Professionals need to develop attitudes and skills to enable them to listen to those people whose interests they are supposed to serve. An essential feature of this is the capacity to see something of what life is like 'in their shoes'.
- It is important to find ways of acknowledging the knowledge and experience that clients have, of developing support for their growing confidence in doing things for themselves and in finding effective ways of pooling and sharing their knowledge and experience with each other.

THE DEVELOPMENT OF TRAINING OPPORTUNITIES AND EXPERIENCES

These should provide the seedbed for the growth of very different professional attitudes and practices from those that are currently fostered. More attention needs to be given to the preparation, training and further development of teachers and adult educators, youth and community workers, social workers and health professionals (e.g. Atkin and Bastiani 1987).

In this area, it is possible to incorporate parental perspectives and experience through the provision of opportunities such as placements, the involvement of parents in discussion groups, simulations and other practical activities. Above all, training can more productively tap the opportunities to learn 'out there', in the real world, in parent-centred settings such as playgroups, family and community centres and in self-led projects and activities. In these ways, important elements of community education can be developed where they properly belong – in the community itself.

Sources of parent data

1 Parents' dealings with their children's schools

THE DEVELOPMENT OF EFFECTIVE HOME/SCHOOL PROGRAMMES PROJECT

Atkin, J. (1985). *Teacher/Parents*. University of Nottingham School of Education.
Bastiani, J. (1983). 'Listening to parents: philosophy, critique and method', unpublished Ph.D. thesis, University of Nottingham.
Goode, J. (1982). 'Parents as educators: a study of parental perspectives on their children's schooling', unpublished M.Phil. thesis, University of Nottingham.
Tizard, B 'Carry on Communicating', *Times Educational Supplement*, 25th May 1977.

Shorter and more accessible accounts of these three studies, written for trainer/probationer audiences, are beng published in the following:
Atkin, J. and Bastiani, J. (1987). *Listening to Parents: an Approach to the Improvement of Home-School Relations*. Croom-Helm.

2 The Diagnosis and assessment of special educational needs

Hanson, E. (1985). 'Parental perceptions of professionals', unpublished M.Ed. assignment, University of Nottingham School of Education.
Newson, E. (1976). 'Parents as a resource in diagnosis and assessment', in Oppe, T. and Woodford, F. (eds), *Early Management of Handicapping Disorders*, IRMMH Assoc. Scientific Publishers.

2 The management of illness by parents of small children

O'Neill, P. (1985). 'Different sources of influence and advice used by mothers of small children', unpublished B.Ed. dissertation, University of Nottingham.
Spencer, N. J. (1979). 'An education for health educators? A critique of the concepts of professionals as the sole possessors of health knowledge', in Anderson, D., Perkins, E. and Spencer, N., 'Who knows best in health education?', Leverhulme Health Education Project, *Occasional Paper 19*, University of Nottingham.

Additional references

Atkin, J. and Bastiani, J. (1984). *Preparing Teachers to Work with Parents: a Survey of Initial Training*. University of Nottingham School of Education.

Bastiani, J. (1985). *Listening to Parents: Talking to Teachers*. Dialogue no. 2, March 1985.

Byrne, P. S. and Long, B. E. L. (1976). *Doctors Talking to Patients: A Study of the Verbal Behaviour of General Practitioners Consulting in their Surgeries*. DHSS. H.M.S.O.

Mayer, J. E. and Timms, N. (1970). *The Client Speaks: Working-Class Impressions of Casework*. Routledge & Kegan Paul.

McConkey, R. (1985). *Working with Parents: a Practical Guide for Teachers and Therapists*. Croom Helm.

Pugh, G. (1984). 'Parent involvement', *N.C.B. Partnership Papers,* no. 2, National Children's Bureau.

Tizard, B. *et al.* (1981). *Involving Parents in Nursery and Infant Schools*.Grant-McIntyre.

CHAPTER 11

The art of the possible: personal and social education and the community secondary school

GARTH ALLEN

Both community secondary schooling in general and the development of PSE within comprehensive education in particular represent significant and congruent educational reform movements. Allen argues that the connections, as well as their inherent ambivalence, need to be more clearly understood. In the process, an important dimension of community education developments within the compulsory sector can be effectively demarginalized. A wide-ranging survey of both internal and external demands upon the comprehensive school indicates why PSE has taken its place within the secondary curriculum and how this parallels the kind of claims made by many community schools. In this respect, Allen's paper is a timely reminder of the centrality of community education to the wider debate about education in schools.

One of the major contributions which recent social scientific research has made to our understanding of social structure and social change is to demonstrate that schools are extremely complex social institutions. We now know that accurately and truthfully to describe and account for the way schools are and how and why they have become the way they are is both necessary, because of the importance of schooling in social life, and difficult, because of the intellectual and financial resources required to be confident that something approaching a truthful and accurate account has been arrived at.

Sociologists of education have played a major role in this discovery, demonstrating the difficulties of rolling back the reality of contemporary mass schooling for all to see. Paul Willis, for example, in his influential study *Learning to Labour*[1] suggests that in order to understand the thoughts, words and actions of teachers and students, we have to engage in three levels of analysis.

First, we would have to examine the public face of the school – how the school publicly defends its aims, effectiveness and structure. This would mean, for example, analysing school prospectuses, speeches at governor's meetings and speech days, letters to the press, to parents and so on, and through talking with teachers and students in order to gather the ways in which people are willing to openly describe and explain the nature of a particular school as they see it.

Second, according to Willis, we need to recognize that what people are prepared to publicly acknowledge is often quite different from an inner or private reality. This, of course, is much more difficult for an outsider to observe and analyse. The distinction between public and private accounts of schooling identifies a twin rationality. Willis observes that teachers' public justifications for words and deeds often constitute a response to a private demand simply to survive in the most convivial and productive fashion. For example, a head teacher might publicly defend a shift in the timetable from 40-minute periods to one-hour periods in terms of needing bigger blocks of time to allow the use of microcomputers across the curriculum. The private reality for the head teacher might be simply a need to shorten the morning breaktime and eliminate the afternoon break because he felt that his staff were not able or willing to control the student's behaviour during breaks to his satisfaction. Willis is encouraging us to recognize that teachers and students need to maximize their welfare and enjoyment during school hours and, to achieve their aims, will choose those public explanations and arguments which they feel are most likely to be persuasive.

Thirdly, Willis introduces what he calls the cultural or social milieu of the school, the interactions between the school and the general social universe it inhabits, made up of prevailing political, economic and social structures and pressures. He suggests that the analysis of schools should take account of the school's social context, of its cultural milieu. This belief, now approaching the status of a universal truth, has taken sociologists of education into detailed historical studies of schools and schooling and into entertaining accounts of the innermost mysteries of youth cultures and the views about society, and schools in particular, held by prominent industrialists.[2]

These three levels of analysis are not mutually exclusive but suggest a systematic research process which acknowledges the difficulties of understanding why schools have become what they have and do what they do and also acknowledges the political requirement to understand how to change them. Judgements about schools, for social scientists as well as the majority of the population, are part of a personal ideology or political belief system. There cannot be a completely neutral social account of schooling. Dewey, in his great book, *Democracy and Education*, pointed this out fifty years ago:

> The concept of education as a social process and function has no definite meaning until we define the kind of society we have in mind.[3]

What we like about schools and what we want from schools determine and is determined by our views about the sort of individuals we prefer to live with. In particular, whether we believe that people are born nice, and often lose their niceness, or are born nasty, and have to lose their nastiness. Also our views about schools influence and are influenced by our views about the social structure we prefer. In the UK this often becomes reduced to a conflict between a demand for individual freedom of expression and a counter demand for social obedience.

The manner in which we deal with conflicts arising out of these long-standing political issues creates the processes and structures which determine any prevailing social context for schools.

The general nature of Willis' suggestions for enabling truthful and accurate accounts of people and their relationships and social institutions and their structures is both intuitively and intellectually appealing. Other approaches to describing and accounting for the nature of schools have been developed, of course, and the number of available case-studies of state schools has grown rapidly during the past decade.[4]

The main theme of this discussion is that people involved in, and committed to, the development of community schools need to understand certain aspects of schools which have significantly changed in recent years (and need to be prepared to act on their understanding). Schools have been subject to a public critique which has required a public defence. The direction, form and intensity of this public questioning of the compulsory school has led to the growth and development of educational reforms which share many features with the ideas and practices of the community school but are not necessarily publicly or privately defended in such terms.

One of the major growth areas in the secondary school curriculum in the past twenty years has been the new Personal and Social Education movement (PSE). PSE has not only had major influence on the curriculum but has affected the nature of the school as a bureaucracy, its rules, regulations, rhythms and rituals. PSE often encompasses activities which have titles such as pastoral care, guidance and counselling, active tutorial work, negotiated learning contracts and pupil-controlled assessment procedures. Arrangements within the school to enable such activities to take place and flourish have helped create schools whose internal organization and curriculum have dramatically changed during the past two decades.

There has been a number of attempts in recent years to produce a conceptual framework for understanding significant features of the ideas and practices of the community school or college. The scheme offered by Angela Skrimshire[5] is built on the premise that the main litmus test for a community school is that it is sensitive to, and takes seriously as 'problematic', its prevailing cultural milieu. She proceeds to create a persuasive conceptual continuum which enables us to make sense of the ways and means by which various types of community school practices have been brought into being. A simplified version of her framework is reproduced, together with brief annotations hinting at the congruence of the Skrimshire continuum with key elements of the PSE movement (see Figure 11.1).

There are other reasons for claiming that people working in and for the community school would benefit from a developed understanding of the recent popularity of PSE. First, community education staff working in or from community schools often have a teaching commitment and this often requires some form of PSE work. Such workers can find themselves teaching fourth and fifth year courses concerned with PSE (usually non-examined) or they are engaged in specific counselling and guidance activities with young people. They may be involved in community service, work experience or careers education. All of these often come within the framework of PSE in the school. Second, the youth service tradition within community education enables community staff in

Figure 11.1 Congruence between community education and personal and social education

Community school	Personal and social education	
School-centred	School-centred	
School as community	Can attempt to create community spirit within the school through explicit and/or implicit values education.	
School with strong home–school links	Can enable parents to be part of a contractual relationship with teachers and pupils so that pupils can be managed through behaviour and performance contracts.	
School with a community curriculum	Can be the main vehicle through which pupils learn in out-of-school contexts (e.g. community experience, work experience)	
The neighbourhood school	Can become a major source of community funding of schools (through fund-raising organized during, e.g. active tutorial work).	
Schools for dual use	Can enable a mixing of ages – e.g. through association with mother and toddler groups, the elderly and the physically handicapped.	
The community controlled school	Can offer pupils the opportunity to elect representatives for an existing schools council or equivalent, or be a focus to get this started.	
The school as a community development agency	Can increase pupils' understandings of political issues which may lead to local political action.	
Community-centred	Community-centred	

community schools to be involved in a whole range of activities which are traditional in the youth service and have been colonized (often without recognition) by the PSE movement. They may be involved in fund-raising activities, in school trips and in activities which require a residential component (accompanying one of the PE teachers on a residential week at an outdoor pursuits centre) and may be encouraged to organize playtime activities (e.g. lunch-time discos). Third, one of the traditions of adult education in the UK has been to work with or on behalf of people (mainly working class) who have failed to benefit from compulsory education. Many workers in community schools, influenced by this particular adult education tradition, are easily attracted or are naturally pushed towards PSE because it is often aimed (in the first instance, at least) at pupils who are identified as being less able.

How can people working in and for community schooling make sense of the recent growth and development of PSE in the UK? Personal and social education in the UK, as far as I know, has not been subject to a major Willis-type analysis or any other type of sustained analysis which has tried to truthfully and accurately account for its popularity and its rapid growth and development in recent years. That is not to say that we have not had a massive interest in PSE. The interest, however, has been much concerned with what it is (philosphers of education) and what it should be (moral philosophers interested in education) and what it could be (curriculum and pedagogic specialists) rather than how it has been brought to its current state of relative prominence. There are few, if any, secondary schools in England who would publicly admit that they did not have a policy towards PSE.

Richard Pring,[6] in his very informative book, *Personal and Social Education in the Curriculum*, offers a personal synoptic account of the phenomenon from the standpoint of a philosopher of education of international repute, but nowhere attempts to specify *why* PSE has grown and flourished. He refers to the H.M.I. secondary survey[7] and quotes the following passage without further comment:

> In recent years these major objectives (namely, 'opportunities and experiences ... that will help their personal development as well as preparing them for the next stage of their lives') have assumed a more significant and conscious place in the aspiration of schools in response to external pressures and to changes in society, and within the schools themsleves.[8]

However, one searches in vain in the secondary survey, in a chapter on 'Personal and social development', of 35 pages, for any further mention of precisely what these 'external pressures', these changes 'within the schools' might be. We have no excuse for not doing this – Willis and others have shown the way. Given the lack of theoretical and empirical attention paid to explaining the PSE movement, the best we can do is to engage in some speculation about the findings of an *imaginary* substantial research effort into the recent origins and growth of PSE in schools.

We do know a little about the nature of these pressures and changes which have had a general impact on public images of schooling in contemporary Western society. T. Husen[9] has broadly characterized the 1960s as a period when formal education, as a universal 'good', was hardly questioned. Any problems in educational systems were to be cured by expansion. The 1970s, for Husen, were a period of less public deference to the structure of major social institutions, such as schools, factories and families. A greater willingness to question the purposes and effectiveness of schools existed amongst greater numbers of people, some of whom had learnt from I. Illich[10] that formal, mass, publicly controlled schooling was neither inevitable nor desirable. The 1980s, Husen rightly predicted, would be characterized by retrenchment, a fear that too much critique and too much change cuts out too much of the good and too little of the bad.

I. Shor,[11] in a new book *Culture Wars*, primarily concerned with the USA confirms Husen's prediction. He calls the 1970s and the 1980s the period of the 'conservative restoration'. Within this fifteen years, he distinguishes three major episodes of reaction in the liberal 1950s and 1960s. 1971–5 was the era of careers education, the beginnings of a freshly articulated demand to improve the fit between school values and skills and industrial values and skills, prompted and professionally controlled by a new brand of teacher, the trained and respected careers educator. Shor's second episode, from 1975 to 1982, sees a shift in emphasis through the prominence of a 'back-to-basics' movement, a revitalized call for schools to stand publicly accountable for failures to achieve minimal levels of literacy and numeracy for all their students. The current period, from 1982 on, he describes as a 'war of excellence', a crusade against mediocrity, with a corresponding obsession with new criteria for achievement and for new forms of assessing it. Shor's thesis, in brief, is that, in the USA, the last fifteen years have witnessed a conservative backlash against liberal, progressive movements in schools and a re-emphasis of vocational, centrally controlled education. There has also been, in his view, an attack on the wastage of egalitarian educational principles and policies and their replacement by new forms of student, school and teacher differentiation in order to provide families with greater freedom through greater choice of school and greater rewards for individual merit.

So far this paper has made three general points. The first is that there are no easy ways of arriving at defensible explanations for major changes in the structure of public sector education in the UK although social scientific research methodologies have progressed sufficiently to enable such tasks to be undertaken, given sufficient intellectual and financial resources. Second, it is assumed that no systematic account has been given of the recent origins and growth of PSE but that this demands to be undertaken both for its own sake and for the lessons to be learnt from such an account by other educational reform movements, such as the community school. Third, it assumes that many of the general descriptive and explanatory frameworks advanced by writers such as Husen and Shor help define the most fruitful areas of enquiry, at least in the initial stages, for teasing out the truth about the reasons behind the popularity of PSE in secondary schools in the UK. PSE has not come about by default or by chance. A 'botch-up' view of school structural change and curriculum development will not suffice.

PSE has grown and developed in certain ways rather than others because of the determined beliefs and actions of individuals and groups who wish to influence what schools do, how they do it and with what effect. PSE has been supplied because of demands for it. These demands can be filtered through Willis' 3 levels of analysis. From within schools, teachers and students have both publicly demanded and defended PSE and privately accommodated it and benefited from it. From outside the school, the prevailing social context, the cultural milieu has provided sufficient conditions to demand and encourage its growth. The following analysis speculates about the specific forms which such demands for PSE have taken. These demands, collectively, represent a coalition of interests. In a pluralist model of social and educational change, such demands would, in principle, eventually lead to counter-claims and demands, to critiques of PSE and to radical or deviant forms of PSE. What counts as radical PSE must be discussed at some other time, although I shall briefly allude to this question in my concluding remarks. The following ten sets of demands seem to me to be intuitively plausible – they ring true, they are what I suspect would be discovered. The list is not exhaustive and is not rank-ordered in terms of importance or chronology. However, they have been simply grouped into demands from 'within the schools themselves'[1–6] and into demands arising from 'external pressures and to changes in society'.[7–10]

The demands of academics

Academics in universities and colleges in the late 1960s, especially philosophers of education, were in disarray. They could not agree, nor agree to disagree, about the meanings of such terms as education, teaching and indoctrination.[12] They could not agree about which forms of knowledge were most worthwhile and hence offered conflicting advice as to what the primary purposes and characteristics of schools should be. Some nimble academics neatly side-stepped this debate and argued that, anyway, schools were too concerned with knowledge and not concerned enough with promoting the affective domain, with feelings, values and skills.[13] The broadening and deepening of teacher training from 3 to 4 years and the simultaneous upgrading of the teacher training colleges into colleges of education staffed by a new model army of academic specialists in education, helped create a flow of young teachers into schools who carried with them this rejection of the dominant position of the cognitive domain. PSE is much more concerned with values education and with the development of interpersonal skills and has become a major avenue within schools for offsetting this cognitive emphasis. This shift has given academics in education departments a new lease of life and has simultaneously enabled a smooth transfer of power over the curriculum to HMI.

Teachers' demands to be less authoritarian

One of the major public controversies about teaching and teachers has been the degree (either too much or too little) with which teachers coerce their students to think or act in ways which the students would not freely choose to do. Teachers of the humanities, in particular, again in the late 1960s and 1970s, were increasingly concerned with the quality of their personal relationships with their students. They searched for a shift away from the authoritative and authoritarian, no longer seeking to dominate students nor intellectually monopolize their students' opinions. Such teachers were influenced by the interest in the late 1960s in new forms of political relationships in society, culminating in the community politics movement and also in the deschooling movement which briefly flourished in the early 1970s and which itself grew out of this more general political movement.[14] Teachers demanded to be able to work more democratically, to be less inflexible and predictable, less expert, and to be able to work with students (and with other teachers) within a less autocratic regime.

PSE offers teachers the opportunity to develop non-authoritarian pedagogies. PSE requires that students and teachers are prepared to get to know one another as people in order to diagnose respective strengths and weaknesses, needs and demands. Full-frontal, teacher-dominated talk and action, as a teaching style, has only a small part to play within PSE. These shifts, from content to process and from teacher domination to teacher facilitation, have been able to draw on initiatives in the youth service, for example on non-directive learning methods, and have created an arsenal of teaching and learning techniques that enable new forms of personal relationships in schools for teachers and students alike.

The demands of head teachers

An increase in the average size of both primary and secondary schools took place during the late 1960s and early 1970s. In secondary education, this was in response to demographic factors, the shift to comprehensive education, the move to educate boys and girls together and the economics of school building regulations. Larger schools, especially large mixed comprehensive schools, created a major control problem for head teachers, especially for those who had previously been the head of small, single-sex grammar schools. Head teachers no longer felt they could control the institution. They had little or no training in managing complex bureaucracies and little inclination to change their ways of working. If teachers and students were too numerous to keep in touch with, if school sites (often split) were too vast to regularly show one's presence in every nook and cranny, how could head teachers be confident that the institution was working and thriving, and that deviant students (and teachers) would be identified and dealt with?

One answer was to create a sense of community. Large schools needed to be places where people knew the part they were expected to play in order to promote the well-being of the institution. Traditional means of creating organizational and group identification, through school uniforms, prefects, house systems and organized competitive sport, were often unavailable or ineffective because they were not always in keeping with the prevailing cultural milieu. Students in large schools must be able to be trusted to work through and for the institution without constant surveillance. They must feel part of a community, part of a collective interest which preserves and promotes the school. Such a control mechanism required a major shift in values for some young people in order for them to put the collective interest above, or at least on a par with, self-interest. PSE can and does confront the question of values in education directly. It can and does encourage students to rationalize their words and deeds in terms of their own current and future welfare and enjoyment and in terms of their personal impact on other people, groups and institutions. PSE can and does create the institutional solidarity which head teachers demand. It makes deviant behaviour more noticeable, more difficult to rationally defend and more difficult to continually sustain. This applies for both students and teachers alike.

The demands of LEA officers

Civil servants, despite the messages of Radio One disc jockeys, do not often set out to deliberately antagonize people. They seek to minimize conflict, not create it. LEA officers want to remain the confidant and friend of all members of the local authority education service. A demand derived from this arose during the period in the late 1960s and early 1970s when many secondary schools changed their image and character.

Many teachers were angry and disillusioned with the extent and pace of change. Many felt they would lose out in any major reorganization. LEA officers were often the target for public abuse and personal bitterness. Large comprehensive schools were often formed by the amalgamation of two, sometimes three, schools, one of these often a grammar school. Senior teachers in the secondary modern schools often failed to get the senior academic posts in the new school, rarely becoming the new head teacher or one of his senior heads of a subject group or faculty. Senior teachers who could see themselves losing out through reorganization put pressure on LEA officers to create new schools with a sufficiently

large senior management team to accommodate themselves within
the new school in a position of rank and substance. These could not
be academic posts – they were reserved for grammar school staff or
for newly imported energetic graduates.

Many local authorities created new schools with a new hierarchy
within them, publicly rationalized in terms of protecting the
individual welfare of students in a large organization, but privately
defended as a response to pressures from disaffected, experienced
teachers. Posts with titles such as Head of Pastoral Care, Head of
Counselling, Senior Careers Teacher, Senior Mistress Girls Welfare
and Community Tutor were offered to redeployed, low-
certificated staff, where loyalty and experience appeared to be more
important than academic credentials. Such teachers were often
from the same working-class background as the majority of the
students they were to work with. Ex grammar-school staff and
new, bright graduates were released from the drudgery of actively
making the institution work and were able to get on with the task
of teaching the brightest and oldest students in the smallest class
sizes. PSE enabled local authority officers to cool out the fears and
anxieties of senior teachers during secondary reorganization. It met
the bureaucratic demands for conflict resolution.

The demands of students

We now know that for many students, school represents a series of
interlocking exchange relationships. For example, teachers offer
knowledge, students exchange deference; teachers offer
certification or the prospect of a job, students offer effort. Such
exchanges, or trade-offs (so much knowledge for so much less bad
behaviour) take many different degrees and forms both within and
between schools. The 1970s, as we have seen, have been
characterized as a period when, in general, there was a significant
loss of public faith in the effectiveness of secondary schools. This
was true for students too. For significant numbers of students,
especially less-able students, existing exchange relationships
weakened or disappeared altogether. For example, unconvivial
learning arrangements were no longer traded for the prospect of a
good testimonial and reference. Increasing numbers of students
resented the traditional authority of the school, an authority
challenged by teachers too and recognized as difficult to enforce by
head teachers. Students demanded the freedom to exert their own
culture on the school, to have recognized the fact that they are

individuals with rights to a democratic and productive environment.[15]

PSE puts into a practice a demand for alternative reward systems (e.g. through records of achievement and personal profiling schemes); stresses the need for a shift in responsibility for actions away from teachers and on to the shoulders of students, recognizing and utilizing their demands to be more self-aware, more self-determined and more adult. Furthermore, PSE allows students to do more of the things in school that they want to do, e.g., talking amongst themselves, engaging in role play, gaming and simulation, watching television, and making unaccompanied visits out of school through community and work experience programmes. More important, PSE allows students to do less of the things they *don't* want to do in school – less study of written materials, hear less teacher-dominated talk, and less keeping quiet and sitting still for the majority of the time. For many students, PSE represents a new freedom to negotiate a new series of exchange relationships and, moreover, the possibility of negotiation with teachers from an explicit position of equal strength, or better.

The demands of parents

Parents generally do not welcome major changes in public sector schooling unless such changes are seen to be directed at improving the competitive position of their own children. Parents compare their own children to other people's children who they know and are happy if their own children achieve their expected place in the queue for rewards which schools offer. The school fails in parents' eyes if children do not match up to parental expectations of achievement judged against the achievement levels of other children who constitute the reference group. PSE offers the promise of a new deal for the parents of predicted low academic achievers. PSE meets parents demands (as well as student demands) for their children to be treated as individuals, to be distinguished from the group and mass of children, to be recognized as having particular attributes and abilities which need to be identified, nurtured and rewarded no more but no less than other children.

Moreover, PSE offers parents an explicit invitation to join the teachers and students to make a triangular partnership, a learning contract, for individual students. PSE, through its pastoral care and counselling work, can enable parents not only to know more about schools, teachers and their own children, but to become active participants. Behaviour and achievement contracts, whereby teachers and students agree on set targets for quality of work, amount of work and time for completion, are one of the hallmarks of PSE. Parents can influence the terms and conditions of such contracts in many PSE programmes. Such intervention roles allow parents to play a direct, purposeful, systematic part in improving their children's current and future welfare through helping to enable their children to reach those minimum achievement expectations, and better.

The demands of economists

Education systems are always cited by economists as a major cause of the failings of the UK econcomy.[16] Whenever there is a heightened feeling of comparative economic decline and crisis, major critiques of public sector schooling re-emerge in more intensive or new forms often led by economists, especially right-wing economists.[17] From the early 1970s, the UK economy was thought to be performing very much worse than its major competitors. One of the scapegoats became the size and distribution of public sector expenditure, especially on education and the welfare state. Educational expenditure is an obvious target for cutbacks in public expenditure because of its size – it makes up a significant proportion of public expenditure so any cutbacks in educational expenditure will have a significant impact on public expenditure as a whole. Similarly, increases in educational efficiency and reduction in 'wasted' expenditure will improve general public-sector efficiency and help minimize public-sector waste. Another scapegoat for economists became the personal qualities of young people queueing for a job or for work. They were seen to be lacking in the qualities that the owners of economic resources wanted and, moreover, placed too high a price on their own labour.

Schools had to become more cost-effective, creating more productive people at lower real costs. PSE helps meet both of these demands. First, PSE lowers the internal costs of schools.[18] For example, space on the timetable for PSE was often found by restricting the science and modern languages curriculum even further for less able students; young, cheap teachers were encouraged to make sure that PSE work was part of their workload, and the predicted better behaviour of less able students throughout the school, as a result of PSE, reduced the costs of all teachers spending significant proportions of their time dealing with disruptive students.

Teaching students how to behave becomes centralized through PSE which avoids the inefficiency of an often unsuccessful decentralized system, operating in all classrooms with varying degrees of success. Secondly, PSE raises the quality of young people in the eyes of potential employers. PSE provides a high-profile, centralized, controlled system of certificated character-building which teachers, and students and parents can more easily sell to prospective employers. Its stress on values education, on institutional identification, on rational decision-making processes and its behaviour and achievement contracts, offers students the possibility of offsetting low or zero academic certification with scholastic good conduct medals. PSE helps in the economic war against our economic competitors and illustrates the knock-on effect which economists can have when suggesting causes and reactions to major public concerns (i.e. the relative decline of the UK economy).

The demands of industrialists

This is a special case of the demands of the economists. Industrialists are offered a major public subsidy through the selection and certification process of schools. Schools offer industrialists a filter which enables them to choose which young people to consider employing and what position and level to employ them at. A major part of the costs of production for any company is labour costs. A major cost of labour is finding the right type in the right place at the right price. Schools offer this service and employers only pay to the extent that they pay state taxes (they, of course, employ their brightest recruits from the education system to advise them on how to avoid paying such taxes).

However, the 1970s witnessed industrial disillusionment with this service. Leading industrialists publicly harrassed the Prime Minister of the day with stories illustrating their lack of trust in the school system's ability to identify, promote and reward the qualities industrialists required. They wanted minimum levels of literacy and numeracy parcelled within the appropriate character wrapping. This disillusionment with schools led to industrialists increasingly introducing their own diagnostic tests and devices to offset the high costs of searching and failing to recruit the right sort of employees (they often, of course, decide to stop employing young people altogether, preferring married women to carry out traditionally young people's work). This meant that industrialists began to bear a higher proportion of the costs of hiring and promoting labour at a time when they were simultaneously claiming that profits and long-term investment programmes were being squeezed by high labour costs.

A quick retreat from such a new burden could be expected. The MSC came to the partial rescue by introducing YOPs and the one-year and now two-year YTS, all of which act as a publicly funded selection service for companies. Within formal schooling, PSE offers industrialists more productive workers, workers who know their own minds, have initiative, are used to working to achievement targets and, at the same time, know the meaning of loyalty and social responsibility. PSE also enables employers to be much more particular in their selection procedures than an array of CSEs, or lack of them, together with a character reference, or lack of it, could ever do. For example, teachers, who, through PSE, know the strengths and weaknesses of their students so much better than they ever did before, pass this information on to potential employers when they believe it's in their students' interests to do so. Students produce highly detailed accounts of themselves, through continually monitoring their own aspirations and achievements through various accounting systems, such as personal profiling. Work-experience courses, frequently developed within PSE, allow industrialists to assess students at minimal cost to the firm and, more important, allow them to cheaply assess the school as a whole. Some firms cut their labour search costs by avoiding school-leavers from some specific schools altogether.

The same is true for the careers officers, representing a public service which is part of the selection and certification subsidy and which, through often being invited into school within the auspices of a PSE programme, can work even more effectively for industrialists (and, let it not be forgotten, for students too who can be more effectively cooled out of particular job aspirations, thereby reducing their own job search costs). PSE meets industrialists demands to maximize profits and the long-term survival of the firm through providing a new way of cutting still further the costs of selecting and grading labour.[19]

The demands of politicians

Just as schools are seen to be able to revitalize a declining economy, they can also be viewed as preventive medicine for the ailments of a decaying moral order. The symptoms of the decay are vandalism, in the early 1970s, together with anti-nationalism in the late 1970s and early 1980s. Schools are seen as both the cause and the solution to social problems, problems which are seen to upset the stability or achievement of a desired political culture. Since 1979, this new political culture has meant a search for a revitalized international political voice in world affairs, achieved through creating a 'strong' economy, itself determined by encouraging people to engage in individual initiatives with energy and gusto, but only in initiatives which support the achievement of international prominence through economic strengths. People-building is a major explicit function of PSE. Within a government controlled and financed system, such as mass schooling in the UK, any people-building exercise will inevitably be conditioned in a major way by contemporary power holders, by governments and government-sponsored and protected institutions. PSE, with its emphasis on a self-examination of the role of the individual in society, becomes the main form of civic education, helping the establishment of the new civic culture, a culture which reflects a new conservative ideology. PSE, in the UK, meets the political demands for a conservative retrenchment both within schools and within the broader social structure.

The demands of the bishops

Religious education, as is well-known, has a special status in secondary education. There is a legal requirement that schools ensure that all students experience some form of religious education. The precise nature which this education should take has always been one of the more public controversies about the aims and methods of secondary schools. Debates about religious education correspond to the general social context of religion and morality, and, in particular, reflect the state of health of organized religion in the UK. Interestingly, there is always the possibility of strong arguments for an extension of religious education in order to either arrest the decline of organized religion or to reflect its growing strength.

Knowledge about religious life is made available in schools through religious instruction or religious knowledge courses, through assemblies and through guest speakers and special events. A shift to the broader idea of morality and moral education beginning in the mid 1960s and growing in strength throughout the 1970s, created new possibilities for student learning but also created associated problem areas. What sort of moral education is appropriate? What is or should be the relationship between moral education and moral development? Can, indeed, morality or virtue be taught (or can it only be caught from saintly teachers)?[20]

PSE offered a partial solution to the bishops' demands to maintain the strengths of the historic relationship between, since 1870, Church, state and mass school. PSE often encompasses moral education (if not religious instruction) and many of the teachers working on PSE courses have been trained as religious instructors. PSE can be interpreted as part of a reaction by governing élites, to the observed and projected problem of a decline in religious interests and activities (and a linked decline in the quality of family life). Head teachers have encouraged the growth of PSE, and encouraged the involvement of teachers trained for religious instruction work. Such teachers are seen as a necessary member of a PSE teaching team in order to offset, in head teachers' eyes, the dangerous moral relativism that the media reported was characteristic of youth cultures in the UK. PSE can and has become a major system for the preservation or revival of virtue. PSE highlights the idea and practice of moral standards.

Concluding comments

This discussion has argued that PSE has become such an important part of public-sector secondary schooling during the past twenty years that this growth demands explanation. It has further been argued that people concerned with community schooling are, in different ways, involved in PSE and should wish and be able to make sense of it. Some tentative suggestions have been advanced, anticipating, in general terms, the outcomes of a major, rigorous enquiry into this growth. An equally important associated question is whether we welcome this growth or not? How do we make judgements about it? Do we believe, for example, that the catch words of PSE – self-respect, personal autonomy, self-actuation, independency and interdependency – can be taught within government controlled institutions in such a way as to maximize real freedom for the maximum number of people? Do we believe that PSE offers a significant beneficial reform of schools? Such questions may not be conclusively answered by any type of major research programme. People will make their own judgements, based on their reading, on their experience and through their own political belief system. One of the great strengths of PSE is that it may be the major curriculum vehicle for ensuring that all students experience a political education. If, however, we dislike and disagree with the nature of the civic culture which is being produced and reflected through PSE in schools, the dominance of PSE as a political educator within school becomes its greatest failing.

This analysis of PSE reflects an ambivalence which, for me, also cuts across many developments associated with community schooling and with community education. The community school can be thought of as a very appealing prototype for the school of the future. Its concern for people's needs rather than institutional growth and survival, for power sharing and empowerment rather than authoritarianism and disenfranchisment and for the cost-effective distribution of public resources, identify principles which attract many of us in to the community school. However, the community school has not and need not lead to the identification and implementation of such principles. Such principles, are, in any case, distractions from real policies and practices and Ian Martin in this volume has already quoted Tawney on the British dislike of principles. We need to identify the principles, policies and practices by which the school is to be judged. For me, the key test for the community secondary school is an examination of the arrangements it makes (and fails to make) for social education. The youth service has already been cited as one educational sector which, at its best, far outstrips the school in the care and attention it has paid to social education. In many local authorities, community education simply means a management structure which brings (or attempts to bring) the youth service, adult education and, less frequently, community work together. In such cases, the possibility of a politically powerful and educationally effective social education for young people seems strong (and its neglect inexcusable).

The ten demands for PSE all produce pressure for change in the same direction – for more PSE. However, these demands need to be related to a detailed account of the forms in which PSE has arisen in the secondary school and public justifications for such different varieties. PSE can, at worse, become a vehicle for repression (keeping both students and teachers in line with a general authoritarian school ethos) or for liberation (allow learners to explore and identify existing and new forms of personal and social knowledge, skills and values through democratic teaching and learning styles).

We face the general welfare policy dilemma of unintended outcomes – liberation for some can result in repression for others. We may also have to accept second-best positions, where, for example, the outcome is liberating but the intention repressing (true of some YTS schemes where young people learn that they don't have to actively search for dead-end jobs, that to become one of the deserving poor is not necessarily a worthy objective). Such awareness of the double-edge of educational policies and movements is one of the prime lessons for the community educator. Moreover, it means that such awareness or sensitivity must be applied when considering whether to invest scarce public resources – for example, the time and budgets of community educators considering initiating or supporting specific forms of PSE. We know that one of the major everyday difficulties facing social workers, community workers and youth workers is how to choose which client or client group to work with or on behalf of. Such decisions that are made should be explicit and, if demanded, publicly as well as professionally defensible rather than unacknowledged and unaccountable.

A secondary school which decides to 'go community' should begin with social education. It should choose those forms of social education which meet the principles already identified (liberating, focusing on people's needs, democratic and cost-effective). It should also choose policies and practices of social education which are fair. This is not the place for a sustained analysis of what we might mean by fairness in the distribution of public resources. However, it seems to me that a politically literate[21] community educator could effectively defend a PSE programme of activities which follow a Rawlsian[22] principle of social justice. This would be based on the fairness of assessing the impact of social policies in terms of their degree of beneficial impact on the worse-off members of the community to be served. This would not mean a 'ghettoization' of PSE. It would mean that all learners in the secondary school would receive the genuine opportunity of engaging in PSE, a policy which just might raise the status of PSE (it suffers from an identification with poor and 'problem' students and teachers) and help identify and create the sort of secondary school many of us would prefer. The community secondary school should be in the front line of this movement, working from principles and taking policy decisions which reflect a political sensitivity to the prevailing cultural milieu. What is pragmatic must and can be good!

References

1 P. Willis. (1981). *Learning to Labour*. Gower Press.
2 S. Baron, *et al*. (eds). (1981). *Unpopular Education*. Hutchinson.
3 J. Dewey. (1944). *Democracy and Education*. Free Press.
4 For example:
   A. Green and R. Sharpe. (1975). *Education and Social Control*. Routledge & Kegan Paul.
   S. Ball. (1981). *Beachside Comprehensive*. Cambridge University Press.
   P. Woods. (1979). *The Divided School*. Routledge & Kegan Paul.
5 A. Skrimshire. (1981). 'Community schools and the education of the social individual', *Oxford Review of Education*, vol. 7, no. 1, 1981.
6 R. Pring. (1984). *Personal and Social Education in the Curriculum*. Hodder and Stoughton.
7 HMI (1979). *Aspects of Secondary Education in England*. HMSO.
8 Ibid., p. 216.
9 T. Husen. (1979). *The School in Question*. Oxford University Press.
10 I. Illich. (1969). *Deschooling Society*. Penguin.
11 I. Shor. (1986). *Culture Wars*. Routledge & Kegan Paul.
12 I.A. Snook, (ed.). (1972). *Concepts of Education*. Routledge & Kegan Paul.
13 G. Chanan and L. Gilchrist. (1974). *What School is For*. Methuen.
14 I. Lister. (1974). *Deschooling: A Reader*. Cambridge University Press.
15 S. Hall and T. Jefferson. (1976). (eds). *Resistance through Rituals*. Hutchinson.
16 M. Blaug. (1971). *An Introduction to the Economics of Education*. Allen Lane.
17 See the many critiques of the mass school published by the right-wing Social Affairs Unit.
18 C. E. Cummings. (1971). *Studies in Education Costs*. Scottish Academic Press.
19 P. Broadfoot. (ed.). (1984). *Selection, Certification and Control*. Falmer Press.
20 M. Warnock. (1979). *Schools of Thought*. Faber.
21 G. Allen. (1979). 'Researhing political education in schools and colleges', *International Journal of Political Education*, Autumn.
22 J. Rawls. (1972). *A Theory of Justice*. Oxford University Press.

CHAPTER 12

Paulo Freire's education approach: a struggle for meaning

PAULA ALLMAN

Many British community and adult educators have taken an interest in the work of Paulo Freire. But how much real understanding and educational commitment has it evoked? Allman argues that Freire's ideas have been scavenged in an eclectic and selective way which has devalued and distorted them. However, this futile attempt to incorporate 'radical' technique in the 'liberal' agenda has been both necessary and salutary. We are now in a position to reflect upon this experience and to re-engage in the 'struggle for meaning' in a way that is consistent with the substance of Freire's philosophy. This paper raises fundamental questions about the nature and purpose of community education as a radical manifesto. In addition, by focusing on the post-compulsory sector, it indirectly issues a significant challenge to the school-based community educator.

Frequently it's claimed that the ideas of the Brazilian adult and community educator, Paulo Freire, have had a considerable impact on educational thought and practice throughout the world. Notions such as student–centred, negotiation, the empowerment of learners and dialogue are common currency in British progressive education and these notions are often linked with Freire. However, the extent to which Freire's ideas have been applied as a total approach to educational work with adults is extremely limited in Britain. The piecemeal, fragmented, and distorted manner in which Freire's ideas have either been incorporated or rejected has to do with the different ways in which educators working within both radical and liberal traditions have made sense of his writings. This chapter is about that process of sense-making amongst British adult and commuity educators. I suspect that what has happened in Britain is not so very different from what has happened elsewhere.

First I will explain the sense which myself and learner colleagues have made of Freire's writings. That explanation will demarcate the critical relations which comprise Freire's educational approach and will provide the background against which the reader can assess my discussion of how and why others have made sense of Freire in quite different ways.

The first and most basic point to make about Freire is that his approach to a philosophy of education, though reflected in his discussion of literacy work, is not reducible to a mere application of the methods he describes. Literacy education is only *a* medium for his philosophy. When litcracy work expresses the whole of the philosophy it involves politicization and political action. Freire uses the Latin American term 'conscientization' to signify that politicization entails greater complexity and commitment than simply a state of awareness or 'consciousness raising'. Freire admits that his earliest publication (which wasn't published in Britain until 1976, i.e. four years after some of his more mature writings) might have been vague on this point.[1] However since then he has made it quite clear that 'consciousness raising', an awareness of a specific form of oppression, can actually serve a manipulative role in sustaining ideological domination. The specific and personal focus of 'consciousness raising' can prevent people from understanding the total structure of oppression and therefore the sources from which these interlinking forms of oppression arise.[2]

Another basic point which needs sorting out is the relative contributions of Christianity and Marxism to his thinking. This is important because many readers will see these two types of contribution as incompatible. Freire, however, does not, but then his concept of Christianity is not exactly a conventional one.[3] Freire says that as a young man he went to work with the urban and rural poor because of his Christianity, but that the people, their conditions of life and most crucially the way they thought about them, sent him to Marx.[4] The assumptions which underpin his approach and the approach itself, are Marxist but his language, his tone is imbued with the language of possibility which characterises the theologies of liberation emerging primarily from Latin America during the 1970s.[5] Rather than being imcompatible I would argue that a Maxist critical analysis is complemented by a language of possibility and vision whatever its derivation.

The first assumption on which Freire's philosophy rests, the foundation from which every other idea follows, is his assumption about what it means to be fully human. Here Freire shares with Marx the analysis that human beings have the ability to think about, or to reflect upon, what they think and how they act.[6] This reflective thinking should lead to people being the originators, the architects of their life activity and the social and economic contexts for these activities. Unfortunately most societies have not been constructed so as to maximize the interests of all human beings but instead to preserve the interests of a very few; therefore our human potential is an unrealized one. Limiting social and economic formations, the relations that arise from them produces a type of conditioning that creates an alienation from our human potential. However, this is an alienation from our possibility of becoming more fully human rather than alienation from a lost or suppressed human essence. For both Freire and Marx, human nature is neither innately good or evil; it does not pre-exist the relations within which it is produced.[7]

Freire and Marx also share the same concept of ideology as a mechanism which makes possible the alienation of people from their real interests. Freire describes a 'culture of silence' in which inner, critical, reflective voice is silenced and as a consequence there can be no external voice which denounces dehumanizing conditions. When people speak they offer explanations that come from and therefore justify the privilege, status and power of their oppressors.[8] Therefore they accept a false ideology, false in the sense that it masks the real relations of power and the material conditions which give rise to them. This dominant ideology doesn't falsify with bold lies but by means of explanations which are partial and abstract.[9] One result is a version of what is real and natural that justifies the status quo and another, perhaps more insidious result, is that the ideology of the oppressors becomes embedded and habituated in our behaviour and emotions producing consent even amongst those who are oppressed by it.[10]

Freire's strategy for dealing with ideological domination is also the same as Marx's. Awareness of the oppressor's ideology is not enough; it will remain until we act to transform the relations that produce it. The task is not to substitute one ideology for another but to develop a dialectic understanding of our reality as a critical tool for informing our action.[11] Freire's strategy for both education and revolution is linked directly to his concern for creating post-revolutionary conditions in which people could become more fully human. His concept of and arguments for cultural action preceding cultural revolution though not as comprehensively developed, bear a striking similarity to those of the Italian Marxist scholar, Antonio Gramsci.[12] Since Freire's concept of what it means to be fully human and his strategy for what is necessary to realize this potential derive from a Marxist analysis of human beings and their material conditions, it is difficult to understand how his ideas can be interpreted within anything other than a Marxist framework.

The second assumption integral to Freire's philosophy follows directly from his thinking about the meaning of being fully human. It locates education as a specific form of both pre- and post-revolutionary strategy. He says that education can either be used to domesticate or liberate; it is our choice.[13] Education for domestication or 'banking' education is characteristic of class societies and performs the ideological function of masking conflict, i.e. our real relations, by depositing certain categories of abstract knowledge in learners, knowledge which has been removed from real conditions and problems. Knowledge becomes just another commodity which can be accumulated and so education is conceived as a possession which can be used to gain access to power, privilege and status.

Education for liberation, which is what Freire as well as neo–Marxist analyses of education advocate, is something altogether different.[14] Its initial aim is a reawakening of the inner voice of reflection as people are challenged to focus on the oppressive aspects of their existence, to 'name' or speak their reasons or explanations for these conditions and then to critically and collectively investigate the reasons given. This, of course, is only the beginning. Participants also go on to develop more accurate and complex explanations and plans of action for social change. Education for liberation has no fixed time limits, but as life activity, itself, a continuous struggle that reaches for a realization of our human potential. Nor is it an education aimed at the individual as it is assumed that individuals cannot be liberated in isolation. Freire's concept of liberation involves the political transformation of social/economic structures and relations; therefore it has nothing to do with notions of liberation that involve the psychological detachment of the individual from other human beings, history and material reality.[15] Individuals are social beings, not autonomous selves, and they must think and act together if they are to create a better world.

The third assumption integral to Freire's philosophical approach is that learners and teachers must struggle together to overcome the oppressive relations of banking education.[16] Education, of course, is only one aspect of a total social revolution. Nevertheless, there are parallels between the oppressive relations in this sphere and those which pertain elsewhere, e.g. the social relations of production between radical leaders or activists and the people. With reference to the latter instance Freire says:

> One of the most difficult problems confronting a revolutionary party in the preparation of militant cadres consists in rising above the canyon between the revolutionary option formulated verbally ... and the practice which is not always revolutionary. The petit-bourgeois ideology that has permeated them in their class conditions interferes with what should be their revolutionary practice. ... In so behaving, all they do is reproduce the dichotomy – typical of a class society – between teaching and learning ... They start by giving prescriptions, 'depositing' revolutionary knowledge ... it is impossible this dichotomy between the militant intent, which is political, and their methods, techniques and processes through which the intent is translated into practice.[17]

Therefore practice must clearly communicate the revolutionary option. Freire assumes that if we choose to engage in creating a form of socialism based on the interests of all human beings, we must choose to overcome any contradiction between what we say we believe in and what we do. However, these oppressive relations have been rendered as the natural state of affairs and the acceptance of their 'naturalness' is well embedded in our ideas about the expectations of education. Therefore overcoming their oppressive nature involves engaging in a struggle to create transformed ways of thinking, acting and communicating. It would be manipulative if educators tried to create and then impose these transformations, themselves; therefore all those involved in the learning experience must struggle together to create transformed relations.

Freire's philosophical approach to education can be clarified by examining his analysis of the contradictions inherent in 'banking education' along with the forms of opposition he advocates for overcoming them. First, however, it is necessary to make three points. I am explaining his educational approach, i.e. not a series of methods or techniques but a philosophical totality which rests upon the assumptions discussed previously. Secondly, to overcome a contradiction does not mean that we eliminate it but rather that we remove the oppressive relations between two opposites so that one no longer suppresses or over-determines the nature of the development of the other. I hope to add further clarity to both of these points in the discussion which follows. The last point is that I will be discussing the contradictions within the context of adult and community education, i.e. non-compulsory education. If we were to include the compulsory sector we could not consider the contradictions without looking at the ways in which young people attempt to resist over-determination.[18] The form which resistance normally takes with adults is non-participation.

The oppressive nature of 'banking education' involves hierarchical power relations wherein one of two elements is placed in a position of domination over the other. This form of over-determination[19] exists within relations between:

1 Teachers and learners.
2 Abstract and concrete knowledge.
3 Mental and practical work.
4 Academic content and critical thinking.
5 Learners and learners.
6 Educational institutions or organizations and learners.

It is necessary to examine the oppressive nature of each of these relations as well as the transformation that would be essential if we are to overcome them.

In 'banking education' on any practice which involves a domesticating educational relation the teacher or leader possesses knowledge which they place as a completed object before the learner. To possess this object, as given, the learner must enter into relations based on dependency and deference. To transform this relation is not to turn it upside down but to recognize that teachers and learners thinking together about, co-investigating, the 'knowledge object' leads to a deeper and more complex understanding.

> ... in education for liberation there is no complete knowledge possessed by the educator, but a knowable object which mediates educator and educatee as subjects in the knowing process. ... Here there is no split between knowing and doing, there is no room for the separate existence of a world of those who know, and a world of those who work.[20]

Therefore this transformation is contingent upon a transformation in the epistemological stance of both teachers and learners, i.e. their theories of knowledge, and as a consequence it depends upon the transformation of relations (2), (3), and (4), above. In 'banking education' abstract knowledge and mental work are elevated to a status that relegates concrete knowledge and experience as well as practical work to an inferior position. And since, in 'banking education', thinking is seen as a derivative of academic content, i.e. it cannot exist adequately prior to the ingestion of content; critical thinking is also relegated to a dependent and therefore secondary position.

The oppressive relations of 'banking education' are not confined to organized education and institutional settings. They permeate every conceivable relation in which people come together to exchange information and ideas. Charismatic, popular teachers or community workers may appear to listen to and request the thinking of others; but all too often, whether they realize it or not, their real role is to soften the direct line of control, i.e. to mediate between the oppressors and the oppressed.[21] They may succeed in enabling people to voice their concerns and to be more participative in their communities, but these activities continue to be framed or defined by those who already hold power rather than constituting real challenges to and transformations of that frame. This sort of practice – even within non-formal community development work – is bolstered by our societal concepts of critical thinking.

In Freire's educational approach critical thinking is altogether different. It is different because it depends upon the reunion of abstract knowledge with concrete knowledge and experience, and as a consequence the inseparable unity of mental and practical work or thinking and doing. Academic content/theory or any other legitimate body of knowledge is not the source or even a delimiting framework for thought but a resource to be used and transformed by learners as they critically reflect on issues and problems which arise for their material conditions. This transformation of the meaning and relational position of critical thinking, means that the validity of abstract knowledge cannot be assumed until it is grounded in reality. Should it pass that test, abstract or theoretical knowledge can never again be elevated and isolated but must remain forever on the testing ground of the historical movement and development of our real or material conditions.

Critical thinking within Freire's approach is, therefore, a permanent critical approach to reality and entails the same method of logic or theorizing developed by Marx in his later works, that is dialectic thinking.[22] This is a logic or conceptual tool which enables a comprehension of things, people, and societies in the process of movement and change.[23] Critical thinking within 'banking education' involves thinking about abstract and therefore static concepts which have been extracted from history as well as the material present and hence their movement.

In 'banking education' the relation between learners is one of competition in which a few gain a superior status at the expense of all the others. This relation must be transformed through people learning in cooperation and interdependence so that all gain together. Freire puts it so well: 'I cannot be unless you are; I cannot be without you.'[24] This is not a rejection of the individual but a recognition that individualism, the concept of an independent, autonomous self, is an ideological one, an abstraction which may exist with the aid of psychological delusion but which has no foundation in the reality of the human condition. The transformation of the relations between learners also demands a transformation in communication patterns, in fact the creation of an oppositional form of communication. This is what Freire refers to as dialogue.

If there is any aspect of the Freirean approach that can be equated with methodology it must be dialogue. However, as I hope to make clear in what follows, dialogue is a transformed type of communication and is therefore not a technique which can be used in isolation from an acceptance of and commitment to the assumptions and resulting approach that comprise the totality of Freire's philosophy. He says it's the seal or expression of all the transformed relations we've discussed so far.[25] Therefore, dialogue requires great expenditures of effort and thought by all those who attempt to engage in it. Dialogue should be considered as a form of action aimed at the transformation of our normal communication patterns combined with continuing reflective evaluation of that action.

A group cannot enter into dialogue without considering how it challenges forms of communication such as discussion. Even with careful consideration, it's not likely that participants will commit themselves to the process of dialogue unless they share a desire to overcome the contradictions discussed earlier, and unless they share a desire to learn to relate to one another in ways which will produce caring, trust and a willingness to question the knowledge they already possess, i.e. to be critical and curious.[26] Since none of us come from previous educational relationships which will have developed these dispositions, we cannot expect them to pre-exist or to function as prerequisites for dialogue. But it is important that they are the prerequisite aims of all those who attempt to dialogue.

I can best explain what dialogue is by beginning with a description of what it is not, namely, discussion. Discussion is a form of group communication in which participants engage in a sharing of monologues. These monologues are composed of sets of pre-existing ideas, knowledge, or questions arising, which participants offer to the group. Sometimes one monologue engages in argument with another and the participants are required to further articulate what they already know. It is from this form of group communication that the principles of group dynamics have arisen as well as a host of techniques designed to minimize the conflict which arises from the interaction of competing ideas and persons. Discussion leaders are necesary to ensure a particular type of power distribution amongst the group, namely, the power of time allocation, so that participants have equal access to a time slot in which they can offer their monologues. Discussion focuses primarily on allowing each person to express or communicate and thus clarify in their own minds *what* they think.

By contrast, dialogue involves an exploration of *why* we think what we do and of how this thinking has arisen historically. It centres on a theme, object or issue of significance in the life experience of the participants. The object, theme or issue mediates the communication within the dialogue, as participants first explore the ways in which they think about or make sense of it and then look critically at that sense making.

Within dialogue critical thinking and its vocal expression, problematizing, can be thought of as a type of evaluation which examines whether current thinking is abstract and partial rather than dialectical, and whether it serves the interests of the oppressed or the oppressors. The oppressors, of course, benefit if our commonsense explanations promote deference, silence and the continuation of oppression. Within dialogue participants undertake a critical analysis of their reality and formulate explanations capable of challenging the conventional ones. They also consider the action that must be taken in order to transform oppressive conditions. This later aspect will lead to action outside the dialogue when the participants have analysed the situation and think there is potential for at least some degree of success. Participants return to the forum and form of dialogue to reflect on their action; to assess and modify it and to resume their continuing struggle to learn and to shape the conditions of their existence.[27]

Clearly dialogue does not fit neatly into time slots of one to two hours that we normally allocate to group meetings. However, it can be worked for within these time periods if participants have agreed to undertake the struggle, i.e. expend the effort, and if they understand that dialogue cannot be evaluated by the same criteria that would pertain in evaluating discussion or any other traditional form of communication. For example, one entire meeting might be devoted by all participants to helping one of them explore the ways in which she or he thinks about the issue under consideration. Of course, the others will speak but their speaking would be primarily focused on the thinking of another person rather than on the expressing of their own pre-formulated knowledge. They would pose questions to help clarify that they have understood the meaning of the person in focus, and they would also help the person to question or problematize his or her thinking. All participants continue to explore their own interpretations but they do so with a type of curious reflectivity that arises from trying to understand how the person in focus makes sense of the issue. Therefore dialogue is intended to be a way of relating, one to another, the effect of which is radical because it produces the development of trust, care, collaboration and commitment amongst the participants rather than competition and individualism. But equally because it develops commitment to or an affirmation of the belief that this form of mutual co-investigation gives rise to more complex and comprehensive understandings, i.e. the creation of the types of knowledge which people need to order to take charge of their lives and engage in the transformation of their society.

Nor does dialogue fit neatly into conventional notions that education is politically neutral. It must be clear to those who initiate this form of educational communication, that they are initiating a form of education which empowers people to want to transform not just their own lives but the oppressive social and economic structures in which they exist. As a consequence participants should be fully appraised that the political nature of this form of education is quite different from the political nature of domesticating education. This point should be made clear to participants when we are working in contexts which are formally recognized as education and also when working in non-formal contexts such as political parties, tenants groups or trade unions. It seems quite obvious to me that Freire's educational approach is 'education for socialism', a thoroughly democratic form of socialism created by and continuously monitored by the vigilant critique of the people it serves rather than a form of socialism imposed by a political or intellectual élite.

Earlier I mentioned briefly that the critical thinking which develops in Freire's approach i.e. within dialogue, is not only different from but constitutes a challenge to traditional concepts of critical thought. In his writings Freire does not examine or describe this form of thinking; he simply refers to it and uses it. To reiterate, it is my conclusion that what Freire is referring to is the form of thought or conceptual tool which Marx fully developed in writing *Capital*. Marx was aware that what he referred to as dialectic materialism was a distinct form of logic,[28] but he never found time to write about his method. I would argue that the dialectic method of thinking will be necessary for the establishment and maintenance of the type of socialism described above. It is unfortunate, in terms of our present stage of human progress, that new and more adequate methods of thinking develop and are used long before those who utilize them develop a level of awareness that allows a description of the method.[29]

My own understanding of the method of dialectic thinking has developed considerably since I first began to write about it, and I have offered a detailed analysis of its form elsewhere.[30] However since it is the type of critical thought which should develop within dialogue, it's important that those who wish to engage in and reflect upon dialogue have some notion of what they are aiming to develop. I will try to recap on the essential features most of which I have already indicated or interwoven in the preceding discussion.

Dialectic thinking enables us to think about things, ourselves and our societies in movement and development because it involves regrounding our ideas in concrete, material conditions. We know that these conditions are constantly moving, changing, developing rather than static. It is contradiction which activates this movement and it is the interaction between contradictions which regulates the changing nature of things, people and societies. For example if we take any or all of the following opposites or contradictions: men and women, master and slave, capital and labour, or capitalism and socialism, it is the interaction between them that regulates their development. Perhaps it becomes even clearer if we consider that historically and currently the former in each of these relations stands in a position of power or domination over the latter. When this is the case the development of the more powerful thwarts or hinders and therefore over-determines the development of the latter. Formal logic or rational thought, our normal method of critical thinking, places the object of our thought in isolation from its movement. For example, we tend to think about men or women, not their interaction, and therefore we conceive of them as separate and fixed categories. This is what creates abstract thought and is also what leads to the mystification or reification of ideas. As a consequence, much of what we think and communicate is stale and partial knowledge by virtue of the fact that it is knowledge which is removed from the historical movement of material conditions and relations. Abstraction works by enabling us to eliminate contradiction, but since contradiction is the dynamic regulator of reality, to eliminate it is to simplify and falsify that which is complex. As a consequence our comprehension is impeded. In dialogue when we subject what we know and even how we feel to critical thinking, when we problematize these things, we do so by reuniting our thinking with the real conditions about which we are thinking. Therefore, dialogue provides a framework which supports the development and use of dialectic thinking.[31]

Dialectical thinking also necessitates a transformed way of existing. This is not easy as our present existence is one in which we want to know, i.e. to possess deposits of knowledge, rather then to engage in a continuous reworking and sophistication of our understandings. Since dialogue is intended to enable the type of continuous thinking and action I've tried to describe, it is certainly not intended as a 'soft option' but is imbued with the pain and rigour as well as the excitement we would expect from collective struggle. It does not, as so many colleagues have assumed, neglect the content of either objective or subjective knowledge but engages participants in rigorously scrutinizing both of these.[32]

The final over-determined relation in 'banking education' is the relation between the educational institution or organization and the learners. When the teacher/learner and learner/teachers have begun the mutual struggle to overcome the opposition nature of the other contradictions, in the course of those struggles, it will emerge that everything they, together, are becoming stands as a challenge to and is oppressed by the institutional or organizational framework and procedures in which they are learning. Some readers may think that they have already overcome this relation because their work takes place outside an institutional framework – as did much of Freire's literacy work in Brazil. However, if we consider the neo–Marxist argument that the source of oppressive relations within an educational institution derives from its role as an ideological state apparatus,[33] then so long as we function within an oppressive state, the problem remains. Regardless of where we engage in learning, the real relationship of oppression is that which exists between learners and the framework of ideas that legitimates the interests of the dominant groups who control the state, i.e. their ideologies. What varies between institutional and extra-institutional contexts is both the concrete conditions or forms which the oppression takes and the timing of confrontation.[34] Within a formal or institutional framework, the first point of confrontation will be with the rules, procedures and traditions of the institution and the concepts of learning and education which they uphold. Whereas from its inception, work within a non-formal framework faces the ultimate struggle with the interest of 'capital'; therefore it can be argued that it is necessary for such work to be closely allied to political organizations. Whether this means that non-formal education is more important because of its more direct influence, or potential for such influence, on social transformation, I do not know. However, I would argue that the transformation to a socialism that derives from a popular mass movement and support must deal with people transforming themselves, their communities, organizations and institutions. Only transformations at all these levels will carry the possibility of a society which can serve and develop the interests of all human beings.

Many of my colleagues argue that it is a waste of time and energy to struggle for real institutional change. And this raises the question of whether radical work can take place within state institutions on state funded educational projects. This question has dominated a great deal of the debate amongst radical educators and has frequently been used to rationalize either piecemeal attempts to ameliorate conditions or to rationalize practice which continues the straightforward domestication of learners.

Much of this debate misses the point. Not many people would claim that the existence of a few transformed, i.e. socialist educational institutions, even if allowed to exist, would be capable of challenging the social-economic structure. This is not the purpose of transforming institutions prior to social revolution. The purpose is one of the preparation of people, through new relationships and new ways of thinking, and of our institutions so that when social revolution occurs it holds much more far-reaching possibilities for humankind than simply an alteration in the source of domination.[35] This sort of pre-figurative work is also intended to create a broad-based will and understanding of the need for socialism.[36] However having said that, the question still remains as to whether, or for how long and to what extent, radical education work would be allowed in state institutions. I don't think this question is answerable at this time. I will be arguing in the pages which follow that we have only just arrived at a state of readiness, through the accumulation and sophistication of both experience and understanding, to undertake such work with any promise of success.

In discussing this final oppressive contradiction, I have not discussed in any detail the exact nature of the necessary transformations. This is because the exact expression of oppression in rules, procedures and traditions will vary from one institution or organization to another. However, there are general points which can be made. Learners or participants would need to undertake 'institutional or organizational critique' or an anlaysis of the ways in which dominant and oppressive ideologies, are embedded in the rules, procedures and traditions of the institution or organization. They would need to pay particular attention to the types of relations which result as well as to consider the nature of the type of transformed relationships they are attempting to create. Any change in structure or practice would always have to be evaluated in terms of the latter consideration, i.e. ways of relating which are devised around allowing people to become more fully human rather than around ways of maintaining our consent to and collusion with oppressive ideologies.[37]

So far I have tried to explain the meaning which I, and others with whom I've been learning, have made with reference to Freire's philosophy and approach. This meaning did not always jump directly off the pages of Freire's writing but has been made through careful study, application and hours of reflection. Freire's works have touched the minds and hearts of many adult and community educators, and I suspect that others have expended an effort equal to or greater than our own in 'making meaning'. However, as is so often the case, those who are actually engaged in radical education work have little time and feel little security in writing about it. Still others have used some of Freire's ideas or alternatively have rejected them. As I suggested earlier, partial or eclectic usage reduces these ideas to techniques and allows for their incorporation within liberal progressive approaches.

In the remaining pages, I want to explore the conditions which have led to either a flawed application of Freire's approach or the outright rejection of it by educators working within and promoting the radical tradition of adult and community education in Britain. This will also entail some exploration of how Freire's ideas have been received by those working within the liberal tradition because, as I will try to show, radical educational thought and practice have often been delimited within a frame which has been predetermined by the liberal tradition.

One would expect liberal and radical education to be two quite different, even opposed, forms of education. However, though the end objectives might differ enormously both in our present circumstances as well as historically, the trend, at least in the twentieth century has been a merging of the two traditions towards one of two centres of focus, namely, content or process. Here I am talking about broad or general tendencies towards polarizing content and process. Increasingly and promisingly there is, within the radical tradition, a recognition of the problem of such polarization; however, I'll come to that later. The consequence of polarization is that those who focus on process or content within either of the traditions may share more in common with the opposing tradition than they do with those working for the same objectives. To assess the validity of choosing to focus on content rather than process or vice versa we must consider that choice in terms of the end objectives.

Very generally, the end objective of liberal adult education is the expansion of the mind through the exposure to and the learning of our great cultural storehouse of knowledge. Within the liberal tradition, it is assumed that 'cultured' or educated men and women will be more effective citizens and better developed individuals.[8] Since the qualities of both the individual and the citizen, their intellect and sensitivities, are seen to derive from academic content,[39] be it great literature, the sciences or history, it seems quite reasonable to argue that content must be given the greater emphasis. A process focus could be seen to be indicative of trivialization, i.e. less serious study and students.

On the other hand, the end objective of radical adult education can be no less than preparing people to engage in the radical transformation of the social and economic structures and relations of society, i.e. the radical transformation of capitalism to socialism. Whether radical adult educators see their role as solely the preparation of people to engage in that transformation or to also participate with people in political action is not central to my point. What is central, however, is how radical educators envisage the transformation taking place. Historically within this tradition, there has been the recognition that a radical, oppositional knowledge base was necessary e.g. Marxist economics.[40] This was valid so long as we thought socialism was mainly about structures; however, once we gave equal attention to relations, e.g. the social relations of production, and reasserted our commitment to a popular socialism, a broad-based democratically created and sustained form of socialism, process became problematic.[41] Could socialist men and women, a major transformation of not only thought but sensitivities, ways of relating and communicating, result from the same forms or processes of education that we had adopted from the opposing tradition, a tradition designed to preserve capitalist culture and traditions?

When this question first arose, the tendency was to utilize new methodologies designed to make education more humanitarian and democratic. However for the most part these methods also had arisen within liberal practice; and the purpose of humanizing and democratizing education in the liberal tradition has much more to do with making education palatable than revolutionary. Furthermore, the concepts of democracy and humanity are also limited by being framed within the liberal discourse of capitalist ideology. This is a complex point but very simply I mean the limited concept of parliamentary democracy wherein first we're deluded into thinking we live in a 'free' society because we choose others to make decisions about how our society is to be run and organized and second we're deluded into thinking that those decisions are the most essential factors in shaping or determining the societal conditions in which we live. These are delusions because they make us think we're in control and prevent us from asking how much real control we have over major issues, such as, poverty, unemployment or nuclear weapons and energy. Humanity defined in terms of individual choice, rights and autonomy is an equally limited way of thinking about human beings because we don't exist, can't exist and were not created to exist as a species of autonomous beings but as beings in social relation and a social and historical context – beings interdependent with one another as well as other species and the total world environment.

It is impossible to consider any educational approach as radical unless it attaches equal significance to content and process. But just as the content must be radical so too must the process. However, during the first period in which process was recognized as important, our ideas remained trapped within the pre-given parameters, the assumptions and methods, of the liberal tradition and especially the notion of progressive pedagogy which had developed within that tradition.

When Freire's writings first appeared in Britain, those in both traditions whose focus was content dismissed the importance of his thinking but for slightly different reasons. The liberal educator could see no value in popular knowledge; whereas though radical educators valued such knowledge, they could see no room for the insertion of content which could provide a challenge to the ever pervasive 'cultural capital' of liberal education. They couldn't see how to include such content within Freire's approach because they failed to see that this approach changes the relationship between content and the learner. Trapped within the ideological assumptions of liberal methodology, wherein content must be transmitted from teacher to learner rather than used and scrutinized by both, radical educators assumed Freire had neglected content.

As mentioned previously, in the early to mid 1970s, the 'process radical' was equally trapped within the frame of liberal, progressive methodology. Like their counterparts in the opposing tradition, they succumbed to scavenging methods or techniques and ideas from Freire and other educational writers. But this response can only be fairly assessed by placing it within the context of what was a major problem for adult and community educators during the 1970s, namely non-participation. Some adults who hadn't participated in either adult education or community development became involved when educators began to align education to their problems and encouraged people to discuss and/or take action relevant to these problems.

Terms such as thematic investigation, coding, decoding and dialogue became popular; sometimes they were used to signify real changes in method while in other cases they were just a new bit of jargon applied to traditional ways of working. That early reading of Freire frequently resulted in the assumption that his ideas gave a name to methods which the professional had been practising for years. A careful critique of practice in light of his ideas was a much less frequent phenomenon. In other cases professionals settled on some vague concept, such as, negotiation, as the essence or sum total of Freire's approach. 'Process radicals' shared with 'content radicals' the failure to see in what way radical content was to play a role within the process. A good deal of attention may have been given to the radical content of people's life experiences; however what seemed an imposition and therefore a problem was the inclusion of radical academic or intellectual theory. The consequence of all of this was that the slight increases in participation had little real effect on challenging the structure of oppression.

But the tendencies described were all part of an extremely important learning process which many of us had to experience. In particular, the experience of those working on the DCPs the other forms of community development and community action[42] taught difficult lessons and created important insights. Alongside this learning through experience, socialist/Marxist thinking amongst many educators was reaching a new level of maturity. Undoubtedly the most important influence on this maturation in thinking was the translation of the works of the Italian scholar, Antonio Gramsci.[43]

One of Gramsci's major contributions to neo-marxist political and educational thought was his development of Marx's ideas about ideology. From the 1920s on, the problem which confronted many radical intellectuals was why the inherent contradictions of capitalism had not led inevitably to working-class consciousness and revolution in the West. In part confusion over this question was due to the failure to recognize that in his mature writings Marx was offering a method of analysis not a dogmatic set of inevitable predictions. The confusion was also fostered because we needed a more comprehensive theory of ideology. Gramsci's writings reasserted the notion of ideology and explained how ideologies which reflect the interests of dominant classes and groups become hegemonic, i.e. consented to even by those who are oppressed by them. However, Gramsci stressed that hegemony could only be established and maintained through constant ideological struggle.[44] Therefore capitalist hegemony is vulnerable and by pointing this out Gramsci was encouraging us to engage in that struggle by challenging their ideology. He also identified the need for a great deal of pre-revolutionary work which was necessary to prepare all of us for a revolutionary future.

Freire's educational approach can be used to break through and reveal ideology and to create oppositional ways of thinking, knowing, feeling and acting. He distinguishes, as does Gramsci, between cultural action which is a preparation and oppositional, and cultural revolution which is a permanent process of creation that takes place within a post-revolutionary supportive framework.[45] However, Freire does not analyse the content of the ideology in his own or other societies. His writings assume a Marxist analysis of ideology, but this is not enough. In our own context of a society with a highly sophisticated form of ideology, one which overlaps and interlocks the ideologies of race, patriarchy and one-nation with the ideology of the dominant class, Gramsci's ideas are indispensable.

To understand what's happening within Freire's approach and to use it to its full radical effect we must come to a comprehensive understanding of ideology. Furthermore it is only when all those participating in the approach begin to understand how ideology works that the full extent and depth of the struggle necessary for education for liberation can be realized. Even though such an understanding is demanding and complex, certain fundamental features can be understood by simply investigating the commonsense explanations of a single theme or issue. For example any such critique of ideology should reveal that it works, i.e. achieves hegemony, not by directly falsifying but by playing on some 'truths' of experience whilst masking or leaving out others and so these partial or isolated 'truths' become our explanation of what is natural.[46]

One clear example of this is the way in which patriarchy confirms the subordinate position of women by focusing on a particular biological difference, i.e. child-bearing capacity, as a rationale for traditional child-rearing practices in our society. Therefore we tend to link and rationalize a social and socially constructed practice with a biological explanation, but we can only accept this argument if we leave out or forget that child-rearing is a socially conditioned practice and varies significantly from society to society. Another example is how currently that dominant capitalist ideology has convinced most people that because of technological advances there will never again be full employment. This plays upon the 'truths' we've all read about whereby a microchip can replace a whole shop floor of workers and the three plus million unemployed that seem to be a technological inevitability. What is left out, however, is this prediction only holds so long as our concept of production exists to create profit rather than to fulfil human needs.

I mentioned earlier that Gramsci was a most important influence on the maturation of Marxist/socialist thought. However there have also been many other influences, some of which have derived from Gramsci, others of which developed independently. Most importantly when taken together they have culminated in a new level of maturity in our thinking about socialism. Just as I could only touch on Gramsci, I cannot begin to go into the substance of these contributions here. However I have referenced this paper extensively in order to offer the reader a guide to further reading. It is only very recently, perhaps just the past three to five years, that these contributions have begun to be more widely disseminated to practitioners.

Wide dissemination of ideas is useless, however, until people are ready to receive the ideas and it is only when ideas meet head on with and so inform experience that we do receive them. Therefore I would stress that this intellectual activity is important because it coincides, at this time, with what radical educators have learned from experience over the past fifteen years. Nor am I speaking only of our experience in adult and community education. Perhaps the most profound experience for many in the 1970s was the reawakening from the spell created by post-war prosperity and the delusion created by the spell that the 'capitalist beast' could be tamed. With the re-emergence of 'economic crisis' in the 1970s, the contradictions of 'capital' could once again be seen clearly. Unfortunately had we looked more carefully during those years of relative prosperity at shop-floor politics, the plight of black people and women and of our brothers and sisters in the exploited nations, the contradictions of capitalism would never have disappeared from our view. As a consequence of our enthusiasm for reform, we all lost valuable time, time in which multi-nationals amassed increasing economic, political and ideological powers as well as power over the selection, ownership and distribution of information and time during which the nuclear arsenals of the world grew as did the degree of exploitation of our natural environment. These consequences are real but need not be insurmountable barriers. To surmount them we will need both really radical education and really radical mass politics, each informing and enriching the other. And the time for a really radical approach to education seems to have only just arrived.

Freire's ideas have been with us since the early 1970s. I have argued that if we rejected them or misused them in the past, it was because we were not ready for them. Freire himself now refers to *Pedagogy of the Oppressed* as a 'sweet little book';[47] he too has matured in terms of his understanding of the structure and ideology of oppression.[48] However, the core, the essentials, of his educational philosophy and approach are in that book. When I say we were not ready for Freire, I mean we could not begin to use his approach in a fully radical way without the experience and theoretical contributions that have accrued over the past fifteen years. Making sense of Freire simply could not begin to happen until we became engaged in several other kinds of sense making.

On the other hand, to say we are now ready to use Freire's approach to its full radical intent, is not to imply a simple or straightforward task. A great deal of hard work, serious and continuous study lies ahead for all of us. But then how could we have ever thought that the creation of truly human, just societies, a world community serving the interests of not only all human beings but of all other species and the total environment – a world in total opposition to the one we know – would be the inevitable gift of history. Only human agency, guided by a complex and comprehensive understanding of reality and safeguarded by permanent critical thinking can promise such a utopian world. And for those who are sceptical of utopias may I conclude with Agnes Heller who shows us what utopias really are.

> The utopian is not the impossible; it is the 'counterfactual', conceived as a realizable alternative to present realities. ... Utopia is one of the constituents of an alternative 'imaginary institution' which should be constrasted to the dominant 'imaginary institution' of the present.[49]

Notes

1 Freire, P. (1985). 'An invitation to conscientization and deschooling', in *The Politics of Education*, Macedo, D. (trans.) London, Macmillan, pp. 167–73. This article was first published by the World Council of Churches in 1975. In it Freire is referring to his stance in *Educaçáo como Práctica de Liberadade* published in 1967 and translated into English under the title *Education for Critical Consciousness*. London, Steed and Ward (1974), and later republished as *Education: the Practice of Freedom* London; Writers and Readers Publishing Cooperative, (1976).

2 Freire, P. (1973). 'Conscientization of liberation', Geneva. Institute of Cultural Action, IDAC Document no. 1 on *The Politics of Education*. Ch. 12, pp. 159–161.

3 Freire, P. (1974). 'Naive and Shrewd Christians', an audio-tape from the series *Thinking with Paulo Freire*, Sydney. Australian Council of Churches.

4 Ibid., 'Christian Faith and Marxism', part 1 audio-tape same series.

5 Giroux, H. (1985). 'Introduction' in Freire, P. *The Politics of Education*, p. xvii.

6   Freire, P. (1972). *Pedagogy of the Oppressed.* Harmondsworth. Penguin, Chapter 1, especially p. 21.
     Marx, K. (1976). *The German Ideology.* London. Lawrence and Wishart, 1941 and *Capital*, vol. 1, Chapters 6 and 7, Fowkes, B. (trans.) Harmondsworth, Penguin.
7   Ibid., Freire, p. 21 and Marx, *Capital*, p. 86.
8   Freire, P. (1985). *The Politics of Education.* London, Macmillan.
9   Marx, K. *Capital*, vol. 1. Marx's mature concept of ideology figures in many parts of *Capital*. As a guide see Mepham, J. 'The theory of ideology in *Capital*', in *Cultural Studies 6* Birmingham. Centre for Contemporary Cultural Studies, (Autumn, 1974), pp. 83–123.
10 Gramsci, A. (1971). *Selections from the Prison Notebooks of Antonio Gramsci.* Hoare, Q. and Smith, G. N., (eds. and trans.), London. Lawrence and Wishart, pp. 241, 326, 349 and 367.
11 Freire, P. (1985). *The Politics of Education.* pp. 154–5.
12 Gramsci, *SPN* pp. 238, 263, 268, 323 and 351–7 and compare with Freire, P. 'Cultural action and conscientization', *Harvard Educational Review*, vol. 40, no. 3, August (1970) pp. 452–477. Also in *The Politics of Education*, Ch. 7.
13 Freire, P. (1972). *Pedagogy of the Oppressed.* Harmondsworth. Penguin, Ch. 2.
14 Ibid.
15 Jacoby, R. (1977). *Social Amnesia.* London. Harvester.
16 Freire, P. (1972). *Pedagogy of the Oppressed.* Harmondsworth. Penguin, Ch. 3.
17 Freire, P. (1985). *The Politics of Education.* London. Macmillan, p. 163.
18 Willis, P. *Learning to Labour.* Farnsborough, Saxon House (1977) and McRobbie, A. 'Working-class girls and the culture of femininity', in Women's Studies Group, CCCS, *Women Take Issue,* London. Hutchinson (1978): two sources which examine resistance in the compulsory sector.
19 Freire, P. (1985). *The Politics of Education,* p. 54 and *Authority and Authoritarianism* an audio-tape in series 'Thinking with Paulo Freire'.
20 Freire, P. (1979). 'Education: domestication or liberation?', in Lister, I. (ed.). *Deschooling.* Cambridge. Cambridge University Press, pp. 20–21.
21 Freire, P. (1985). *The Politics of Education.* London. Macmillan, p. 79.
22 Ibid p. 85.
23 Engles, F. (1959). *Anti-Dühring.* Moscow. Foreign Languages Publishing House, p. 169.
24 Freire, P. *Authority and Authoritarianism.* An audio-tape same series.
25 Freire, P. (1974). 'Education: domestication or liberation?', in Lister, I. (ed.). *Deschooling*, p. 21.
26 Freire, P. *Authority and Authoritarianism.* Audio-tape.
27 Freire, P. (1972). *Pedagogy of the Oppressed.* pp. 53–9 and *The Politics of Education*, (1985) Ch. 7.

28 Coward, R. and Ellis, J. (1977). *Language and Materialism*. London. Routledge & Kegan Paul (1977) p. 83.
29 Althusser, L. (1969). *For Marx*. Brewster, B. (trans), Harmondsworth. Penguin. p. 174.
30 Allman, P. (1983). 'Adult thinking potential', in Tight, M. (ed.). *Adult Learning and Education,* vol. 1, London. Croom Helm in association with the Open University and 'Dialectic operations: our logical potential', Aspects no. 26, Sprint (1984).
31 For a more detailed discussion see Allman, P. 'Gramsci, Freire and Illich: their contributions to education for socialism', in Lovett, T. (ed.). *Radical Initiatives in Adult Education*. London. Croom Helm, in press.
32 For the best treatments of the idea see Giroux note 5 and Jacoby note 15.
33 Althusser, L.
    There are problems with Althusser's original formulation of this concept; I use it here to indicate that whether ideology is expressed directly by the state or through the apparatus of civil society, it expresses the formation of the essential social relation which are constituted in the sphere of production.
34 Earlier I referred to resistance and cited studies by Willis and McRobbie. Here I've used the term confrontation drawing on Perry Anderson's argument that human agency must be guided by critical consciousness: see Anderson, P. (1980). *Arguments Within British Marxism*. London. Verso, p. 23.
35 Gramsci, A. *SPN* pp. 12, 238, 263, 323, 351–7.
36 Education Group, CCCX. (1981). *Unpopular Education: Schooling and Social Democracy in England since 1944*. London. Hutchinson in association with the Centre for Contemporary Cultural Studies, University of Birmingham.
37 The dominant capitalist ideology viz. liberal democracy is cross-cut and supported by other oppressive ideologies e.g. Patriarchy, Race, One Nation, etc. For an excellent explanation see Hall, S. Unit 21, D102 The Open University Social Science foundation course.
38 Wiltshire, H. (1976). 'The great tradition in university adult education', in Rogers,A. *The Spirit and the Form*. Nottingham. Dept. of Adult Education, pp. 31–8.
39 Ibid.
40 Brown, G. (1980). 'Independent and incorporation: the Labour College Movement and the Workers' Eductional Association before the Second World War', Ch. 5 in Thompson, J. (ed.). *Adult Education for a Change*. London. Hutchinson.
41 For insights into this point see Hall, S. as in note 37 and Anderson, P. 'The antinomies of Antonio Gramsci', *New Left Review,* 100, 1976–7.
42 Thompson, J. (ed.) (1980). *Adult Education for a Change*. Foreword by Jackson, K., Ch. 7 by Evans, D. and Ch. 9 by Yarnit, M.

43 Especially *SPN* cited previously; however for a good introduction and also a guide to reading. *SPN* see Simon, R. (1982). *Gramsci's Political Thought: An Introduction.* London. Lawrence and Wishart.

44 Gramsci. *SPN* pp. 238–68.

45 Freire, P. (1985). *The Politics of Education.* London. Macmillan, Ch. 7.

46 Hall, S. Unit 21 – D102, Open University, Milton Keynes.

47 Freire, P. *Christian Faith and Marxism.* side 1. an audio-tape same series.

48 For these advances the best source is *The Politics of Education.* especially Ch. 12.

49 Heller, A. in Wright, P. 'A socialist in exile', an interview with Agnes Heller by Wright in *New Socialist*, no. 29. July/August (1985).

CHAPTER 13

Liverpool's parent support programme: a case study

JOHN DAVIS

In this paper the participants, parents and professional workers, speak mostly for themselves. As Davis suggests, this kind of case material is very difficult to pin down and anatomize in terms of the conventional classifications and distinctions of educational discourse. Indeed, perhaps the most significant characteristic of the learning process described here is precisely the way in which the usual barriers are broken down: between, for example, learning and doing, process, content and product, adult and child, professional and lay person, instruction and negotiation. Ultimately, however, people are learning from their shared experience in a very real sense and, as a result, are developing both personal confidence and collective awareness.

In 1979 Liverpool initiated a scheme which, with inner city partnership funding, has established parent centres in thirty inner city primary schools. Each centre is based in surplus classrooms which have been attractively furnished, decorated and provided with cooking facilities, a toddler play area, and equipment for parent and toddler activities. Each parent centre is permanently staffed by a teacher keyworker (who must be a qualified teacher) and an outreach worker. Both are directly responsible to the head teacher and work a flexible timetable, promoting formal and informal activities inside and outside the centre.

As with its precursor Education Priority Area Project, run by Midwinter in the late 1960s, the aims of the scheme have to do with pupil underachievement in areas of deprivation. The original funding proposal states:

If it is true that levels of attainment generally are lower in the Inner City than elsewhere, it is not because the Authority has starved its Inner Areas of staff or other resources. Social environment and particularly levels of parental interest and support are major elements in the determination of pupil attainment. The primary schools offer a natural focus for the development of parent support and parental education programmes designed to help parents in their several roles and in particular in understanding how best to help in the education of their children.

The difference between this scheme and the EPA initiatives is that the latter, with the subsequent social priority (SP) and positive discrimination (PD) designations, provided additional resources for the school while in the parent support programme (PSP), the resources are used to support and reinforce the responsibilities of the parents 'in their several roles'.

These centres are places where, free of charge, parents and others from the community can 'drop in' at any time and where they are encouraged to develop their own ideas and interests, to have confidence in their own abilities. Clearly the PSP scheme is aimed at response rather than prescription:

> It is vital that the units should be seen to be geared to local needs and heavily reliant on self help .... It follows that each unit should be allowed to develop naturally and flexibly.

> While this scheme has its distinctive features it follows no blueprint, offers no prescription. Schools have been given the freedom to pursue what they feel is important for their group of parents.

It is natural that Liverpool's patchwork of self-contained local communities, and the interests of the teachers and workers in the schools themselves, have led to substantial differences between parent centres. Nevertheless the work has a number of aspects which are common to all: parent-toddler activities, the use of the rooms as drop-in centres which lead to a wide range of social and adult education activities and also to contact and support from an extensive range of agencies and services.

From the beginning the adult education aspects have been given definition through an allocation of five hours paid adult tutor time per week in each centre, also funded with partnership help. Through the activities of the PSP workers this resource has been substantially supplemented by help from voluntary agencies and from individuals in Social Services, Health, Education and other departments, and it has also resulted in an increasing reliance on outreach tutoring from FE colleges. For these college lecturers and adult tutors the clientele is not the same as they would normally meet in FE or evening institute work, and they find themselves sidetracked from their specialism into a more general education process as relationships build. For tutors, as for the PSP workers and their teaching colleagues in school, the development of a responsive approach to work with parents is a learning experience. The following account sets out to illustrate something of what is taking place, by focusing on a flow of activities in one of the PSP schools – Abercromby Nursery – that started as an attempt to involve parents in their children's education.

In the summer of 1982 the workers organized a course for parents based on a dual process in which the parents tried out some of the common printing techniques used with the children and then worked with small groups of children in the nursery to see how they learned the same thing. In fact this idea was suggested by the teachers when they were considering how they might build on the practice – which had been established for some time – of encouraging parents to sit and work with the children when they brought them to school in the morning. It was the staff who decided that art and craft would be the best kind of activity to start on, and they selected standard printing techniques that they used with the children: bubble prints, blow prints, potato prints, hand and finger prints, marbling, string patterns.

> We decided that the best thing was to have this taught to the mothers as a technique by the art and craft tutor (adult education) who they already knew and liked, rather than by the staff – so that they didn't feel that they were being, you know, patronized.

The purposes behind the scheme were several, and by no means altruistic, as Jo Baillie (the head) explains:

> It is a double experience. They do it themselves so that they can experience what it is like to be a child, before they work with the children, because they (the parents) don't just pick things up from you explaining it to them, they don't necessarily do the thing with the children in the way you hoped. They see that it has got to be very well prepared, and there's got to be quiet in order to succeed. Also the parents see that control is needed to work with children.
>
> Quite selfishly we saw it as a way of ensuring that proper help from parents was acceptable help for the teachers.

So, on eight Friday afternoons, the group of parents (all women) worked on a series of printing techniques, led by their art and craft tutor who, to the amusement of the staff: 'Had to look up how to do all these things for a start, and found it wasn't quite so, sort of, primary as you'd imagine'.

In these sessions Lyn Carey, the teacher keyworker, also talked to the parents about the activity in relation to child development and to the language that went with the activity:

> It gave them the opportunity to discuss which processes of this technique could be accomplished directly by the child; which needed instruction by the adult and which were variables that didn't matter at all when the child didn't do what you thought they ought to do – because you might get more interesting results anyway. So that they were really thinking about the kids' capabilities, and their creativity, in this way.
>
> As well as that, the other strand was down to basics like why you let them go to town with the scissors but were perhaps a bit more cautious with the glue – which is the reverse of what they would have expected.

When they had gained sufficient confidence, which seemed to take two or three weeks, the idea was for a pair to work in the nursery with a small group of children, and this used to take place on a Monday or Tuesday. The staff had shown them where the items they needed were kept but they were expected to prepare and set up everything for themselves: 'As though it was a wet day or everybody had got 'flu, and they'd come in to help'.

Lyn explained why they wanted the parents to do everything for themselves:

> We thought that was really an important part of it, both the preparation and going over it afterwards. Part of the aim was to show the running of the nursery as well as the actual techniques.

While the mums were working in the nursery Lyn hovered in the background, explaining various things:

> Like, well, the ages of the children, because when we'd done it in our room we were doing it as adults. And although we'd talked about how the children had different skills at different ages I don't think it really went in, until the children were there.

The following Friday, at the beginning of the craft session, the pair of mums would report back on how things had gone with the children. Running through both elements of the work was the understanding that they would mount a selection of their own and the childrens' work as a frieze at the annual South Liverpool Arts and Crafts Festival in the Phoenix Centre – which also pleased the teachers, who usually did that job themselves. I asked the mums how they felt about it all:

> *Me*: So there you two were, struggling with three or four kids. Were they good?
>
> Pretty good, yes.

> *Me*: And how did you feel about it afterwards?
>
> I enjoyed it. I liked working with the kids.
>
> They were so good anyway, so you're amazed by how controllable they were.

> Me: What sort of things did you find out about them, and their work?
>
> The different ways they did it. Some of them put the paintbrush in the water and some of them the paintbrush in the paint – which was different. Some of them wanted to go on all the time.
>
> When I was in there they all just came to the table, so you had to say "You'll get a turn" so they could watch. It was knowing not to give them such a big selection of colours – two was it, we had? Once they had done a picture they were satisfied, not even ten minutes some of them. And some of them would just use the one colour, whereas another one would use the two. And the way they would go about doing it – one might start at the centre, another one at the side. And different textures of paper as well, we didn't just give them the one type of paper.
>
> Older ones were tidier, whereas the younger ones would splash.
>
> It's the way, their peculiar logic on some things. If they're printing and they've got the sky and the ground with nothing in between, well so why? And talking to them and trying to find out why they've done things.

As well as thinking and talking about the way children work, and using the printing techniques as a vehicle for developing language, the mums are being extended in other ways: by the experience itself:

> The first day we did painting I was that excited, because I had never worked with paints as a child. I didn't know what they felt like,

because you got a tin of paints, in the little squares. I really enjoyed that painting, I was even doing that – feeling the paint. And I'd never blown paint out of a straw in my life.

Or in terms of attitudes:

> *Jo*: The immediate spin-off was that the mothers realized that when their children come to them with these wet and grubby offerings, that in fact it represents a lot of hard work both on the part of the child and the teacher. Even leaving the children aside, they found that those techniques required a lot more skill just in preparation, apart from doing them, than they ever reckoned on.

Some of the notions the mums are faced with are quite fundamental, as Lyn explains:

> We talked quite a bit about letting the children do what they wanted to do, because I think as adults we felt we had an idea of what we wanted it to look like before we started. Also we were putting all these things together to make a frieze about the sea, so we'd got an idea in our minds of what we wanted the children to do. And I think that was quite difficult, just to leave the children to get on and do what they wanted.

These notions are being reflected back in what the mums say or do:

> They would look at the thing they had done and say 'It's like a cow' and I was all excited because I had seen a cow, although I wouldn't dare say it. I was delighted because I had seen the same thing.

Although one can never be sure that these things have been learned as a result of this course, statements like this do provide an important indicator of the level at which the mums are thinking. Certainly, too, these ideas and activities are being used at home:

> Well, I was cheeky. Whatever was left over of the paints I took it home and I had my children doing that. I've done everything with the children at home now. Except I didn't do the marbling because the morning I started, I mixed it all and everything was perfect, and my son was sick.

> *Me*: Have you done much painting at home before?

> Oh yes, I love painting, but I didn't know how to ....

> *Me*: You use different techniques now? Do you work with him in a different way?

Well, for instance, if we're painting, there's two children so I just give two colours at a time. And what I do now is I bring in certain cars that he has, with certain types of wheels, and let him put the wheels in the paint. Or blocks, or even his fingers rather than his hands. He'd already done paintings in the nursery with his hands and his feet.

Me: With his feet!

Oh yes, but I mean they love it. But getting him to use his fingers rather than the brush, because they love the brush, or a straw. But even with only the two of them I find the preparation is the worst. I could spend a full hour sellotaping paper down on the table where they're going to paint, and the space where I'm going to put the work they've done, and then mixing the paints, and aprons on. And Donahan, ten minutes, he's done a blob in the middle of the page and he's decided that's enough.

The value the mums see go beyond the activities themselves:

They're learning to count, and the different colours.

With my eldest, Christine, who is four, I actually involve her in preparing things.

They want to help, to do things. I think when they get older they will be doing things themselves. Like if you let them make the beds, when they're old enough they can do their own beds.

I think maybe they're also developing a sense of the consequences of things. If you're painting and there happens to be a cake or bottle of milk close by you don't go and splash it around otherwise you'll end up not having any milk for breakfast. They're developing, almost, a sense of responsibility or thinking about what's going on around them. Not being quite so self-centred.

I think its sharing things. And you're learning from them, you're learning how they see things.

And then the play

The exhibition rounded off the work on printing towards the end of the summer term, and Lyn hoped the group would move on to work on language. The course was also intended to result in mothers being attached to members of staff and spending some time working in the nursery, but so far only one mum has done this. She works with one of the nursery nurses on one afternoon a week, taking a group of children for printing. Eventually the idea is that she will work on her own.

> *Lyn*: Really the idea was for more people in the group to do that, but because the group changed and various things happened it didn't work out like that. At the end of our course on printing we got on to talking about how it was possible to get the children together, once they'd practised a skill, to talk about what the skills were used for – to make a picture, or something. So in talking about what we were going to do this term, and because we'd been doing things about stories in books, and how to tell stories, we talked about that and came up with the idea of making puppets for the children. And then the cycle started: all the preparation, the actual doing of it, and the show at the end.

It sounds more straightforward than it actually was. Lyn had been working for some time with a group of parents who were doing English and Steph, the art and craft tutor, felt that this work should lead up to some point, such as a play, which like the exhibition would provide a vehicle for putting the skills that had been learned into action.

So the English group started writing a script. None of the printing group were doing English, but they decided to continue their craft work and produce costumes, puppets and scenery for the play.

> *Lyn*: All the strands came together, really. Can I tell you the story, because that's how it all tied in? It's about this tree, which is very unhappy because various things have happened: boys have come along throwing for conkers, the leaves have all dropped off, and she has a friend, an owl, who lived in her branches, but the owl left – chased away by the cat. So the children have somehow got to bring the owl back, and cheer the tree up. They decorate the tree, and sing to the tree, and then when she's all happy again the owl comes back.
>
> So the children, with the staff, made decorations to hang on the tree, and actually the mums worked with the children there, because they made decorations with some of the children. One of the teachers wrote the music and the songs, and the other songs are the Christmas songs that the children sing anyway. And the parents, with me and the craft teacher, did everything else. And we wrote the story in the English group.

Actually the English group rewrote the script a number of times. The first version was a story in 'written English' which had to be cast in a form suitable for four-year-olds and turned into 'spoken English':

> I got involved in the language, and having to remember that we were sort of on so many different levels. It was going to be for the children, and for ourselves. Annette was going to be the girl who was narrating it, dressed up as a clown. So it had to be ideas from the script put into some cohesive form, then it had to be rewritten so that Annette could say it without sounding as if it were me trying to write something for her.

> *Jo:* I've walked in and out and listened while they've been slogging away at it. And they've worked enormously hard.

> Making an owl. Making a tree.

> Making puppets and finding out how to articulate them, how to operate them.

> I've learned about the craft of making this enormous thing, three-dimensional thing (the tree) and I've learnt not to feel embarrassed inside it.

After the play

I asked them what they were going to do next. The craft group had thought they might use the puppets as a basis for working on particular language skills with the children, but several of them have got involved in making a videotape about women's health.

> *Me:* Has that come out of the group?

> That's me. I said something … it was about, well, I breast-fed my son. I just said this to the people who were sitting down having a cup of coffee, and it opened the flood-gates then. We realized we were not the only ones who had these problems, and we want to be positive about it and help other people. We've had a series of health talks where invited people came in, doctors and that, and we had a talk about the health service. Most of us had bad things to say about it, but in talking it turned out that there were more good things than we thought there ever were about it, so we're going to try and bring that out.

Not only is there a flow of ideas among the people who attend the centre but they cohere in different groupings in order to pursue a particular interest, as and when they wish:

> I got rather dragged into it, because I'd been around having a cup of coffee when the idea for the play had been discussed, but I'd got exams so I was left out for a while. When I came in they were actually at the stage of writing the play.

Although they did learn to handle the equipment and started work on the health video this project was never completed. I asked Lyn why this was, and she felt it was partly about leadership. The tutors, a group from a community-financed workshop, were trying to offer a facility because they felt women hadn't access to the technology for making films or videos, but they expected the mums to work out their ideas themselves. But the parents had disparate ideas and needed help to discuss these out and reach decisions in order to make progress. Part of the problem was that the community tutors weren't used to that, but Lyn also felt that they weren't sufficiently open about their own role either. They talked about ways in which the Health Service was unsatisfactory, but not why they were involved in the project. To the mums it looked as though they were looking for the film to have impact, that negative things would be portrayed, yet the mums were actually feeling quite positive about the Service and weren't inclined to be 'used'.

The dragon

While the regular timetable of activities and flow of initiatives – like producing a community magazine which involved working with several departments in the local FE college – continued, the next stage in this particular sequence of development was probably the production of a dragon for the International Garden Festival in May 1984.

Lyn and Ester (the outreach worker) had been to a meeting for schools in which the idea of a Day of the Dragon had been discussed, and they saw this as another opportunity for a shared project between school and parents. The art and craft group was still going, although mostly with different people now, and the parents were given the task of producing designs. These soon covered most of the wallspace in the parents' room, and they worked out how each of them might be constructed. Steph, still the tutor, had made life-sized puppets with a travelling show and wanted an upright design, and although they didn't think it would work they agreed on Dave's dragon and sorted out how to build a bamboo cage that a man could carry. The most difficult bit was making a jaw that could be opened from inside, and they never did work out how to get smoke or flames.

Being upright and with extended wings the dragon grew too big for the room and they had to move into a community room belonging to the church. Different groups took on different bits. Staff brought in pictures and articles from magazines, and techniques used with the children in the Nursery were used for the various parts – the scales, for instance, were made with paper plates. The children had done Christmas cards with pasta and paint in the nursery one year and ideas like this were fed through to the parents by the workers, rather than the teachers explaining directly, as it was felt that the parents would feel more free to choose what to do. The idea was that parents would work with groups of children, and the staff picked children who could glue and paint without making too much mess.

Neither the parents nor the adult tutor, Steph, felt they wanted to have to explain to the children what they would be doing, feeling rather intimidated about how to convey ideas to such young children, so this was undertaken by the workers. What they did was to take about eight children at a time and, in front of the parents, set the scene by telling a story. They then discussed the dragon with the children – bringing out ideas about the lumpiness of the scales, and so on. The plates and the pasta were given out and the work, new to the parents but not to the children, began. At first the parents tended to want either to do it for the child or to direct them, but they began to realize that some of the children already had good ideas and they learnt to stand back and let them do what they wanted. Ester and Lyn took it in turns to start groups off. So that the head and the wings would catch the sun they were made by glueing coloured tissue paper to plastic and peeling it off when dry. The body and tail were made of calico, first tied and dyed and then printed with sponges and bright colours. The parents became very wrapped up and committed to it all, working on the dragon themselves in the afternoons. The teachers helped with suggestions like using gold paint, but the project was definitely the parents', not theirs.

Lyn explained that they had decided to do it this way because the dragon was too big to do in the nursery anyway. And when the parents had worked in the nursery before, with a small group, things tended to become a bit uncontrollable for the parents when other children swarmed round them, wanting to take part. They had to repeat what they were doing so that everybody could have a go, and they were also under the teachers' eye there. They were more at home in the parents' room, and some of the parents working on the dragon Lyn felt wouldn't have been prepared to go into the Nursery rooms.

Doing it this way the workers spent a lot of time talking to the parents, about whether the children were old enough to do this or that, how to get the best out of them – not to rush them, not to wipe off every splash, not to point to where to stick the pasta. They could see and appreciate the child's contribution, and some of the 'wildness' of the printing was good – not limited in the way it would have been if the parents had controlled it. They could see through the children's eyes what was happening: the fantastic world of their imaginings, the creativity that freedom allowed when things were not set or rehearsed.

And, for that matter, the same applied to the parents. One of them, loud-mouthed and aggressive, stood back at the beginning passing destructive comments: 'It looks like a cow' and so on. And she swore. But she had ideas, and some were taken up by the group, so she too got wrapped up in it all. In the parents' centre one can make allowances for her, and others, which would not be possible in the nursery with its rules and routines. As Lyn said:

> We were catching the paint pots as they fell, smoothing out the difficulties as they arose. The staff in the nursery are not ready for that yet, and the standards then perhaps have to be more rigid anyway.

On the day of the procession the parents were dressed to kill. The staff collected the children, and when the procession arrived their dragon was leading it: 'Well, it went in order of the childrens' age, but anyway theirs was very evidently the best.' I thought it was, too.

Some considerations

Inevitably these anecdotes illustrate a number of matters, and the reader will no doubt bring perceptions other than my own: about the role of the two workers as facilitators and as intermediaries between parents and school, about the kinds of things that the parents are learning that may influence their relationship with their children – like the balance between the need for control and the need to stand back and create space for the children to try out their own ideas; the need to be open to new ideas like experiencing the feel of paint and blowing it through a straw, and of the preparation that has to be done both to stimulate the child's imagination and to set up the conditions under which the child will work. Or the kinds of link being made here between the children's work in school and the parents' curriculum.

Or, indeed, the nature of the adult learning that is going on here. For me there are several aspects of this which seem significant. Decisions about the curriculum are substantially their own: although the professional worker will act as broker for ideas and will provide a focus for consensus, the chances are that it will not be her decision. While the initial idea about parents and children working together on printing techniques came from the school staff, only one mum (so far) subsequently became attached to the nursery to work with the children, and the group did not go on to use puppets as the basis for the language work. Instead the printing and the English group collaborated on the play, and then the mums became interested in health topics and started to make a videotape. The fact that some ideas are picked up fairly spontaneously, like the interest in health, must depend on the responsiveness of the workers in finding people to give talks on particular concerns, but other activities will be the result of a more protracted process of negotiation in which ideas are put forward, to be picked up or not, in an atmosphere which is relaxed and supportive. For these parents to be prepared to express anxieties and problems they must feel comfortable and confident, and the centre provides a part of the school which is 'theirs', a 'neutral' environment in which they can relate to visiting 'experts' on a basis of greater equality.

But it is clear from the anecdote about making the video that while the work needs leadership it also requires open and honest discussion. The parents are not inclined to be driven, nor will they let themselves be used, and in order to get their commitment it is necessary to face any underlying reservations they may have about the subject, or themselves, or you. It is about trust, being able to take risks, and such confidence is a collective as well as an individual thing. The succession of activities undertaken in the centre represents a pattern or regrouping through which that confidence is developed. The progression from the early work on printing techniques, to the play, to the health video and the dragon constitutes a flow of individuals who are not just joining or leaving an activity from a series of offerings but a regrouping to pursue common interests, and group processes are deliberately fostered by the workers – both through choice of appropriate tasks and by encouraging open discussion about what is going on in the group.

In such a context much of the learning that takes place is informal, and the breadth is considerable. Although the parents become very involved in, committed to, their projects the learning occurs as much spontaneously, from what people pick up in conversation, from interest in what they see going on, as from the courses or projects they undertake:

> It's all a sort of hotch-potch really. I mean there are so many different types of women who come to the centre, and so many different things going on that the centre has to offer, that you come in and kind of become part of some bigger thing. It sort of rubs off on each other. I might be involved in this film thing that's going on, and other things I might not be completely aware of, only that so and so is doing them. But it kind of all rubs off at the same time, and then you go back to your family and I find I can bring back things that have been going on. Little things and big things. Like doing Ethiopian cookery – a different cake to eat, but from a different culture. And bigger things, like how to cope with my younger daughter who is telling lies, and my son who won't go to sleep. I hear what other people do, and it's like having a roomful of aunties to talk to. We all help each other, no matter what it is – it could be anything.

> That's right. To talk over the things that were going on between me and my family. And looking at the Open University material (*First Years of Life*): that became for me, more important.

> If you mention anything here it's disastrous. That's the catalyst, and it starts something off. It's got massive: there's also the newspaper, and a recipe book. The response you get is 'Oh, that's interesting, what can we do about that?'.

They are learning from each other, valuing each other's contributions, valuing their own experiences. Learning about how to cope with bringing up children, with husband, family and neighbours. And learning about how to deal with Housing, DHSS, Health Service and other agencies. The curriculum consists of the real problems of life as much as with the acquisition of knowledge and skills that will take them on to a job or to Further Education. In practice these centres are a significant stepping stone to further study for women in this area (Toxteth, Liverpool 8). Few of the people attending these centres left school with any qualifications and few would normally attend evening classes or take up further education at FE college. Yet in the spring term of 1985 over 250 parents were attending classes run by tutors from one FE college, either in school or at the college.

Having said that it is nevertheless apparent that education isn't what these parents, mostly women, come to the centres for:

> What I mean to say is, as well as the skills that you pick up in here, like how to paint with your child, how to make play-dough, and so on, that's not the most important thing. The most important thing is gabbing to Linda, or whoever's in, you know what I mean, about what's going on in the house. Because if you're in the house on your own what have you got? A lot of people in here, their parents live a long way away, I know mine live a long way away, so you can't go rushing back to your family for help. Normally this area has quite a high turnover of people, so you don't really get a close relationship with your neighbours until it's too late. And you're just in your house, on your own, with nobody to, sort of, turn to.

> Yes, it's the same with me. What I come for is basically companionship.

> Also we get into contact with people that we never would have before. Like Therese, her accent alone would put me off. And there's Rose, hers would put me off the same, you know what I mean. And Barbara, whom I always thought too upper crust for me to mix with ...

> You're not talking about my Irish ... [uproar]

> When I come to sewing class on a Wednesday there's a lot of Asian women in here, well not just Asian. And I mean you would not just go up to somebody in their costume and stuff and just say to them 'By the way the local supermarket is there, in that street' because you

wouldn't have the nerve. And yet that's what they want to know – where the cheaper shops are, and everything.

So if they are coming for companionship then content is in a very real sense secondary, it is merely a vehicle. The work is essentially a process of constructing and maintaining the warp and weft of social fabric. The evident enthusiasms generated by the play and the dragon have to do with collaboration as much as with craftwork. The work is about developing the self-disciplines of being supportive and tolerant, of collaborating, of taking decisions, solving problems and surmounting difficulties together, it is the collective success as well as the personal success that provides the satisfaction. After the play it was evident what the performance had unleashed: like any cast after the first night these parents were high on their experience, jubilant as individuals and proud as a team.

Now I haven't asked these people about their social life and background, since to do so might well prejudice relationships that the workers have laboured to construct. The quotations hint at the isolation they feel at home, and at the therapy they get from discussing problems. The workers can see changes in the parents:

> Well, these people *have* changed. Ros and Sue used to be rather offhand with their children, and now they're different. Some, like Tess, have gone on to do other things and they see what's in it for them and they appreciate that that is also the case for the child. They apply what they've experienced in their own learning – for instance they've been talked to differently as a learning adult and they do that with the child – like praising because they've been praised.

We know, too, that the social groupings persist outside school in terms of holiday activities with the children and for mutual help. With these people friendship means help, so perhaps we are talking about a broader spectrum of friendship and an enlarged range of resource contacts. Apart from such practical aspects of community, activities like the community magazine and welfare rights courses look outwards to the needs of the community, indeed much of the work on health, ethnic cultures and even children's reading books will develop an increased awareness of the local situation. Whether this will in practice lead to 'empowerment' we have yet to see – Liverpool's present politics do not help and there is an unwillingness among these parents to put themselves forward, be it as chairman or for other kinds of responsibility. It seems that they don't like to be seen as trying to be different, and they don't like their children to be different either. Yet there are signs in Abercromby that such things may develop. One mother who has had a caesarian birth and is pregnant again heard of a support group in Manchester, and has established a group in the centre which includes the local health visitor in order to support other mums.

Inevitably these processes take time, and that is also true of the involvement of their teaching colleagues in school. As it happens, Abercromby was one of the seven primary schools in Midwinter's EPA project, four of which are currently in the PSP scheme, and that was by no means the beginning of the movement. Jessie Reid Crosbie received an MBE for her work with her mothers' fellowship – which she began in 1905. While none of the staff at Abercromby were in the school at the time of the EPA project the notion of support for work with parents persists as a kind of general willingness in several of those schools. But in Abercromby the two workers are now the longest serving members of staff, apart from the head who has been hospitalized and will shortly retire. Work with staff, as with the parents, is a constant cycle. Yet, because of the importance of relationships and of the appropriate approach to this work, continuity is important. In Abercromby the art and craft tutor was with them from 1982 to 1984, and the FE tutor working with them on the community magazine has done so since 1983. In another centre an FE tutor has developed family woodwork sessions into collaborative dockland and local environment projects with infant and junior classes over a period of four years. Which raises for them and for the tutors questions about what constitutes a 'course' and, indeed, what their 'expertise' really consists of. In practice they are retained because they work well with the parents, and they remain because they find it:

> ... a breath of fresh air, it gives me the flexibility to be different. It's a lot more relaxed, informal, the people don't have to be there but they want to be there. It requires more of my time but it is easier to do when people approach you for the learning.

In practice there are distinct parallels between the adult education in PSP centres and new curriculum developments in secondary schooling. Are not the parents already engaging in what is in effect a real alternative curriculum, with experiential learning, content and practices that are negotiated in a relaxed atmosphere, emphasis on life skills and on group interaction, vocational elements in partnership with adult education and FE mutual support and collaborative skills that solve problems in the school and which, through elements of the curriculum like welfare rights and community magazine, look outwards to the needs of the community?

The modular systems currently being developed by examining boards in response to TVEI, GCSE, CPVE and LAPP programmes also offer potential accreditation to these parents, as would the possibility of an open college system which Liverpool is currently exploring. Yet most of the parents are not involved in order to acquire certificates, or because they need to pass exams in order to get a job. They are doing things because they are interested, but they don't come with that interest – they get interested, often because they join in with others in whatever happens to be going on.

It isn't like school because there isn't any pressure, you don't have to come at all if you don't want to – though about a quarter of the parents only miss two or three days in a month and a further half are there regularly three times or so a week. Obviously these centres have distinct advantages: in being able to get out from under timetabling rigidities, in size of groups and their few but continuing relationships with professionals, in having time to devote to their own interests and concerns and to the group process, of norms which treat lengthy discussions as worthwhile and are prepared to consider working on the spontaneous as probably more effective than sticking to a programme, of having a base which is 'theirs', and so on.

Much of this, of course, is by no means new to adult education, although the PSP workers do seem to have learnt it for themselves. The strength here, though, is in the platform, the backbone, that adult education provides for the range of other activities that go on in PSP. It affords the basis for developing the individual's confidence and in the fact that the education system has something to offer that they value, and it provides a vehicle to develop the necessary relationships for effective work on the parents' skills in parenting and as educators of their children. It offers a bridge that can link with the school curriculum, and that may teach staff in schools more about the community they serve. That teachers are a major target of this scheme is not something that will be found expressed in the original Education Department proposals to inner city partnership. It talks rather in terms of 'identifying and reacting to the educational needs of the community' and of 'generating in the indigenous population of the inner areas a sense of community and pride' and of 'making the process regenerative'. Yet one wonders whether, behind the apparently necessary phrases that accompany bids for funding, there was a vision of reopening a door to something that was already there, to which the education service had become blind. The notion of supporting parents is but one of the facets of a more general movement of parent involvement, and behind it there is clearly the idea that in the present climate the education system needs their support. To do that it must itself be responsive.

CHAPTER 14

The dilemmas of self-help: a perspective on community education from Africa

JOHN AND JEAN ANDERSON

Community education today needs to reassert and reappropriate the positive traditions of communal self-help, self-determination and voluntary action which are deeply rooted in its history. We have much to learn from the experience of developing countries in this respect. This paper demonstrates how the development of self-help educational initiatives in Kenya prefigures some of the contradictions and dilemmas of choice now being confronted by the more formal education systems of Western societies: in terms, for instance, of the relationship between school and community, local and national priorities, education and production. The logic of local self-help in the wider context of inequality and the maldistribution of resources illustrates both the positive potential and the unresolved ambivalence of many community education approaches.

> Lazy people do not get cows,
> One finger cannot kill a louse.[1]

In the introduction to the centenary edition of Samuel Smiles' bestseller *Self-Help*, Asa Briggs wrote 'few books in history have reflected the spirit of the age more faithfully'.[2] In extolling the virtues of labour, cheerfulness and perseverance it is easy today to recognize 'Victorian values'. The phrases still ring: 'Heaven helps those who help themselves.' 'Help from without is often enfeebling in its effects, but help from within invariably invigorates.'[3] At first glance they seem to epitomize the free market, individualistic approach to development rather than notions of community development and cooperation. Smiles was a socially concerned radical, but whilst he continued to support such causes as public education and public libraries, he appeared to draw a distinction between self-help and socialism, advocating the former in opposition to the latter.

The two are not necessarily opposed: the rise of industrial entrepreneurship was paralleled and buttressed by a vigorous community self-help movement. Agencies such as the Friendly Societies and Sunday Schools paved the way for a welfare state based on the idea of a partnership, bringing together government and voluntary community action to the advantage of all. However, today as building societies compete with banks, polytechnics ape universities and voluntary hospitals give way to BUPA, the significance of voluntary action through community self-help appears lost to our understanding. Worse, it is being perverted, as more and more institutions founded to serve the community as a whole, and in particular the poor, have turned to serve the well-to-do, leaving those disadvantaged by industrial decline to their own devices. Unlike the nineteenth-century monetarist, his twentieth-century counterpart has forgotten the methodist.

Today it is the countries that face the most pressing needs to achieve social and economic development that exhibit the most telling examples of community self-help. The implications of classifying nations as 'developed' or 'developing', 'first world' or 'third world', are made clear by John Samuel.[4] But one characteristic associated increasingly with the new nations is the emphasis placed on the mobilization of peoples and the responses generated. Whatever the prevailing ideology, efforts are being made to bring communities together, to establish learning strategies and thus enable people to tackle their own problems.

In the 'third world', particularly since countries achieved independence, there is an ongoing debate about the role of schools and what constitutes relevant education for community development, particularly in rural areas. Much emphasis has been placed on self-help and self-reliance to expand and improve education provision. In the UK, as has been demonstrated elsewhere in this reader, community-oriented schooling has taken on various forms in response to varying needs – village colleges in Cambridgeshire to combat rural drift and increase educational opportunity, the post–Plowden measures focused on the issue of deprivation and enhanced home/school relations. Now there are alternative forms of schooling to combat inadequate provision for minority groups, to build closer links between school and work, and to control the effects of youth unemployment. Vocational skills are increasingly perceived a relevance, and throughout the world, 'community education' is increasingly becoming associated with the search for relevant education in terms of employment, and development.

Self-help is often the means of provision employed, though as will be demonstrated, self-help endeavour does not always seem to be harnessed to either relevance for economic development, or the particular needs of a specific local community, and therein lies a tension.

This chapter draws upon the work of a number of African students, mainly from Kenya, studying at the College of St Mark and St John, who have carried out research in their own home areas, on vacation, into school and community relations, whilst studying community education developments in Britain. What several have done is to compare developments and initiatives in their homeland with those in the United Kingdom. We don't very often do this, and there are lessons to be learned!

This chapter tentatively suggests that by examining a number of initiatives in Africa, particularly Kenya, we can learn that the self-help factor is not necessarily a capitalist ploy, but a complex operation which can be effective in differing ideological contexts. But unless it is harnessed sensitively it may inhibit or misdirect, rather than develop, appropriate community-oriented education.

One of the conclusions drawn by Sinclair and Lillis is that relevance programmes for school-going children are not an appropriate vehicle for the rectification of social and economic ills partly because children are not well placed to influence their elders, and partly because social and economic problems cannot be solved by one agency alone.[5] They draw on examples and models from Mexico in the 1930s, from Turkey and India in the 1940s, from Tanzania in the 1950s and from the Upper Volta in the 1960s. Similar conclusions might be drawn from the UK by highlighting the limitations and frustrations of EPA and CD schemes in the late 1960s and 1970s, or more recently by examining the confusion about curriculum developments in technical and vocational education: 'The comprehensive curriculum may well be more relevant to the twentieth century. But it is still the old style academic curriculum that guarantees university entry and, ultimately, access to power and status.'[6]

Current education strategies, in whatever location, no longer can hope to achieve a sudden breakthrough to economic growth. Increasingly, access to, and the expansion of, schooling appears to be creating a mismatch between institutionalized learning and a community's needs.[7] Yet as the energies and ingenuity of disadvantaged peoples across the world focus upon the immediate practical problems of improving living conditions, water supplies, preventative health measures, functional literacy, they are almost inevitably focused on the establishment of schools as well, often overshadowing the issue of what needs to be learned.

The 1920s were a watershed for community education both in England and Kenya. Henry Morris saw the end of the First World War as the opportunity to bring together a range of ideas and earlier experiments to establish at least in Cambridgeshire, a comprehensive community college programme. The unsettling nature of the War in Africa increasingly led Africans to question colonial authority. As a consequence Thomas Jesse Jones was asked to lead the Phelps Stokes commission to review African education in British colonial Africa.[8]

Morris sought to extend the advantages of education across the community but failed to attract significant government support. Jones, borrowing the Jeannes school model from earlier experiments with freed slaves in the southern states of America, sought to limit education to the technical and vocational requirements of rural development.[9] He was supported by colonial governments, who saw such policies maintaining the hierarchies on which they depended, but at the same time promoting rural development. Perhaps the real significance of the Phelps Stokes reports was that they catalysed amongst the African population pressure for the advantages of full and comprehensive education which Morris, not Jones, had intended.

The focus which formal education took, played a key part in Kenya's struggle for independence. For as leaders like Kenyatta argued, once Africans could take their place in the legislature and argue cases in the courts they could, by England's own parliamentary and legal principles, claim their birthright. They could also dispel the 'myth of trusteeship' often used to justify colonial authority.[19]

Formal education in Kenya has its origins in the traditions of its

African peoples. These differ, reflecting a rich diversity of cultures, both settled and nomadic. Yet in general, traditional forms of education developed as part of an integrated pattern of life in small-scale societies, involving the key institutions of family, neighbourhood and age grades. Education was recognized in a formal sense through initiation ceremonies and the periods of training associated with them. In certain communities specialist skills, such as smithing and medicine, were acquired through a form of apprenticeship, and such training was recognized. Often in non-hierarchical groups in particular, forms of selection set in train at initiation periods resulted in recognition in later life, when the successful were identified and underwent further training to serve as elders on various councils.

Based on this understanding of education, African responses to Western forms of schooling initially offered by missionaries, were cautious but curious. Often schooling was rejected, but as colonial power became established interest developed and formal education opportunities rapidly became an issue of important concern. Initially a coincidence of interest occurred with missionaries providing teaching whilst the local population used their cooperative community techniques to build the schools and pay the teachers, a practice common in much of colonial Africa.

The curriculum soon became a point of conflict. The skills of reading and writing and eventually academic learning were perceived as valuable as they appeared to underpin European success. But many Europeans, particularly settlers, sought to offer only practical skills and the moral precepts of the 'good labourer'. This was the dilemma the Phelps Stokes commission was asked to resolve across much of British colonial Africa. The Jeannes Schools were advocated, by the Commission because in a number of respects, they were models of community education, focusing upon local needs, relating curricula to community life, and involving teachers in community development. They attracted supporters with imagination, commitment and dedication and at their best created an approach to learning that recognised both the practicalities of life in the local community and the more immediate requirements of its members.[11]

To some extent they paved the way for the community development movement developed in most of British colonial Africa prior to independence. But, as models imposed from outside, they reflected colonial thinking and were never perceived by Africans as an answer to educational aspirations. Africans quickly distinguished between 'real' schools which offered young people credentials to find wage employment in the emerging modern sector, the growing towns and administrative system, and 'Jeannes schools', and community development centres which failed to offer transferable skills and credentials. Indeed such institutions often appeared to fail in their own terms for instance by promoting the back-breaking task of soil conservation but having no impact on a colonial agricultural policy that prohibited Africans from growing cash crops such as coffee and tea.

To utilize education to improve rural life made economic sense, but it generated little enthusiasm amongst local people who saw the supposed benefits as limiting their real opportunities to power and condemned them to second-class citizenship. Such sentiments can be found in minority groups in Britain today, as they consider attempts to ameliorate the educational disadvantages in inner cities, but perceive few tangible results.

The African response in the colonial era was first to work within the context of missionary and later colonial government provision to press for academically oriented education, and refuse to cooperate with practical training. Second, and more significantly, they developed schools of their own. Across the country African communities realized that it was their own self-help efforts that had built and supported mission stations and their satellite schools, and they began to demand a say in their control, particularly of the curriculum. When this was not forthcoming, groups began to break away and establish their own institutions. The most significant developments were the Kikuyu independent schools. These grew rapidly during the 1930s, eventually including secondary schools and a teacher training college. The four hundred or so schools represent the commitment and capacity of community self-help, but even more significantly, they represent both the drive of parents to obtain advancement for their children and the efforts of communities to determine their own future. The political lesson was not missed for these schools, and the independent churches with which they were associated grew with, and supported, a new political consciousness, creating a vital network which helped to launch and sustain the struggle for independence.[12]

When Kenya finally gained independence in 1963 Jomo Kenyatta, now President, turned again to African culture, summoning the community self-help ethos present in each of the various ethnic communities into a national development movement – 'Harambee' – the swahili word for 'pull together'. The coincidence of interest was re-established and throughout much of the country community self-help groups began to support government policy, building up the rural infrastructure by constructing roads, dams, cattle dips, and in particular health centres and schools. The techniques which had previously been employed to build primary schools were now directed towards nursery provision and particularly secondary schools. One account illustrates this pattern.

Kirimara School, situated in a prosperous area of central province, but also an area of high population growth which put land and services under strain, can trace its origins to the 1940s when local people determined to build a primary school free from mission influence. Even at the outset there were dreams of a secondary school, but the ban on independent schools imposed during the so called 'Emergency' takeover halted these plans. It was not until 1959, during the period of land consolidation, that a title deed was granted and another primary school was established on the Kirimara site. Dreams of a secondary school were revived by the local primary headmaster and politicians; in the early 1960s the four locations in the area were called upon to construct classrooms, teachers' houses, bring in electricity and water and finance laboratories. Local taxes were levied, those unwilling having to forfeit a good, for instance an axe or a hoe, and labour was obtained on a voluntary basis in particular from women's groups and local masons. In many ways this is a model success story: the primary headmaster refused a move, and the local community paid his salary to retain his services, to develop the secondary school. It received support from the local community development association and developed activities of its own to raise funds, such as a coffee plantation and milk production. The government started to give aid to the school in 1969. This has been matched by continuing local support, and the recruitment of volunteer teachers from overseas, to supplement local staff.[13] Here is an example of a community initiative marrying with government support, and as long as tangible results can be perceived by local communities such marriages can, and do, work.

Secondary education, above all, was seen in Kenya to be the route to social and economic advancement, and in the early days of independence, when Africanization programmes were being

Table 14.1: The development of second-level schools for African pupils in Kenya, 1945–68

	Aided	Unaided	Total
1945	4	–	4
1957	21	4	25
1960	33	8	41
1963	82	13	95
1964	154	90	244
1965	186	181	367
1966	199	266	465
1967	226	336	562
1968	232	369	601
1969	265	443	708

(14)

implemented and some industrial expansion being undertaken there was a buoyant job market for the secondary school leaver. The self-help response was outstanding (see Table 14.1).

However, although Harambee secondary schools were very much the product *of* the community, their service *to* the community in any local development sense soon became questionable. These schools were established to emulate the government and missionary schools and, as such, they sought to offer the same curricula, enter the same diploma race, and award the same prizes to their contestants. So the net effect was to offer another route out of the rural community, into the wage-earning sector in the town for the winners, just as the grammar school, and assisted places, have done in this country. In order to carry out this function Harambee schools had to charge high fees and so began to serve more prosperous members of a commuity or, in order to attract government aid, had to widen their catchment areas to attract 'good' primary passes, and so raise standards. Sadly, therefore, it could be argued that in some cases community self-help was not so much supporting the community as exploiting it on behalf of the fortunate few.[15]

Communal effort certainly provided services which the central government could claim were part of a successful national development plan. At a local level, the situation became increasingly complex. Successful communities improved their immediate surroundings and then used their success to build further and to strengthen their national negotiating position. Less successful communities soon recognised their relative disadvantage and began to complain.

One young schoolboy commented, when answering an examination question related to national development 'Self-help is a disease which is badly affecting my country ... some big people are helping themselves well, but mostly the poor people suffer badly from poor roads and schools and not having hospitals.'[16] The views of that one young school boy must be kept in context but the forcefulness of his metaphor highlights the dilemma of communal self help policies where communities have to deal with very different economic circumstances. There is no doubt that in many areas Harambee education endeavour brought tangible benefits to local communities. But in secondary school provision, inequalities were revealed particularly in relation to employment prospects: wages for the few and 'relevance' for the many.

Along with similar initiatives in other countries, the Harambee schools of Kenya rapidly became overtaken by the school leaver problem, youth unemployment, and narrowing opportunities for secure wage employment. By 1968 unemployment amongst secondary school leavers in Kenya began to rise steadily.[17]

Although the Kenya government has recently sought to change both the structure of the school system and curriculum, aiming to redirect pupils towards more practical and vocational studies, the general popular response after independence was a continued pressure for academic education. The dilemma of Phelps Stokes had re-emerged and now faced the new independent government. Interestingly, the churches, which had done much to pioneer education initiatives in the 20s and 30s, now began to turn their attention to the school leaver problem.

Many had already been instrumental in establishing and supporting Harambee schools. However, even in the early years of independence, the national Christian Council for Kenya, had published a report 'After School What?' which identified the youth unemployment issue at the primary level, and advocated experiments in non formal education for school leavers who could not find work. This led to the establishment of a small group of ad hoc experiments in various parts of Kenya, projects which came to be known as 'village polytechnics'.[18]

The early polytechnics received little community support, being largely established as a result of individual or church initiatives. No government support was forthcoming until 1970. They relied on charity from external funding and only when tangible results were seen, for example in providing skills to service community needs, or providing routes to skill qualifications, was community support forthcoming. The NCCK recommendations had focused upon providing young people with training which would enable them to play constructive roles in rural development, emphasizing the notion of self employment. But two features need to be noted: there was a continuing need for a dynamic programme, to prevent saturation of certain skills in local areas, and there was a demand from local areas for institutionalization and opportunities to acquire recognized qualifications.[19] A case study illustrates the dilemma clearly.

Bushinahgala village polytechnic following a position established by neighbouring institutions was started by an American teacher working at the local secondary school in the late 1970s and support was received from the local church, which donated land for a workshop, and from the local self-help committee. Two skills were offered, tailoring and carpentry, and later masonry was added when a Danish volunteer came to the area. He generated support from Denmark, which resulted in a workshop and a metal workshop being initiated and, more recently, under local leadership, home economics has been added. In order to maintain local support, formal classes leading to government trade tests were established, though at the same time locally oriented agricultural training has continued to be compulsory for all trainees and attempts are made to generate improved agricultural practices in the local community. A study of the leavers however, indicates that most go to urban areas to look for work. A number of the skills offered, are no longer marketable as saturation develops and changes take effect. For instance, metalwork has become questionable as plastic replaces metal kitchenware and soldering skills become obsolete. Yet the development of more sophisticated skills is hampered by a lack of resources and facilities. Although there is an apparent demand for welding, the necessary equipment and power supplies are not obtainable.[20]

The practice of creating employment by identifying local needs, and then establishing programmes and, where necessary, capital and business skills, was a key goal identified by the NCCK, and there are success stories, such as the sponsorship of apprenticeships with local craftsmen and businessmen, loans to establish cooperatives. But the innovative element has proved difficult to sustain and the pressure to provide certification resulted in the formalization of village polytechnics.[21] As in the case of Bushiangala, the incentive to search out potential markets and evaluate community needs tends to take second place as the demand for 'academic qualifications' again assumes precedence. As the fees for Harambee schools rose, parents who couldn't afford them looked to the polytechnics for opportunities for their children, but saw them as a 'second chance' to gain credentials.

By 1970 the government, via the Ministry of Cooperatives (later Culture) and Social Services, brought the polytechnics into a pre-vocational training scheme linking them to the older youth centres, designed mainly to cater for children from families who could not afford school fees. The implications of this have now been recognized and a separate Department of Village Polytechincs has been established. However, although the government anticipates that village polytechnics can offer skills required in the labour market or self-employment, local communities are not as enthusiastic about sending children to them. Enrolment has not been high, nor has Harambee support been anywhere near as significant as it was for secondary education. Indeed, self-help effort in the technical/vocational field has been largely directed towards district or provincial level, Harambee Technical Institute offering modern sector technical training.[22]

Against a background of pressure to balance rural development for the great mass of population with the limited possibilities of urbanisation this may seem shortsighted. It must be remembered however that rural community life depends to a great extent on farming. To develop cash crop farming requires land, capital and business skills. Consequently many who struggle to maintain subsistence farming on limited land feel that the best chance for their children lies in wage employment. Moreover, fathers who own land know that if just one son can find secure wage employment he will create a source of capital to allow his brothers to work the land very much more effectively.

Implicit in this situation is the competitiveness and self interest often associated with capitalism. It can be argued that in countries with a more explicit and determined commitment to socialism than Kenya, communal effort might be better used, that education will be less competitive and academic and better focused towards the needs of its local communities. Tanzania is in many basic social and economic respects similar to Kenya and is often cited in comparison. At the instigation of its president, Julius Nyerere,

Tanzania embarked on a policy of community based socialism and the Arusha declaration of 1967 'Socialism and Self Reliance', attempted to provide a framework for development through the establishment of socialist villages, (Ujamaa vijijini). These ideas stirred the imagination of the world, and are an important reference point in community action. But it is now clear that the success of an Ujamaa village depends very much on the commitment of the villagers as individuals. No matter how carefully the communal philosophy is argued, attempts formulated by central planning agencies do not achieve success unless the villagers themselves see the project meeting their requirements.[23]

There are two important similarities between Kenya and Tanzania in relation to community self help. First, notwithstanding ideological considerations, community self help traditions and techniques have, in both countries, been turned to advantage. Improvements to the infrastructure: roads, water supplies, schools, health centres, cattle dips, all lie within the capacity of committed community groups, particularly if an external agency can provide scarce capital items. The ongoing provision of services requires a more careful and sensitive integration of communal and national effort, for it is the provision of scarce recurrent items, fuel, drugs, science materials, that normally stretch beyond the capacity of local groups. The interplay between the central and the local is critical in maintaining and developing communal self-help effort. Second, the tradition of communal support for schools is strong in both countries but so is the view that school provision provides access to mobility, wealth and power. Thus, in both countries, formal schooling, especially at the secondary level, tends to emphasize academic, credential oriented curriculum. If anything, the more structured social and political philosophy of Tanzania has reinforced central control more strongly than in Kenya. This, for instance, has enabled Tanzania to re-shape the formal school curricula more readily and to make more explicit the requirements of rural development and the values of co-operation. Yet, in comparison with Kenya, the strength of the centralisation has tended to reduce the capacity of particular communities and schools to generate or respond to local initiatives.

It is arguable that the European mind leaps too readily to contrast Kenya and Tanzania on its own terms, and to conclude that Kenya's apparent economic success negates the philosophy of the Tanzanian socialist experiment. Such observations may or may not have justification, but they miss the point that both Kenyatta and

Nyerere knew well the frailties of capitalism and socialism as exhibited in the West and the East of Europe. Both sought more appropriate, less orthodox pathways for development using African based community self help methods and both countries now offer further insights for the rest of us.

It is interesting that Kenya's recent moves to a new pattern of education 8:4:4 appears to be borrowing some of the ideas of Nyerere, whilst the communal village policy of Ujamaa is being adapted to allow for individual ownership and initiative. There may be differences in the emphasis but, notwithstanding the need to balance individual and communal gain, Kenya and Tanzania both demonstrate that in Africa, nations faced with rapid transition can use community self help to good advantage.

Beside the question of ideology there is also the question of sensitivity. A final example may illustrate the point. One of the neglected areas of Kenya, the North Eastern Province, has recently been recognized by the government as one of disadvantage. Ignored by the missionaries, who saw little point in evangelisation in a largely Islamic nomadic area, viewed with initial suspicion by the independent government as an area inhabited by groups whose allegiance appeared to lie northwards, it is now being regarded as a priority area and resources for development are being channelled in its direction. Yet the traditional forms of self help in this area have not been recognized. It is possible to adapt schools to people whose lives are nomadic, for instance to design a mobile resource based unit. It is possible to focus the curriculum towards the understanding of nomadic people, for instance by relating it to livestock rather than arable farming. It is not possible to establish a static community school and expect a nomadic community to support it, even if its material resources are second to none.[24]

What has happened is that others from outside the region have seen the material resources being put into the North East Province boarding schools and have therefore sent their children there to be educated. The percentage of local people still remains low, and the curriculum is not geared to the environment. But then, how many purpose built community colleges and leisure centres in England designed to serve the needs of their local populations, are failing the residents of the inner city and large housing estates in favour of those from the leafy suburbs. Wherever central authorities seek partnership in provision with local communities there must be a full appreciation of the views and habits of local residents.

This chapter began by emphasizing the potential of community self help as a method of school provision. It has sought to show its significance in the context of Africa today and to reflect on lessons this might have for the United Kingdom.

Wherever they are founded community schools are expected to serve a number of purposes – the social and economic needs of the neighbourhood, the requirements of national policy and the aspirations of parents and pupils. Yet, as community members, as national citizens and as parents, people tend to have very different expectations of formal education.

Such different expectations make the school and particularly the curriculum a target for manipulation and pressure. The tension between national and local government policies is well known, not least in the United Kingdom. But the context for this struggle, is a world where education is the key to social mobility and schools have to maintain credibility with parents who seek to maximize opportunities for their children.

It is significant, that faced with the need to improve the learning opportunities for their children, black British communities in inner city areas such as Brixton and Handsworth turn for inspiration not to the tradition of evening classes that had served education development in British cities in earlier times, but to the urgent mobility oriented educational self help now growing so fast in Africa.

Community self help is a method of voluntary taxation. It is open to exploitation. The individualist, market oriented philosophy and the centralist, socialist philosophy can claim community self help as an appropriate technique. In the end however it is the people who do the work and provide the initiative that are the key to successful development. Methods of control that prescribe too strictly tend to kill the goose that lays the golden egg. Yet methods that leave aside national planning, economic circumstances or questions of equity and justice deny the very cooperation which communal effort implies.

The basic sentiments of self help, community service and learning lie at the very heart of man's creative capacity. We need to understand them better if community education is to combine them effectively as the basis for constructive self determination.

Notes

1   Kikuyu proverbs, reflecting self-help and cooperation.
2   Smiles S. (1959). *Self-Help*. Centenary edition, John Murray.

3   Ibid.
4   Samuel J. (reference within this reader)
5   Sinclair M and Lillis K. (1973). *School and Community in the Third World*. Croom Helm.
6   Wilby P. 'Classes of 83'. *Sunday Times* 22.5.83.
7   Fauré E. (Chairman). (1972). 'Learning to be', UNESCO, Chapter 1.
8   Jones T. J. (1926). (ed.) Education in Africa Report of the Phelps Stokes' Commission, Edinburgh House.
9   King K. (1971). *Pan Africanism and Education*. Oxford. Oxford University Press.
10 Anderson J. (1970). *The Struggle for the School*. Longman.
11 Dougall J. W. C. (1930). 'School education and native life', *Africa*, vol. iii, no. 1.
12 Anderson J. (1970). op. cit.
13 Karumba M. (1984). 'The self-help factor in Harambee schools', B Ed dissertation. College of St Mark and St John.
14 Anderson J. E. (1973). 'Organization and financing of self-help education in Kenya', UNESCO, IIEP.
15 Gichunku J. (1986). 'Educational opportunities for children attending self help schools', B Ed dissertation, College of St Mark and St John. Taken from a Kenya Junior Secondary Examination paper 1969.
17 Dore R. (1976). *The Diploma Disease*. Allen & Unwin.
18 'After school what?' (1966). Report of the NCCK Nairobi.
19 For two views of the development of village polytechnics
     1 Anderson J. E., 'The Village Polytechnic Movement: an evaluation report', IDS, University of Nairobi.
     2 Court, D. (1971). 'Dilemmas of development, the village polytechnic movement – a shadow system of education in Kenya', IDS, Nairobi, Kenya.
20 Wabuko E. (1986). 'Youth unemployment', B Ed dissertation, College of St Mark and St John.
21 Anderson J. E. (1974). 'The formalization of non-formal education: village polytechnics and prevocational youth training in Kenya', The World Year Book of Education, Evans.
22 Anderson J. E., Ibid.
23 Von Freyhold M. (1979). 'Ujamaa Villages in Tanzania', Heinemann Educational Books.
24 Ibrahim A. (1986). 'Nomadic Education in N E Kenya', B Ed dissertation College of St Mark and St John.

CONCLUSION

Community education and educational reform

Community education, as this book has shown, exists in many forms and contexts. It is popular but it deserves to be more popular. This diversity has not coexisted with a lack of identity. Community education is fundamentally about responding to people's needs and wants. It is concerned with people's happiness and despair, with the reallocation of resources and power and with establishing the vision and reality of genuine progress for most individuals, but especially with the welfare of the worse-off members of society. Identifying and developing these themes in theory and in practice is the main contribution which community education is making to contemporary debates concerning preferred alternative educational futures.

The United Kingdom is facing a dual crisis in public education. First, the rise of the New Right has questioned the efficiency of education, the democracy of education and quality of learning produced by the education system, and found it lacking. Education is criticized for wasting scarce public resources, for being too insular from public accountability and for either failing to deliver what the public wants or for delivering too much of what the public does not want. Second, there appears to be no energetic, popular educational movement which is consistently creating alternative educational vision and strategies. Community education should and can step into the vacuum created by this dual crisis because it can simultaneously promise more efficiency, more democracy and more consumer sovereignty as well as creating a culture which is supportive of radical innovation within public education and, more generally, within welfare state capitalism.

Criticisms of the educational establishment in the UK have come from the same culture which has thrice elected a government publicly committed to reversing the perceived political, economic and moral decline of the United Kingdom in the 1960s and 1970s. The New Right has identified and fuelled a wide range of intense discontents and at the same time has launched programmes of 'reform' of the welfare state in general and education in particular. That is not to say that most people are in some sense naturally inclined to criticize the educational establishment. Rather, education occupies an ambivalent and sometimes paradoxical place in people's lives and utopias. Public education can be a major vehicle for progress, both individually, in terms of social and economic mobility and collectively, in terms of national strength and prestige gained through a generally educated and specifically trained population. People are concerned with the ways in which education creates disappointment. Education can be associated with failures to lead to employment, with the cause of street violence and with an associated belief that professionals in education are underworked and overpaid. The great strength of community education is that, as Professor Ian Lister outlined in a speech delivered to the Northern Consortium for Community Education in March 1985, it begins where education acknowledges, understands and interacts with the social or community culture of people, with their economic or work culture and with their political culture.

The social or community culture

Community education recognizes that people have needs, that these should be identified or diagnosed and that these needs are diverse. Needs-orientated education starts from a vision of humanity rather than a structure of knowledge. This distinguishes community education from the sterile debate about 'better schools' which is raging at the moment. Within community education there is no one blueprint for the design of methods which support people in the identification and prioritization of their needs nor a consensus on how to resolve conflicts which arise from disagreements about needs. Needs-directed educational planning has to face decisions concerning the resolution or acceptance of conflict over unfair resource distributions, has to decide to aim for harmonious social life or for an explicit acceptance of individualism. Many community educators have been attracted by the renaissance of the education of persons approach of recent years, a debate of longstanding interest in social work. Whether these needs and wants are responded to at a political level or at an individual level, the actual activities of community educators reflect conscious or subconscious decisions about styles of professional interventions appropriate in specific contexts.

A concern with the personal and the political involves values. Few discussions about the nature of community education get far before people start identifying the value position of others and a defence or reformulation of their own value positions. Needs and wants both determine and are determined by values. One of the great strengths of the community education movement is that its activists and supporters incorporate self-awareness and awareness of others as part of their procedural values. Many community educators work at community education because it provides an educational front for combating racism, sexism, classism and ageism and other negative discriminatory policies, structures and practices. There is no room for a moral vacuum in community education. Moral matters are not simply matters of opinion; human communities are more than the individuals that make them up; and there are ways of telling between right and wrong. These procedural values are essential to assert yet their nature needs continual verification so that community educators continue to walk the tightrope between moral and political neutrality and moral and political dogma and closure.

The economic or work culture

The development of any educational reform movement in socialist or capitalist welfare states is subject to the same economic pressures which constrain public services generally. In the UK since 1976, and more intensely since 1979, education, like the economy, has been seen to be in decline. The future economic culture, in the short and medium term, will not radically alter (assuming continuities in super power and North–South relationships). The internal scrutiny of education by HMI, professional assessors and governing and managerial bodies will continue in an economic climate that will bring no extended showers of public resources for education. Centralization of financial control and devolution of political control at the local level will coexist; education will continue to be pinpointed as both actual cause and potential solution to pressing social problems. Generally, education will be subject to claims for a redefinition of purpose and method. These claims may well appear to point to policies and practices which are mutually exclusive and which are irreconcilable given the general lack of productive interaction between theory and practice in education and the lack of time to make direct democracy effective. Community education will need to continue its drive for a coherent set of procedural values, a technical competence and an imaginative resource base in order to maintain or increase its momentum.

The political culture

Roger Scruton, Caroline Cox and other members of the so-called 'Hillgate Group' have dominated agenda setting in recent years. They have tapped into an attractive critique of education through stressing the need for 'good schools', where teachers teach real skills and genuine knowledge, keep order and discipline rather than encourage free expression and idle play and offer children a firm moral and spiritual basis.

The New Right Hillgate Group style is to produce the kind of manifesto-type statements which are not matched by a similar vitality on the left. Such statements can receive widespread media coverage and public support and fit the climate of national decline perfectly. Not only those who work in and for community schools need to have responses to the Hillgate Group commands. There is a general message here for all involved in community education.

What we in community education want is what Fred Inglis has summed up as 'criticality' combined with the delivery of tangible immediate gains in welfare. Our political culture is characterized by an ideology derived from an insistence on efficiency leading to resource cutbacks; expert authority, vested in politicians rather than professionals; rationalization, shifting control and the responsibility for resources from the state to the market and increase discipline, education *for* a new economic and moral order rather than education *about* it. This ideology is not conducive to the flourishing of criticality.

The future for community education

Criticality, according to Inglis, is the critical imagining of alternatives. Any major social system is always subject to critique.

Community education is currently expanding at a time when most aspects of schooling and welfare are undergoing reactionary retrenchment and regression. Community education has maintained momentum because it has always stood as a positive response to more long-standing criticisms of public education systems. The twentieth-century rise of community education can be understood in part as a rejection of relative deprivation (education creating a few winners and majorities of losers), a rejection of a self-maximizing culture where power and material resources are advertised as the only desirable products and a rejection of the iniquitous arrangements for the distribution and rewards for work which arise from the mutually supportive systems of labour markets and educational credentialism.

Community education is piggy-in-the-middle between the New Right and a political tradition (Labour Party) which sees the welfare state as the main success story of the struggle by the organized working classes to wrest concessions from governments and corporations. It appeals to both left and right but it can transcend this ideological pluralism by aligning itself with other alternative education movements. For example the establishment of the International Community Education Association suggests an internationalism which is stressed by the human rights education movement. Human rights education, like community education, offers a framework for the recognition and celebration of cultural diversity, which accepts that to be able to conceive of utopia is to be living in a utopia and is working for the identification and acceptance of human rights which appear to be truly universal.

Community educators are fond of labelling themselves and others: conservative, reformist, radical and the '-isms' are still the main labels. Yet we know such labels often have little illustrative power and that, in practice, community educators, as Colin Fletcher has argued, chart a middle route between passivity and high-profile innovation, between anonymity and annoying announcements. Such 'annoying announcements' can be identified and systematized in alternative educational agendas. The issue for community education is that it must not allow the New Right to create a retrenchment in public education through emphasizing the failures of public education. Community educators have to consider their position with respect to the 1976–1987 conservative restoration of education for national pride, economic strength and a new moral order. They also have to put into practice an alternative agenda derived for the examples provided by the contributors to this volume.

The community education movement can and should work at different levels. These levels, contextualized by institutions and geography, include the production of published accounts of successful innovation of community education in theory and in practice; the arrangement of regular opportunities for discussion and debate and self-evaluation through, e.g., the regional, national and international community education associations; and more research on the conditions under which community education flourishes or fails to take off. Above all, community educators should seek to evolve methods by which they are able to work for the extension and fusion of critical belief and material conditions which leads to real human progress.

This will entail the maintenance of the progressive human-centred educational aims and methods which is the hallmark and legitimization of community education. It will entail working for the elimination of unjust and inefficient delivery systems through exercising the imagination in favour of recognizing equality of need and universality of right. Above all, community education exists and must continue to exist and expand as one of the major educational innovations which promises to deliver and can deliver a fairer distribution of what Bertrand Russell referred to as the amenities of civilized life.

Name index

Index of Themes